KEAN

EDMUND KEAN AS SIR GILES OVERREACH

KEAN

BY

GILES PLAYFAIR

GREENWOOD PRESS, PUBLISHERS
WESTPORT, CONNECTICUT

Library of Congress Cataloging in Publication Data

Playfair, Giles, 1910–
    Kean.

    Reprint of the 1st ed. published in 1939 by
E. P. Dutton, New York.
    Includes bibliographical references.
    1. Kean, Edmund, 1787–1833.
PN2598.K3P5   1973   792'.028'0924   73–10878
ISBN 0–8371–7047–8

Originally published in 1939 by E. P. Dutton & Co., Inc.,
New York

Reprinted in 1973 by Greenwood Press,
a division of Williamhouse-Regency Inc.

Library of Congress Catalogue Card Number 73-10878

ISBN 0-8371-7047-8

Printed in the United States of America

FOR   CAROL

PREFACE

THE facts stated in this book are based on careful and (I hope) accurate research. I have a horror of footnotes, so I have argued controversial points in an appendix. The vexed question of the date of Kean's birth, however, deserves special notice. I do not claim, for one moment, to have settled it, but my arguments, so far as they go, are contained in the following letter which was published in *The Times* on May 10, 1938.

SIR,—In Mr. Ifan Kyrle Fletcher's exhibition of Edmund Kean relics appear two very rare playbills whose significance, I think, has not been appreciated.

Both belong to a theatre in Store Street, and the first, dated March 17, 1801, announces that "The Celebrated Theatrical Child, Edmund Carey [the name by which Kean went in those days], *not eleven years old*, will for one night only . . . give his inimitable performances." The second, dated March 24, 1801, announces that "The Celebrated Theatrical Child, *only eleven years* old, will," etc. According to the direct evidence of these bills, therefore, Edmund Kean was born between March 17 and March 24, 1789.

The date of Kean's birth has up to now been an insoluble problem. In general, two dates have been preferred—November 4, 1787, and March 17, 1789. All Kean's biographers have, it is true, favoured the former, including Mr. Hillebrand, whose very scholarly book was published only a few years ago. But did they ever see the Store Street bills? Certainly Mr. Hillebrand did not or he would have said so. And I think it extremely unlikely that his predecessors did—Cornwall, Hawkins, and Molloy.

The March 17th birthday was originally derived from Miss Tidswell, the actress-guardian of Kean. She was very definite because she remembered "it was St. Patrick's Day"; and personally I have become—in the course of my research —more and more disposed to accept her word.

First I discovered in the library of the Garrick Club a passport belonging to Edmund Kean, in which he gave his age as twenty-eight. The passport was issued in Dieppe in 1817. Thus he recognized officially his own belief that he was born in 1789.

Secondly I happened on some family papers, now in the strong-room of Charles Kean's firm of solicitors. Among these are a few scribbled notes written some time in the late 1820's or early 1830's. They were obviously intended as material for a biography of Edmund Kean, though not set down in his own handwriting. Once again the birthday is given as March 17, 1789.

In the same lot I found the original statement which Douglas Jerrold wrote for Barry Cornwall, Kean's first biographer. Jerrold had it that when Kean came to Sheerness in 1804 he was still in boy's costume. That is quite likely if he were then only fifteen years old; but absurd if he were really seventeen.

For me the matter is finally decided by the Store Street bills. I know it may be argued that even in 1801 Kean (or his mentors) wished to lie about his age. But the month please mark, is given as March, not November. And the day is as near the 17th as makes no difference. Those facts are altogether too definite to be mere coincidence.

This letter drew forth several replies, including one from Mr. Boas, who endorsed the views I had expressed, and one from Mr. Landa. Mr. Landa argued that because Edmund was brought up by his uncle Moses (that is embedded in the Kean tradition), and because Moses died in December of 1792, therefore Edmund must have been born considerably before 1789. My answer to Mr. Landa, though set up in proof, was never actually published. It is as follows:

"In my vanity I thought I was the only one aware of the date of Moses Kean's death to which Mr. Landa has now called attention.

"Personally, I am quite satisfied that the supposed association of Edmund Kean with his uncle is pure myth. In any case its beginning is traditionally placed in 1795 (see F. W. Hawkins' *Life* and *The Dictionary of National Biography*), when Moses had already been two years in his grave!

"There is certainly no reference to Moses Kean in the family papers which I mentioned in my previous letter. According to these Kean was, at different times, with Ann Carey (his mother), Miss Tidswell, a Mr. and Mrs. Duncan, and a Mrs. Clarke. It is impossible to give an ordered account of Edmund Kean's childhood. But I think it feasible to suggest that Miss Tidswell first took him to live with her at the beginning of 1793 when he was not yet four years old and was virtually defenceless and alone in the world. We know that she had reason to do so because she had been his uncle Moses's mistress. We know that when Kean reached his seventh year he was capable of earning a little money for himself. We know that Ann Carey abandoned her son when he was a useless infant but reclaimed him when he was a talented boy. We know that Kean's father (whose Christian name was also Edmund) died very shortly after his brother Moses. And we know that Mrs. Price (Kean's paternal aunt) frequently saw her nephew, but always refused to give him a home."

There, for the moment, I must leave the matter, though I may add that most of the baptismal registers, within a reasonable distance of Gray's Inn, have been searched without result. I append the pedigrees of Kean and Darnley which have been compiled for me by Phillimore & Company.

For reasons made clear in the Appendix, I owe obligation to the following: Mr. C. Harold Ridge (of Phillimore & Company); Mrs. Gabrielle Enthoven, whose collection of playbills is at the Victoria and Albert Museum; the librarians at Gloucester, Cheltenham, Cardiff, Swansea, and Carmarthen; Sir Ambrose Heal; Mr. R. N. Green-Armytage; Miss Grace Lane; Mr. Ifan Kyrle Fletcher; Mr. Horace Collins; and Mr. Derrick A. Sington.

GILES PLAYFAIR

January 1939

ILLUSTRATIONS

These illustrations are reproduced by kind permission of Ifan Kyrle Fletcher, in whose collection they may be found.

KEAN

CHAPTER I

RICHMOND TOWN was once the home of kings; and then the home of noblemen and of the mistresses of princes; of politicians, poets, and novelists.

To-day (so it appears to me) it has almost degenerated into an up-to-date suburb. I write "almost" because there are still a few fine relics of the past for those who choose to look for them. And about the Green, despite the increasing number of ugly buildings which flank it, there is an atmosphere of historic seclusion which no power of Victorian vandalism or twentieth-century ruthlessness has been able to dispel.

It is a sad fact, nevertheless, that, while the modern blocks of offices are very clean and the modern shops very prosperous, those features of the town which distinguish it from Ealing or Hounslow are obviously neglected. They are suffered to appear like poor relations who have outstayed their welcome. Far from being cherished and shown off, they are hidden and forgotten in the hope, perhaps, that they will die a natural death.

It may have been necessary, in the name of progress, to tear down most of the distinguished houses and all the inns of long memory. But surely there is no reason why the courtyard of King Henry VII Palace, which yet remains, should be allowed to resemble an official refuge for litter.

And why has the graveyard of the old parish church, in which so many celebrities of the past were buried, become a dark and overgrown plot of grass decorated only with a few crumbling, disfigured, and lopsided tombstones?

Edmund Kean lies somewhere there.

That one may learn from the memorial tablet, erected by his son, which has been moved to the interior of the church. But the exact place of his grave is no longer known.

The house on the Green and the eighteenth-century theatre adjoining it, which both belonged to Kean, were pulled down in 1850 in order that the road might be broadened. (Why was it necessary to broaden a road where so little traffic passes?) In their place has arisen a red brick building of loathsome appearance. It is labelled "Garrick Villa." Enough for Kean that a small and cheaply inscribed plaque, nailed to its wooden gates, commemorates the facts that "on this spot once stood the New Theatre and the Lodging House in which Edmund Kean died." It takes the English to perpetrate such an unconscious piece of irony!

In a similar way, I suppose, has the modern Royal Borough of Richmond treated the memories of many of its famous residents. But in the case of Kean the significance of this is doubly pathetic.

He came to live on the Green in 1831 and spent there the last two years of his wasted life. When he arrived he was already a chronic and incurable invalid. He had to live in the country air for the sake of his health. He would have preferred, of course, to have retired to his island estate at Bute in Scotland. But that he could not afford. He was obliged, by financial considerations, to remain within measurable distance of the London theatres.

In Richmond, as in no other part of England, Kean was beloved. His fellow townsmen detected a certain nobility in his character and forgave him his weaknesses of which they had heard such frequent and such lurid accounts.

Had he simply impressed them as Edmund Kean, the tragedian, acknowledged throughout America and the British Isles as the most celebrated actor of the century, he would have been a notorious figure, an object to be stared at as he left his house not revered. But he did more than this. He won their gratitude because he was believed to be a man of generosity to whom no one in distress appealed in vain. And he won their respect because, for the first time in his life, he acquired a definite, if pathetic dignity.

It may have been a dignity which he could not help. He swallowed his quantities of brandy and water at home now —under medical supervision. He was constitutionally unable to make a habit of drinking himself silly publicly at the Castle Inn or one of the other taverns.

The inhabitants of Richmond saw him only when he went for walks on the Green or when he climbed the hill to gaze at the view from the terrace. There was something venerable about this man who, even on warm days, wrapped himself up in a fur cloak, and moved so slowly. One would have been astonished to learn that he was still in his forties, the prime of life. He looked years older, in his dotage. And there was something almost supernatural about him as well. For the two black eyes which shone out from his death-pale face had lost none of their piercing lustre.

He became, as it were, a part of the life of Richmond, so that when he died his fellow inhabitants were sorrowed by the loss of a beloved neighbour and hastened to pay honour to the shade of a distinguished townsman. They crowded to pass, in silence, by his coffin while it lay at Mr. Piggott's, the undertaker. On the afternoon of his funeral they closed their main shops and walked behind the official procession to his burial service at their parish church. They were anxious even to spend their money on raising a memorial to him and would have done so had not Charles Kean claimed that right as his own.

People in other parts of the country did not mourn him half so genuinely. They regretted, it is true, the loss of Edmund Kean, the actor. For as such he had been to them an institution; decayed, battered, perhaps a discreditable institution; but an institution nevertheless, and one which, during the past nineteen years, they had in turn lauded and abused and always, in their hearts, cherished. Now that he was gone it seemed—to use his own lofty phrase—as if the last great "representative of Shakespeare's heroes" had been taken away from them. No matter how deeply dissipation had submerged his talents! They had crowded to see him as long as he had had enough breath in his body to speak and enough energy in his limbs to move.

But for Kean, the man?

Well, there had been a few far-sighted intellectuals ready to excuse his weaknesses, and a few loud-throated vulgarians eager even to eulogize his excesses. But the majority of English playgoers had little tolerance or understanding of his character. Conventional sympathy excepted, they parted from him without regret.

There was undeniably pomp and ceremony enough on the day of his funeral. The official procession had been elaborately arranged, and conscientiously puffed by a suddenly sentiment Press. Famous actors, singers, scene-painters, clowns, equestrians, and dramatic critics walked in it, and humble members of the London theatres as well, so that it was fully representative of the *corps dramatique*. Yet to the discerning it could not have appeared as a spontaneous tribute to the memory of a well-loved friend. William˙Macready, himself a great tragedian, was one of the pall-bearers; and his presence may, on the face of it, have appeared touchingly appropriate. But Macready would far rather have stayed at home, and had only been brought to Richmond by his chronic fear of public opinion. This reluctance to honour a departed colleague had not been prompted by any lingering thoughts of professional jealousy. On the contrary; Macready had often admitted his admiration for Kean, the actor. But for Kean, the man, he had had nothing but hatred and much-vaunted contempt. Now that the object of his malice was no longer of this world, he still regarded him with feelings equally pronounced and bitter. A year later he was to record for posterity "that Kean was the greatest disgrace to the art of acting of all the disgraceful members that ever practised it."

Perhaps there was no other who walked in that procession with prejudices quite so violent. But assuredly there were many who could pretend to no great affection for Edmund Kean. They, with Macready, must have welcomed the carriages which, at the end of a long and tedious afternoon, "bore them swiftly back to London."

Kean had enjoyed the devoted friendship of a few. Two such—John Lee, his secretary, and Sheridan Knowles, the dramatist—supported Charles as chief mourners. But, all in all, the man who had struggled so miserably for recognition, who had triumphed so suddenly and so completely, who had found such bitterness in success, and who had died so tragically had never been popular either with the general public or with the members of his own calling.

He were best forgotten. The actor had been worshipped. But his career was over now. And his name would soon count for little except among Old Stagers with a passion for the past.

The church was, indeed, crowded on the afternoon of May 25, 1833. But only the inhabitants of Richmond, who sat silently at the back, saved all the outward show of grief from empty mockery. They, in truth, were sorrowfully conscious of the solemnity of the occasion. They shared the emotional feelings of their parson, the Rev. Mr. Campbell, as he read the burial service. They believed it rightly proclaimed:

> His Body is buried in Peace,
> But his name shall live forever more.

I

In December of 1792 Charlotte Tidswell's second lover died. Now there was nothing to which she could look forward with pleasure. At the age of thirty-two it was unlikely that she would become a wife and certain that she would never advance in her profession. Life seemed already behind her and even her memories were not particularly gay and exciting.

About her childhood she could recollect very little. She

never knew her mother, though her father, she said, was a native of Ireland, an officer in the British army, a man of means and position. By him she was brought up in elegant and luxurious circumstances and was sent over to France for her education. But these halcyon days did not last long. Her father lived extravagantly and died young and bankrupt. So Charlotte, still in her 'teens, faced the world alone, without money, without parents, and without home. It was then that she came under the protection of Charles Howard, eleventh Duke of Norfolk, known to his intimates as Jockey. He was her first lover.

She did not have very fragrant memories of this affair, for Jockey had not the art to inspire affection. He survives in history as a Whig politician of ability and courage, but as a man he was totally inestimable. His family remember him with shame as the only Howard who ever renounced the Catholic faith. And the rest of posterity may fairly judge him by this epitaph:

What Norfolk has been
you may learn from this placard

He lived like a beast
and died like a blackguard.

He was grossly fat and revoltingly dirty. The fat resulted from consistent over-eating; the dirt from a constitutional dislike of water. Only when he had drunk himself into a state of insensibility were his servants enabled to wash him. Mercifully that occasion was frequent.

Charlotte Tidswell was neither his first nor his last mistress. She was one among too many. As a seducer he was frequent, indiscriminating and indelicate. Indeed, it has been estimated that with the exception of Charles II "no man of procreative memory diffused his Maker's image through the land more than he." Certainly, during the whole course of his manhood, he became the father of a steadily increasing number of illegitimate offspring and consequently was obliged to pay annuities to a growing bevy of discarded paramours. Someone has left a vicious picture of this squat, drink-sodden, excessively corpulent old aristocrat sitting in the back parlour of his bank, watching, through a peephole, the former objects of his sexual indulgence as they came to cash their quarterly cheques. He would pass remarks on each of them. Of one he would say, "I'faith she looks as young as twenty years ago"; of another, "What a dowdy"; of a third, "What an old hag." And so on with indelicacy.

Jockey had the best of Charlotte's youth. And when she was twenty-three he did not put her on his list of pensioners but, instead, used his influence to obtain her an engagement at Drury Lane. And so without training she became an actress, and without previously serving an apprenticeship in the provinces she joined the permanent company of one of the two great Patent Houses, which in the ordinary course of events would have been impossible. She made her first appearance on March 18, 1783—as Leonora in *The Mourning Bride*. She faced a large, distinguished, and enthusiastic audience who frequently interrupted Congreve's second-rate tragedy with thunderclaps of applause. But these were not for her. They were for Mrs. Siddons, who had chosen the occasion to show her admirers how grandly she could act "Zara."

Miss Tidswell's début was inconspicuous enough, to be sure! Though she spoke two lines--"It bore the accent of a human voice" and "Hark"—which are included in the paragraph selected by Dr. Johnson as being "the most poetical from the whole mass of English poesy," the part of Leonora the attendant is not exactly a telling one. Nevertheless, it was a fitting prelude to her subsequent career of forty years as a London actress. She never rose far above Leonora. And she never earned more than £3 per week.

Of course, she was an amateur when she first joined the Drury Lane company—untrained and quite inexperienced, but she had sense of a kind not usually found in amateurs.

She was strictly aware of the limitations of her own powers and she had no illusions about the future. She realized that she had been driven to the stage by necessity, not drawn to it. Although in time, of course, she became quite a competent and useful performer, she remained humble. Humility, in fact, was her strong point. She was ready, without a murmur, to support any kind of subordinate part in any kind of play—comedy, tragedy, farce. By her colleagues of the Green Room she was immortalized in these lines:

> Such Tidswell's modesty that she's content,
> Even immodest parts to represent.

Immodest parts were hotly shunned by most actresses of her day. But Miss Tidswell contrived to portray even wantons in a ladylike manner. And the critics of the late eighteenth century, who were already showing signs of prudery, praised her "for not displaying those gestures which would prove extremely offensive to female delicacy." In other words for not acting a prostitute as a prostitute.

Her reticence in this respect was appropriate to the unsullied reputation which she eventually enjoyed outside the theatre. Unlike most of her kind she was said to maintain in private life "a highly respectable character." But that was really all that was ever said about her. She had no personal following and was never by any chance singled out for praise or blame in the newspapers. Indeed, during the whole course of her theatrical career she had but one full-blooded admirer, an anonymous correspondent to an ephemeral dramatic magazine. He complained that the critics had neglected to appraise her talents at their proper valuation, and declared that she was beautiful in features and person, chaste in character and the greatest actress in England. But he wrote this panegyric in 1817 when poor Tidswell was approaching her sixtieth birthday. And since he selected her performance of the Gentlewoman in *Macbeth* as a particular instance by which to justify all his sweeping eulogies, one is forced to the unhappy conclusion that his letter was simply intended as a rather cruel jest.

Already in 1792 Charlotte's position was one of obscure security. Year after year she had acted the same kind of part in the same kind of play for the same money. And so she would continue to do. Now when Drury Lane closed down for the summer vacation she joined the company at the Theatre Royal, Liverpool. She would lose this annual engagement in 1794, being one of the victims of an economy drive. That would be her only setback. There would be no advancement.

Yet she never complained. She seemed quite content to maintain her reputation of being a humble, useful performer and a respectable spinster. She remained balanced and level-headed. She kept her own counsel. Above everything she was reticent.

For herself she had no ambition and no interest in the profession which had been forced upon her. She was only eager to maintain the tradition which, as time went by, became, in its small way, associated with her name—the tradition that she was born a cut above the station of her calling, that she bore her lot patiently and well, and that she guarded her primary virtues from the besetting temptations of the stage.

Perhaps that is why she did not openly acknowledge her second lover, whose name was Moses Kean and who belonged naturally to the world which she had entered by misadventure.

Though Moses was the son of a tailor and was himself ready to do a bit of tailoring in his spare time, he came from an Irish family whose roots were in the theatre. So that there was no cleavage with tradition when he went on the stage. On the face of things, Charlotte might well have been proud of him, for he was brilliantly successful compared with her. He was not just a small part actor, but a specialist—a mimic who gave performances at Covent Garden, Drury Lane and the Haymarket, and had a show of his own called the Evening Lounge which he toured round the provinces. Indeed, there was quite a little public for Moses Kean, and because he was one-legged and always thumped on the stage with his wooden stump before entering, they likened him, somewhat sentimentally, to Samuel Foote, greatest of all English mimics. He was well known enough to be parodied once by a rival and so well loved that the audience resented the parody.

In private life he was a handsome man, tall, well built, with black, bushy hair. And, out and about in his own Bohemia, he was rather a picturesque figure elaborately dressed up in a scarlet coat, a white satin waistcoat, black satin small clothes, a ruffled shirt, a Scott Liquid dye blue stocking (on his one leg) and a long quartered shoe with a large buckle covering his foot; on his head a cocked hat and in his hand a switch or cane.

Still, in spite of his histrionic gifts and his flash appearance, he was a poor match for an army officer's daughter. And so Charlotte Tidswell, though she allowed herself to be known as his wife in family circles, never married him and never went to live in his house. And when the death of Moses Kean, "celebrated for his efforts in the Lounge," was announced in the Press, no mention was made of his widow or of his family.

Charlotte surveyed the future. What was there for her now that Moses was gone? Years of plodding along in a profession for which she had no natural aptitude, retirement one day in the distant future, and then a lonely and impoverished old age? Perhaps. But at least she had an interest in the small boy, not yet three years old, who was left in her care. He would be consolation for the dull drabness of her existence and the frustration of her spirit. Though he was not her own son, she would love him as if he were. He was the bastard nephew of Moses and she called him Edmund Kean, after his father.

2

Actually Edmund Kean was the illegitimate son of the young man whose name he bore and of a young girl called Ann Carey. Charlotte was not even related to him, except, of course, in a very unblessed way through her association with his Uncle Moses. But because of her position in the Kean family she knew all about the circumstances of his birth. And the following is the gist of the account which she gave twenty-three years later when the world was agog to hear it.

> On March 17, 1789, at half-past three in the morning Edmund Kean, the father, came to me and said. "Nance Carey is with child and begs you to go to her at her lodgings in Chancery Lane." Accordingly I and my aunt Mrs. Byrne went with him, and found Nance Carey near her time. We asked her if she had proper necessaries? She replied: "No, nothing"; whereupon Mrs. Byrne begged the loan of some baby clothes and Nance Carey was removed to the Chambers in Gray's Inn which her father then occupied; and it was there that the boy was born.

I have already argued the vexed problem of the date of Kean's birth and have tried to show that Miss Tidswell probably stated it correctly. But there is no need to prove the substance of her story, for it has never been seriously challenged. True, a contemporary rumour suggested that Miss Tidswell was really Edmund's mother and that she lied to protect her respectable reputation from the embarrassment of a bastard child. But this rumour—for reasons later made clear—was chiefly fostered by Kean himself and is supported by none of the established facts. Moreover, Charlotte, who loved Edmund, would never have chosen such a sordid fabrication behind which to shield her own virtues. And Charlotte, who was passionately possessive, would never have let Edmund out of her sight if in truth she had had a legal right to keep him with her. She did not actually take charge of him until he was near two years old —at a time when he would otherwise have died of starvation

and neglect. Though he had relatives besides his parents
—a maternal grandfather, a paternal aunt, and two paternal
uncles—they were with one exception of precious little use
to him. Indeed, he was obliged to his family for nothing
more material than the blood which flowed through his
veins. And that in itself was a pretty poor inheritance.

George Saville Carey, the grandfather, loaned his attic
in Gray's Inn to his wayward daughter Ann for her confine-
ment. That was certainly his major and probably his only
contribution to his grandchild's welfare. He was himself a
man of some distinction in the artistic world, being both
an author and composer, though chiefly famed as a public
lecturer, which meant that he provided a species of light
entertainment very popular in his own day. In halls and
sometimes in theatres he gave humorous talks and recitations, debated and imitated the singers, actors, politicians,
and statesmen of contemporary note. Audiences loved him
for his melodious voice and for his handsome head and for
his black eyes which were very expressive. Really he was
in the same line of business as Moses Kean and, indeed, on
several occasions they joined forces and together performed
a double act. But intellectually he was considerably more
advanced than Moses, for he was the posthumous son of
Henry Carey and had been blessed with a modicum of his
father's talents.

Even to-day Henry Carey, the lyricist, musician, and
writer of burlesques, is not entirely forgotten. His best-
known song, "Sally in our Alley," is considered finely
representative of its period. Those with a taste for academic
discussion still argue his claim to the authorship of "God
Save the King"; and those with a heart for such things
lament the cruel irony of fate which drove him to commit
suicide in the prime of life and allowed him to be found
afterwards with only a halfpenny in his pocket.

Perhaps George Saville Carey, who was improvident and
irresponsible, followed too religiously in his father's footsteps. Alive he earned considerable prestige and just enough

"Uncle Moses"

MOSES KEAN IN ONE OF HIS IMITATIONS

income to maintain, according to one opinion, "the appearance of a decent, honest man." But when he died, in 1807, he left behind him nothing more material than his literary works, his songs, and an authoritative essay on mimicry! And he was given Christian burial at the expense of his friends.

Ann Carey inherited her father's vices, his physical beauty, and none of his mental equipment. She called herself, delicately enough, an itinerant actress and street hawker. But actually she had the natural instincts, if not the commercial acumen, of an ordinary prostitute.

She was an attractive, good-looking wench, with a fine pair of dark eyes. But she made her appeal to the dissolute; and she got herself up to look precisely as virtuous as she was. Her gradual degeneration into a low, dissipated old woman was inevitable. Illegitimate children were the unfortunate consequence of her pleasure, and to these she eventually grew quite accustomed. There is no telling how many bastards were hers. But, besides Edmund, she certainly gave birth to a daughter and to a son whose father's name was Darnley; and as late as 1830, when she was but three years from her grave, she still had a young boy in her charge.

Hawking and acting were sidelines to her chief occupation in life, mere means of making money while she indulged her promiscuity. And in neither capacity was she remotely successful. As a hawker her beat was limited. For many respectable families fought shy of receiving a tradeswoman whose cheeks, even in the daytime, were highly rouged! Her greatest histrionic triumphs were scored after her distinguished son had become the star of Drury Lane, and was thereby enabled to exert influence on her behalf. For example, in 1817, at Kean's instigation, Tom Dibdin engaged her to walk on at the Surrey Theatre. But previously she had not risen above small parts in the very lowest grade of travelling companies—and she must have been a vulgar, rank-bad performer.

All in all she lived a hand-to-mouth existence, often

facing complete destitution and never in her palmiest times
earning more than a few shillings each week. Perhaps she
eventually acquired, through experience, some kind of
capacity for motherhood. But in 1789 she was near the
beginning of her career and then she showed absolutely no
inclination to look after her babies.

The brothers Kean—Moses, Aaron, and Edmund—
lived together at 9 Little St. Martin's Lane, and their
widowed sister, Mrs. Price, kept house for them during
the hours she could spare from her professional duties of
mantua making. It was an erratic *ménage* and she was the
steadying influence. Moses, the successful mimic, bothered
her least, for though he could be fairly dashing and intem-
perate when he chose, he was, compared with his two
brothers, rocklike in his stability. Aaron drank so enormously that he was distinguished for nothing else. And as
for Edmund—well, luckily his time on earth would be
short-lived.

He was still in his 'teens when first he paid his devoted
attentions to Ann Carey, and he was a smart, handsome
young man then with black hair and rather Semitic-looking
features. He was ambitious, too, and not altogether without
accomplishments. Though his chief purpose in life was to
become an architect (he had got himself apprenticed to a
fashionable surveyor), he also possessed the family flair for
histrionics. At school he had entertained his fellow pupils
with recitations and later had learned how to debate, and
was thus able on occasions to assist brother Moses
professionally.

But Edmund was temperamentally quite unfit to be a
father, and it was perhaps fortunate that he only survived
his son's birth by three years. He had a mania for alcohol
which caused his brief and promising career to be consistently retrograde. First he lost his job as surveyor's
apprentice and was reduced to the degraded post of copying
clerk. And then he sank into a deranged state of mind and
became a useless member of society, a burden on the family

dau. of GEORGE SAVILLE
CAREY, *b.* ?
May 27, 1833, at Richmond,
Surrey

AARON KEAN
of London.
? tailor

dau. of (? HOWARD)
MBERS of Waterford, Ireland,
actress, *b. circa* 1780,
at Stroud, Glos., by banns,
July 17, 1808.
at Keydell, near Horndean,
s., March 30, 1849, aged 69.

TREE
actress *b.* ? 1805.
St. Thomas, Dublin (by
ice 284/1842), January 29
(? February) 1842.
47, Queensborough Terrace,
n, August 20, 1880, *bur.* at
rington, Hants. Will dated
24, 1869. Proved January 8,
1881.

O GORDON LOGIE
rgeon-Major, Royal Horse
Guards.
gust 25, 1820 (? in Moray-
e), M.D. Edinburgh 1840.
47, Queensborough Terrace,
n, April 6, 1886. Will dated
nber 13, 1876. Proved October 11, 1886.

ES HARRY GORDON LOGIE.
ember 16, 1876, at 47, Queens-
gh Terrace, London. He is
have died in his early twenties,
married, of consumption.

FAMILY OF DARNLEY

ANN CAREY is said to have had (by
an unknown father) a son named:

HARRY DARNLEY, who married and
had a daughter:

HELEN DARNLEY, who is said to have
married James Cooper, a theatrical producer. Cooper probably
died before 1865 leaving a
daughter:

POLLY COOPER, who was born
about 1846 and is said to have
married at Dover about 1865,

WILLIAM DENISS MCCARTHY of
Cork, who served in the army and
was at the relief of Lucknow. He
died about 1918 and left issue:

HERBERT WALTER MCCARTHY
(known on the stage as Herbert
Darnley) was born in 1872 and is
still living (1938). He married
Winifred Mary Blundell at
Glasgow, about 1905 and had
issue:
(1) HERBERT DARNLEY BLUNDELL
MCCARTHY, who was killed in
the war of 1914–18 and is buried
at Mons. He did not leave issue.
(2) A DAUGHTER, who died young.

MOSES KEAN
ventriloquist and entertainer of
London.
d. about December 19, 1792.
Charlotte Tidswell, actress, *b. circa*
1760 and *d.* September 3, 1846,
aged 86, was his mistress.

EDMUND KEAN & ANI

? actor. Apprenticed to Wilmot, a
surveyor of London, in 1783—his
clerk in 1787.
Committed suicide soon after the
death of his brother Moses in 1792.

bur.

*Church Registers searched for the
baptism of Edmund Kean, November
1787 to December 1790* :—
Gray's Inn Chapel.
St. George, Queen Square.
St. Andrew, Holborn.
St. Paul, Covent Garden.
St. Martin-in-the-Fields.
St. Dunstan-in-the-West.
Arundel, Sussex.
St. Saviour, Southwark.
Christ-Church, Southwark.

EDMUND KEAN *m.* MAI
CI

b. ? Gray's Inn, London, in chambers of George Saville Carey,
March 17, 1789, being St. Patrick's
day (? November 4, 1787). Passport
issued in Dieppe agrees with date
1789. See also letters to *The Times*
mentioned in the text. He died at
Richmond, Surrey, May 15, and
was buried there May 25, 1833.
Administration July 24, 1833,
granted to William Halton, creditor.

m

d
Ha

HOWARD ANTHONY KEAN
b. at Swansea, South Wales,
September 13, 1809.
d. at Dorchester, Dorset, November 22 and *bur.* there November 24,
1813.

CHARLES JOHN KEAN *m.* ELLE
actor, F.S.A., F.R.G.S.
b. Waterford, Ireland, January 18,
bap. January 26, 1811. Educated
at Eton.
d. at 47, Queensborough Terrace,
London, January 22, and *bur.*
January 30, 1868, at Catherington,
Hants. Will dated June 30, 1866.
Proved March 25, 1868.

m.
lic

d. a
Lond
Cath
July

MARY MARIA KEAN *m.* COS
b. at 119, Park Street, Mayfair,
September 18, 1843.
m. Christchurch, Paddington,
February 23, 1876, by licence.
d. at 13, Earls Avenue, Folkestone,
January 4, 1898. Will dated December 10, 1896. Proved February 2,
1898.

S

b. A
sh
d. a
Lond
Nov

CHA
b. D
boro
said
u

at 9 Little St. Martin's Lane. At the age of twenty-two, a few weeks after the death of brother Moses, he put an end to his own life by walking off the parapet on the roof of his lodgings.

And so the small boy in Miss Tidswell's care was the bastard son of a strumpet and a lunatic. He could scarcely have entered on a more wretched inheritance. No doubt his ability (which he developed later) to play the piano by ear and to compose a little in the same untutored fashion was native. No doubt the theatre was in his blood. But these were poor recompenses for prodigality, irresponsibility, waywardness, and dipsomania.

He came to be known as the greatest actor of the nineteenth century and to be remembered as one of its most tragic figures. The former distinction was won in spite of his heritage. The latter was due to the sad fact that he proved himself, in many ways and instances, a true Kean and a true Carey.

3

No one knows how he spent the first few months of his life. Miss Tidswell and Mrs. Price rescued him from his mother when he was near two years old, and Ann Carey was not at all reluctant to be rid of her half-starved, sickly, and wholly neglected infant. Mrs. Price was an amiable woman, with a family conscience, and she knew that something had to be done about her wretched brother's child. Still, she thought her responsibility as an aunt would be sufficiently discharged if she kept an eye on her nephew from a distance, had him to tea in her back parlour occasionally, and generally helped in his education and upbringing. It would be better far if Miss Tidswell actually took charge of him. And thus it was arranged.

Edmund's earliest memories were of living with Miss Tidswell, and though he was told to call her "Aunt" Tid, he suspected that she was really his mother. It is true that on £3 per week she could not be lavishly generous in her treatment of him, but for all that she seemed passionately interested in his future and expected from him a filial devotion in return.

Charlotte was determined that Edmund should be given every chance in life and that he should grow up with the instincts and qualities of a gentleman. He would have, of course, to be an actor, for the stage was her only environment and would be his. She lived at 12 Tavistock Row, Covent Garden, within a few minutes' walk of Drury Lane, and she had no influence, no connections even, outside the theatre. But at least she would teach Edmund to be an aristocrat in his profession. She had marked him out for greatness and she would see that he became a great tragedian, like Garrick, and, unlike the ordinary run of vulgar, illiterate players, a cultured, polished, and scholarly man.

As soon as Edmund was old enough "Aunt" Tid sent him to school; and she also had him taught singing by Incledon and fencing by Angelo who, in their particular crafts, were both masters at Drury Lane. Charlotte herself, after ten years' experience, had learned enough of the tricks of her trade to be a good tutor, and so she gave Edmund his first groundings in the study of Shakespeare, encouraging him to feel as well as understand the lines he repeated after her and making him rehearse his speeches for hours on end in front of a mirror.

At the age of eight Edmund was already something of a prodigy and had appeared on the stage of Drury Lane in several small parts. But though an apt, receptive, and intelligent pupil, he was temperamentally a difficult child —in Charlotte's own words, "active, forward, prone to mischief, and neither to be led nor driven." He had little power of concentrating on things which bored him, and he did not scruple to shirk his school lessons just as often as he felt inclined. He was restless and independently minded, and at nights would sometimes escape from the bed where

"Aunt" Tid had left him to lead the wild life of a gutter-snipe in the streets round Covent Garden. He had, too, a considerable idea of his own importance and was rather vain and egocentric. When Miss Tidswell took him with her to Drury Lane he liked to go up to the Green Room because there, surrounded by a circle of sentimental old players, he would recite and declaim and be applauded and told what a clever little boy he was. But when he was actually engaged at rehearsals and was just one among a whole bunch of child actors he did not enjoy himself half so well. Far from worshipping at the shrine of John Philip Kemble, who was then manager as well as leading tragedian of the theatre, he deliberately set out to be cheeky and tiresome and insubordinate. On one occasion he was caught behind the scenes amusing the stage hands with a parody of the great actor's mannerisms. And Kemble, a man without much humour, was extremely irritated.

Charlotte tried her best to teach Edmund obedience and good behaviour. But she was an unsubtle disciplinarian. Though she beat him, locked him in his room, tied him to his bedpost, and—more ingenious—encircled his neck in a large dog collar which she had inscribed with his name and address, she could not persuade him to conform to a normal, routine existence. And then something happened which made all her efforts seem vain and futile. Ann Carey turned up to reclaim her son.

Perhaps Charlotte would have kept Edmund in defiance of his mother's wishes if he himself had really wanted to stay with her. But he was a wild, precocious child to whom the word home meant nothing and who resented the stick and all the other restrictions which "Aunt" Tid put upon his natural inclinations. Ann Carey, in a negative way, held out hopes of change and freedom and what he called adventure. These were the things for which he craved—and so gladly he went away with her, and heedlessly too.

He was eight or nine years old when he left "Aunt" Tid, to embark on a life in which there was no order, no security, and no permanence. In Ann Carey's charge he became the child vagabond and the street arab, owing loyalty to none but himself. How could he feel any affection for his mother? Obviously she only wanted him for the material assistance he could render her. She made him run messages and she exhibited his youthful histrionic talents for profit and she commandeered his earnings, but in return she gave him nothing except an occasional beating—no kindness, no praise, no disinterested instruction. And when it suited her she was quite prepared to leave him in the care of strangers. She seemed a strange, hard, unsympathetic woman.

Though Edmund was not brought up by Ann Carey, he shared her life and was thus the victim of circumstances which helped to develop his character and attainments. He learned what it was like to run around loose, to be lonely and hungry and cold. He went with cheap travelling companies to barns and stables and fair-grounds, and became expert in the lowest tricks of his trade—tumbling, clowning, riding a horse bareback. And, most important, by the time he was fifteen, he had learned, in his rough and ready way, how to fend for himself. Though his knowledge of the classics was woefully deficient, though he had probably never heard of Mr. Pitt and could not tell the difference between a Whig and a Tory, he had all the assurance and all the accomplishments necessary to face his own little world unaided—as a strolling player.

And yet Charlotte's influence on his early years—too soon cut off—had left its indelible mark. Now he regarded 12 Tavistock Row as home, and often he had returned there for brief intervals, not, it is true, in the spirit of the prodigal son—but because he realized that "Aunt" Tid was the only one in the world who really cared for him and on whose assistance he could count. She had given him a veneer of good breeding—easily dispersed—and certain instincts that were fundamental. He did not know why he longed so passionately for success or why he was so aggressively determined to be treated as a gentleman of consequence. And yet these yearnings, alien both to his fortune and environment, were irrepressible.

In the course of his haphazard childhood others besides himself had noticed that he was possessed of qualities and characteristics that were unusual in a Thespian gutter-snipe. Why else should Mrs. Clarke, for example, have taken him for a while to live with her?

She was a lady of means and position, rich enough to keep a butler and well connected enough to be blessed with at least a couple of titled relatives.

By disposition she was extremely benevolent; and because of this she became one of Ann Carey's few customers, paying double the proper price for Maréchale powder, Jessamine Pomatum, genuine Eau de Luce, and occasionally presenting the dilapidated hawker with some of her own cast-off fineries. She first set eyes on Edmund at a time when he was acting as his mother's errand boy. And she was attracted to him immediately. There was much, of course, about him to excite her pity. He was slender, pale, and small in stature—so small that he seemed not more than nine years old, though she came to the conclusion afterwards that he must have been eleven; one of his legs was in irons; his clothes were wretchedly shabby, and the hat, which he carried in his diminutive hand, was too tattered to be fit for outdoor wear. Altogether he seemed grubby, unkempt, half starved.

But pity unaided does not usually persuade rich ladies to bestow their patronage on street urchins. And Edmund appealed to other emotions besides in Mrs. Clarke's large maternal heart. He was, in spite of his poverty-stricken appearance, a strikingly beautiful child. His auburn hair was a rich mass of tangled curls; he had his father's handsome Jewish-looking features, and his dark eyes were even larger and more noticeably brilliant than his mother's.

He had, too, an air about him which astonished Mrs. Clarke; for it was, she thought, touchingly inappropriate to his age and environment. Admittedly his manners were a trifle theatrical (especially the way he bowed), but they were at least graceful and courteous. He knew how to behave in a lady's house. Moreover, he was already accomplished. He could act scenes from *Richard III*, *Hamlet*, *Macbeth*; and he could play the Clown and Harlequin into the bargain.

In short, Mrs. Clarke found him just the sort of child to be, for her, a first-class pet. And as much from this motive as from mere generosity, she persuaded Ann Carey to give him up and herself took charge of him.

Edmund was much beholden to Mrs. Clarke after he had become her protégé. She clothed him as a respectable little boy, sent him to school, and treated him occasionally to an evening at the Play, when the Kembles were performing. In addition, she placed the amenities of her well-kept house at his disposal. She gave him good food to eat and a comfortable bed in which to sleep. The bed particularly appealed to his fancy. He called it "his bed of roses," in honour of a floral design printed on the cotton curtains with which it was draped.

In return for such kindnesses Edmund entertained Mrs. Clarke and her friends with regular displays of his histrionic gifts—not that he found these exhibitions in the least arduous or embarrassing. On the contrary, nothing delighted him more than the chance to act alone in front of a grown-up audience. The excitements of transforming a section of Mrs. Clarke's drawing-room into King Richard III's tent, of fastening a belt, with a real sword attached to it, round his small waist, of dressing his head in a large feathered riding hat, and finally of performing scenes from his favourite play entirely by himself—all these were only excelled by gratification at the applause which greeted his efforts.

He might have continued to live indefinitely in these propitious circumstances, where his material wants, his spiritual needs, and his childish vanity were alike satisfied; for, as a result of his attractive personality and his exemplary behaviour, he built up quite a position for himself in the Clarke *ménage*. Mrs. Clarke fussed over him; and he was equally popular with her servants and her tradesmen. He even contrived not to get on the nerves of her husband, who was an active member of the Society for the Suppression of Vice.

But unfortunately Edmund's first lapse from grace was his last.

It happened that a country gentleman, his wife, and their two small daughters emerged from some rustic retreat in order to stay with Mrs. Clarke, who was an old friend. Edmund, as usual, was called upon to parade his talents before the guests. But the country gentleman, unlike Mrs. Clarke's other friends (who were presumably town bred and broad-minded), did not consider good behaviour and histrionic virtuosity atonement enough for social inferiority.

At any rate the country gentleman thought it quite wrong that Edmund should be included in the party which Mrs. Clarke had arranged, for the entertainment of her well-born visitors, to take to Drury Lane. And at dinner beforehand, while Edmund was amusing the two small daughters with animated details of the play they were about to see, the country gentleman spoke his mind.

"What!" he exclaimed, "does *he* go with us in the boxes?"

Mrs. Clarke had no occasion to answer. Her protégé rose from his place at the table and made for the door. His cheeks were flushed and his eyes, which could express any emotion, were eloquent of outraged dignity. Mrs. Clarke caught his hand as he passed and told him to get a seat in the pit. Like the hurt child that he was, he shook his head, left the room, and a few minutes later slammed out of the front door. Mrs. Clarke saw him from the window, hurrying down the street. But he did not go to the theatre that night. And for the next seven days he was missing.

He was eventually brought back to Mrs. Clarke by a friendly ostler, who reported that he had found the boy lying insensible on a neighbouring dunghill. Apparently

Edmund had taken the insult from "that unfeeling" country gentleman so much to heart that he had determined to go away for ever, and had begged his way to Portsmouth for the purpose of joining the Navy. But his offers to become a sailor had merely met with repulses, rude treatment, and beatings. So he had returned to London with the resolve to die, a martyr to his sensitiveness, as near Mrs. Clarke's home as possible.

Poor Mrs. Clarke! She forgave her erring young friend, tended him, and restored him to physical health. But obviously she could keep him in her care no longer. She did not attempt to understand how he could have repaid her manifold kindnesses so ill! The little urchin whom she had virtually rescued from the streets had really had no right to his outburst of human feeling. She would, if she had had the heart, have scolded him severely. After all, there was, to her way of thinking, little difference between his impulsive display of wounded pride and a sudden tendency on the part of a favourite dog to snap at strangers. Both instincts were equally alarming to have about the house. And so she parted with Edmund as she might have with any other dangerous pet—regretfully. Benevolent soul that she was, she did her best to find him a good new home. And it was not her fault that his early years were just as checkered after he left as they had been before he became her protégé.

Such was the boy Edmund Kean—a waif, a charmer, a prodigy, an individualist, a complex character quite incomprehensible to those who knew nothing of the conflicting influences which moulded it.

Now, at the age of fifteen, he looked back on his childhood as an old man does on crowded years that have gone before. And he could fit none of its incidents into a chronological form. He had been buffeted and caressed, ordered about and left to his own devices, praised and insulted, and in sum he had learned that the world was cruel and relentless and had to be fought back hard. He did not really know who his mother was. Other men gave definite accounts of their birth and parentage, and it was rather degrading that he could not do the same. He would have to build up his own out of fancy. If mothers were supposed to love their children, then Ann Carey could not possibly be his mother, whatever she said. Much more likely "Aunt" Tid, who seemed so fond of him. He had listened to the lewd, esoteric gossip round Covent Garden, and he had heard of "Aunt" Tid's affair with "Jockey." So perhaps he was really the son of a Duke and had been born at Arundel Castle and had spent the first years of his life there. He would like to think so.

Really Edmund's childhood was a record of wasted opportunity. He might have fared far better if he had had more regard for "Aunt" Tid's authority or had swallowed the insult from Mrs. Clarke's country gentleman friend. And there were others besides who interested themselves in him and from whom he broke away—a Mr. and Mrs. Duncan, for example. And yet at fifteen Edmund himself did not regret the past. After all, it was a great deal to have learned how to dance and sing and fence and throw somersaults. Besides, he had reaped the rewards of these accomplishments. Already he had seen himself billed as a wonder child and had listened to applause and had known that he had the power to sway an audience or to hold them spellbound. He had tasted what he liked best—the fruits of success.

Even Ann Carey had helped him in this respect—though admittedly to suit her own purposes. With her he went to Carmarthen and acted *Hamlet* before Lord Nelson and Lady Hamilton. With her, too, he went, as a member of Richardson's travelling company, to Windsor where the Eton boys asked permission of their headmaster to hear him recite and where his fame reached as far as the Castle, so that he gave a command performance before their Majesties and received from King George III, great patron of the drama, a couple of golden guineas. And in London also he performed under Ann Carey's auspices. For example, on March 17, 1801, a playbill announced: "The celebrated Theatrical Child, Edmund Carey, not eleven years old, will for one night only, for the benefit of his mother at the Great Room, No. 8, Store Street, Bedford Square, give his inimitable performances which have been received by the Nobility and Gentry, with uncommon approbation. Talents so rare in so juvenile a frame was scarcely seen before. Part I. To open with an Address, Pizarro, and Blue Beard. Part II. King Richard III, etc." In May of the following year—still greater triumph—he recited Rollas' address to the sun at Covent Garden.

His mother took his money. But eventually he became exasperated by her predatory habits and ran away from her, cut adrift. He had grown wise enough to realize that what he could earn for Miss Carey, he could earn for himself. And he proceeded to do so, still as the wonder child, by reciting and performing acrobatics in assembly halls, public houses, anywhere where they would pay a few pence to see and hear him.

"Aunt" Tid, who had trained him to be a tragedian, hated these scapegrace displays which delighted the vulgarians; and a little later in his career Edmund would come round to her way of thinking. But at the time he did not consider that any show which brought him money and—better still—prominence was beneath his dignity. Applause from the lowest kind of audience was gratifying enough to satisfy his youthful vanity. That was what he really loved—applause. Money served to buy food and clothes—but for nothing else. Money was the means to maintain life, whereas success and recognition were life itself.

And now at the age of fifteen and looking older than his years, he could call himself an infant prodigy no longer. It was time he started on the real business of his career, time he set out to achieve his ambition, which was as simple as it was consuming. He wanted to be *great*. And he would pursue greatness in the theatre because to him the stage was quite literally the world.

So, like almost every actor who had ever become a star of Covent Garden or Drury Lane, Edmund began to serve his apprenticeship as a poor and unknown strolling player in the country. "Aunt" Tid would still be there, at 12 Tavistock Row, watching over him from a distance, ready to use what little pull she had with provincial managers, and ready to lend him a few shillings when he really needed them. But otherwise he would be quite alone.

He had practically no influence behind him, no background, and no advantages either of education or of upbringing. And yet in a way he had been spoiled. For those small successes as a child wonder gave him a false confidence in the future. They made the long, cruel years of disappointment which followed even harder to bear.

CHAPTER II

I

IT is a soft, pampered, respectable life in the theatre nowadays. Success comes easily to the lucky ones without any tears and with precious little work. Something as simple as a gold medal award at the Royal Academy of Dramatic Art or a short sojourn with one of the so-called repertory companies or an outstanding performance in a try-out show may quite well lead direct to a West End engagement. And even those who are not stars live comfortably enough with the films and radio and commercial broadcasting, and so on. It does not matter much that the provincial drama is as dead as a door-nail. There are plenty of other sidelines.

But when Edmund Kean set out to make his name, the provincial drama was very much alive. It was kept alive by strolling players with bleeding feet and aching bellies, who looked towards London as their Mecca. Some acted in the large, well-equipped Theatres Royal, others in the play-houses of the smaller towns, others still in barns and stables where often grass had grown up through derelict floorboards and where the air was always rank with the smell of burnt oil. The plight of provincial players varied according to their status. But in the social scale they were one and all incorrigible rogues and they worked like navvies for managers who never rewarded them with more than a living wage and who quite frequently paid them less.

The country was the only school of dramatic art. It was a harsh, merciless school, and yet no one who sought fame and fortune on the stage could avoid it. True, David Garrick had gone straight to the top. But Garrick, the diplomatist, the scholar, the shrewd financier, the man of means and good breeding, was quite exceptional. Now that he had gone, the Kembles—John, Philip, and his famous sister,

Sarah Siddons—ruled in his place. But they had not come
into their estate without first serving a long apprenticeship
in the provinces. And as for George Frederick Cooke, the
latest idol of the Town and Kemble's most dangerous rival,
he had been twenty years a stroller before fate had given
him the chance to capture a Covent Garden audience with
his bold, original acting in *King Richard III*.

Cooke's story was, perhaps, an extraordinary example of
patience and endurance. And one cannot be surprised at
the sequel which was so tragic. After twenty years of
struggling in the provinces, Cooke had unfortunately earned
the right to debauch his success and to drink himself into
an early grave. Yet he followed the only possible path to
greatness. It was professional suicide for an ambitious actor
to accept a London engagement unless it carried with it
the promise of a leading part. For stars were born overnight
or not at all. Miss Tidswell was humble, and others like
her might be content to go on year after year as obscure
members of the Drury Lane or Covent Garden company,
earning £3 per week, perhaps a little less. But they would
never advance unless they chose to abandon their security,
and they would retire eventually into oblivion.

Mrs. Siddons had first come to Drury Lane back in 1776,
when Garrick was still alive. But then she had failed to
impress the critics of London who had judged her acting
to be more effete than divine. So rather than court obscurity
by accepting small, insignificant parts, she had returned to
the country and there she had waited seven years for a
second chance to triumph in the metropolis.

The theatre of the early nineteenth century offered prizes
in wealth as well as in prestige, but these were given only
to the great. An actor could always justify his choice of
career by succeeding, even though it was prima facie folly
and wickedness to go on the stage. For in London the
Theatres Royal Covent Garden and Drury Lane were
patronized by highly intelligent audiences, who had a
knowledge of and an enthusiasm for the histrionic art which

to-day is quite unparalleled. The successful actor's standing was much akin to that of the modern boxing champion. He earned, in various ways, a great deal of money, he was news in the Press, he was a hero in his own class, and he was taken up and gaped at by the best people. If, like poor Cooke, he showed himself rampant with all the sins expected of him, he still commanded the attention of educated Englishmen whenever he appeared on the stage, even though he might occasionally be booed and made to apologize for his more obvious lapses from grace. If, like the majority, he proved himself in private life clean, moderately sober, and well behaved, the public were agreeably surprised. And if, like Garrick and the Kembles, he had exceptional social qualities, then, though he would never be admitted wholeheartedly to the ranks of the gentry, he could nevertheless rise to a position of dignity and respect in a society which was rigidly aristocratic.

But every stage player, no matter his social standing, was encouraged to consider himself a person of some consequence in the world; and he had the right to feel that he had earned over and over again whatever favours were now bestowed on him. Comfortably he could look back on his strolling player days as on a penance which he had been compelled to serve in order that he might enjoy his present prosperity.

In the provinces they starved and suffered and hoped. But a few of them at least learned how to be great actors of a kind which we shall probably never know again. Even Edmund Kean came to recognize this towards the end of his life. In 1832 he gave evidence before a select committee appointed by the House of Commons to investigate the chaotic state of the theatre, and he urged that committee, in a brandy-soaked voice, to keep the *status quo*. It was curious advice from a man who had more reason than most to remember his experiences as a country actor with bitterness. Those experiences had shattered his health, had robbed him of his youth, had damaged his character irremediably, and had helped to shape him as he then was—a mental and physical wreck. Yet he spoke from his heart, for there was nothing complacent about Kean. It was a part of his tragedy that even in the luxury of the present he could not forget the hardships of the past and was thus continually afraid of the future. At that moment he must have realized what was true—that he had sacrificed his well-being for a brief period of unimaginable greatness on the stage. "Keep the *status quo*," he said. "In London we should see not the School but the perfection of the Art itself "

The *status quo* was just as it had been twenty-five years earlier when he first became its victim. It hit every young actor pretty hard. During the winter months the Patent Houses—Drury Lane and Covent Garden—had a monopoly of presenting legitimate drama. When they closed for the summer vacation the Haymarket opened in their place by licence of the Lord Chamberlain. But plays were performed nowhere else in the metropolis. There were other theatres —minor theatres as they were called—such as Sadler's Wells, the Surrey, the Pantheon, and the Olympic, but they were restricted to exhibiting pantomimes, ballets, equestrian shows, burlettas, etc., and thus they offered no scope for a straight actor to display his talents. Audiences might crowd to Sadler's Wells to applaud a famous clown like Grimaldi but they never went there to see a player of the Kemble or even of the Munden class. Indeed, if through the pressing needs of the stomach a straight actor accepted an engagement at one of the minor theatres, he virtually put an end to his career. For the Patent Houses, jealous of their rights, regarded the minor theatres as potential pirates and automatically blacklisted those who played there.

So it came to this. All the honours which could be won in legitimate drama were given to the few who shared between them the leading parts in tragedy or comedy, at Covent Garden, Drury Lane, and the Haymarket. The rest of the theatrical profession had either to be resignedly humble or hopefully poor. It was a rigid system which certainly ensured that London saw only the perfection of the histrionic art. It was also a cruel system which probably caused much good talent to be wasted and burnt out.

Edmund Kean was nine years at school—a strolling player in the provinces. And he suffered agonies—of mind at least—which in the history of the stage have hardly a parallel. Yet those years not only perfected his art but created and developed it.

2

But his was by no means an isolated case of relentless ill-fortune. Though his health was partially ruined by strain and malnutrition while he served the drama in the provinces physical privations—of a kind almost inconceivable to-day —were the common lot of strolling players. There was nothing out of the ordinary about the actual hardships which Edmund endured. The bare facts of his struggle for recognition could be told, with few variations, of almost any of his famous contemporaries—with the exceptions of Young and Macready. In fact, though Edmund fared worse than some, he fared better than a great many other members of his cruelly precarious profession. During the nine years that he was a stroller he advanced steadily from strength to strength. He began somewhere about 1804 in a common-wealth which was the lowest form of theatrical enterprise. (Strange that to-day it is frequently being revived as a brand new notion!) According to the terms of his engage-ment in the commonwealth, Edmund was entitled to a share of the weekly receipts after the manager had paid himself a salary and also the outgoings—rent, rushlight, scenery, and costumes. Quite often Edmund's share amounted to precisely nothing and very seldom to more than three shillings. So that in order to survive at all he had to beg, borrow, or steal. Nine years later, in 1813, he was leading actor at the Dorchester Theatre—with a fixed salary of two guineas per week—and from there he went direct to London to become at the age of twenty-five the star tragedian of Drury Lane. Comparatively speaking, that was by no means bad going. Consider, in contrast, the fate of Ann Carey, who spent nearly her whole life in commonwealths and the like of them.

But Edmund's miseries were caused as much by his own actions as by circumstances which he could not control. He encountered experiences which were not in themselves abnormally harsh, but which hurt him particularly because of his individual reaction to them. He suffered so acutely that it is easy to lose all sense of proportion in describing his strolling player days and to forget (as he did) that there were others whose lot was infinitely worse than his own and very few whose lot was much better. He should be pitied, certainly. But more for what he was than for what happened to him. Largely he shaped his own tragedy.

In many ways he was well equipped to be a strolling player. He had been brought up to the life and had drifted into it inevitably. There was nothing pampered about him, and he was not in the least scared of poverty and the things which poverty meant, for he had never been well off. He had, too, the kind of qualities which provincial managers —always hard put to it to make ends meet—welcomed in a young man. He was competent, versatile, hard working, and energetic. From the outset he had no difficulty in finding jobs and in keeping them for as long as he wished.

But he had none of the right virtues of temperament. A stroller needed to be either very tough or very philosophic, whereas Edmund was proud, sensitive, and extravagantly impatient. He was easily cast down and wounded in his feelings. He was lonely and humourless and had no interests apart from his knawing ambition. He had precious little capacity to enjoy life even at the best of times.

It is sadly revealing, in the light of after events, that he did not hate the stroller's life from the beginning. He saw no reason to fear the future when on Easter Monday of 1804 he joined Mr. Samuel Jerrold's company at Sheerness.

There then was still much of the prodigy about him. He was dressed in boy's costume and, though only fifteen, he was engaged to play leading parts. He opened as George Barnwell, and thereafter he continued "to play the whole round of tragedy, comedy, opera, farce, interlude, and pantomime."

He did all this for a salary of fifteen shillings per week, and no doubt a modern actor would quail at the very thought of it. But audiences in Edmund's time were not as easily satiated as they are to-day. They took their seats at 6.30 p.m. and expected, in one evening, to see at least three full-length pieces presented—for example, an opera, a tragedy, and a farce, with perhaps an occasional song or hornpipe thrown in to complete the bill. The London Patent Houses, it is true, retained the services of leading performers who were exclusively tragedians, comedians, or singers. But provincial managers could not afford to maintain so large a company, and consequently one stroller had to play many parts. It was not at all unusual for Edmund to do a quick change from Hamlet into Harlequin.

Samuel Jerrold, ancestor of so many Jerrolds distinguished in literature and on the stage, was by no means in the first flight of country managers. But his Sheerness theatre, fitted up as it was with boxes, pit, and gallery, was better equipped than the exalted barns and stables which served the drama in most of the small towns of the United Kingdom. And though it was surreptitiously used by smugglers for the secretion of casks of hollands, it was also well patronized by playgoers. The Napoleonic war was having a good effect on theatrical business in Sheerness. The town was full of sailors, and nautical drama was particularly popular.

Edmund, at any rate, was perfectly content. He did not mind hard work, for he liked to show off his versatility. And as for the salary of fifteen shillings—it was enough to live on and was handsome compared with that which could be earned in a commonwealth. Money was a trifling con-

sideration. Prestige was all that mattered. And now he was
the star attraction, playing nice fat parts before audiences
who applauded him generously. Indeed, he was making
quite a name for himself, "among the tasteful critics of
Sheerness," with his rendering of a comic song called
"Unfortunate Miss Bailey." He knew, of course, that the
London Patent Houses did not recruit new talent from
Samuel Jerrold's companies. But he was young enough and
vain enough to believe that his self-imposed task of con-
quering the world would not be a very long one or arduous
one. And he thought that if he could be a favourite in
Sheerness, he could be a favourite anywhere else in the
United Kingdom. For the moment he asked no more of
life.

He did not begin to find out his mistake until the following
year when he joined a company of players in Belfast. The
Belfast theatre was a Theatre Royal and was directed by
Michael Atkins, one of the best-known and most influential
of provincial managers. Edmund might well have been
proud to think that, still in his 'teens, he had got a job with
Michael Atkins, and he might have come to the right
conclusion that he had travelled a long way since his
Sheerness engagement only twelve months ago. Belfast,
after all, was very prominently on the theatrical map. The
stars from London came to play there (for an appropriate
fee) when the Patent Houses were closed down for the
summer vacation. And it was an honour for a young man
of very light experience to act with the great ones and to
watch them at work. For him it was an honour even to be
attached to a Theatre Royal.

But Edmund could not regard his present state in that
philosophic light. Now the realization of his ambition seemed
infinitely further away than it had seemed at Sheerness. He
was no longer the petted prodigy, with the pick of the best
roles in tragedy, comedy, interlude, and pantomime. He
was just a very junior member of a company of players in
Belfast, unnoticed by the manager and "scarcely permitted

to deliver a message." He was a supernumerary ordered to play whatever walk-on parts happened to be going and shoved on to the stage dressed in any old, faded costume that might be left over from the theatre wardrobe. For him there was no glory and no applause. He was simply a poor strolling player of whose existence the public were scarcely aware.

He hated being insignificant. It hurt his pride unreasonably, and it appeared to him that everyone was set on humiliating him. He became gloomy, silent, morose, and introspective. He roamed about by himself, day-dreaming, wondering how he could make men realize that he was destined for greatness. But it was an impossible task to impress now that he was denied the opportunity of lauding it on the stage. He was a young man without much wit or intellect, and superficially he was very unattractive. He had no personal charm, no natural conviviality or *bonhomie*. Through shyness he avoided his fellow actors, and naturally they did not go out of their way to bother about him. So that with reason he imagined himself despised and deliberately ignored. Sometimes he went to the tavern, for he found that drink loosened his tongue and enabled him to be more self-assertive. But mostly he was alone with his thoughts and his feelings.

He tried to blind himself to his insignificance. In August (1805) Mrs. Siddons, specially engaged by Michael Atkins, came to play a few nights at the Belfast Theatre. Years later Edmund told the completely fictitious story that the great actress opened in *The Mourning Bride* and that he was chosen to act the leading part of Osmyn to her Zara; that unfortunately he was drunk when he appeared on the stage and that consequently he disgraced himself and ruined the effect of Mrs. Siddons' performance; that on the next evening Mrs. Siddons was horrified to learn that once more he was to play opposite her—as Norval this time to her Lady Randolph in *Douglas*; that at first she refused to act again "with that dreadful little man," but that she was eventually persuaded to give him another chance; that she did not regret her leniency because on this second occasion he acted so brilliantly that he was almost as successful with the audience as she; and that Mrs. Siddons, generous in her praise of him, murmured at the end, "You have played very well, Sir, very well. It's a pity—but there's too little of you to do anything!"

That story, though a complete fabrication, is infinitely pathetic. No doubt Edmund had convinced himself of its truth long before anyone was interested to hear him tell it. For one can imagine him so easily—an awkward, shy, diminutive figure—standing by the wings enviously watching Mrs. Siddons' performance, thinking that it was really his right to be the hero to her heroine, imagining how he would outshine her and how he would leap at once into prominence. And so he elaborated the day-dream until it became in his mind a reality. Most young actors, whatever the extent of their own fame in after years, would have remembered how magnificent Mrs. Siddons was, how devotedly they had worshipped her, how timid they had been in her presence. Not so Edmund; he was always the hero of his own adventures, true or imaginary.

Actually Edmund did attract Mrs. Siddons' attention, and though he would never have admitted it, he set out deliberately to do so. Mrs. Siddons, as was the right of the great, commanded the Belfast company to her lodgings to run through a play before the evening performance. Most of the actors gabbled through their parts in an expressionless undertone, as they do now at a word rehearsal. But Edmund, determined to be conspicuous, spoke his few lines with all the power at his command. When he had done, Mrs. Siddons complimented him: "Very well, Sir, very well. I have never heard that part given in that way before."

Mrs. Siddons was not the only one whom Edmund went out of his way to impress. Leading roles were denied him —unfairly as he thought. But at all cost he had to shine and so he determined to make small parts stand out beyond their real importance. He still had so much confidence in his own powers that he thought the public would single him out for applause even though he had only a few lines to speak. Not at Belfast, of course, where they were dull and coarse and provincial; but in London, where they were intelligent and discerning, where as a child they had sung his praises. It was very important that he should get to London as soon as possible. Until then he would continue to suffer the ignominy of being ignored.

After another year of wandering in the country he had his way. In the summer of 1806 he came, at Miss Tidswell's recommendation, to the Haymarket Theatre. He was engaged only as a junior member of the company and he played such parts as a Servant, a Clown, a Goatherd, an Alguazil, Rosencrantz in *Hamlet* and Carney in *Ways and Means*. But naturally he did not make the slightest impression in any of these. What could he possibly do with such poor material? It had simply been one of the arrogant illusions of his youth that he could rise up suddenly from the ranks of the supernumeraries. He used to complain afterwards that once at rehearsal when he was trying to speak his few lines as well as possible the actors regarded him contemptuously and one of them sneered, "Look at the little man, he's trying to make a part of Carney." That wounded his sensitive pride. But it probably hurt him more to realize that even in London audiences were not nearly as generous as Mrs. Siddons had been. To them a small-part actor was just a small-part actor, and it was waste of his time to attempt to be anything else. If he looked ridiculous or spoke absurdly, then they would laugh at him, and if he forgot his lines or reeled on to the stage intoxicated, they would hiss him. But otherwise they would treat him as if he did not exist. They came to see the leading performer, and on him they would bestow all their praise or censure. It was the duty of the small-part actors to play up to their star, to keep well out of his way, and in no circumstances to intrude themselves.

Edmund loathed being subordinate, and he found it
particularly galling that at the Haymarket he had to kow-
tow to Alexander Rae, who was entrusted with many of the
"leads" in tragedy. Rae was a young man—only a few years
older than Edmund—and he had had a comparatively quick
rise to fame. A little while ago Mrs. Siddons had played
with him at Liverpool and she had thought him very
promising. Now he was firmly established as a London
actor, and though he was not remarkably talented and
would never be considered really great, he would remain
until his death moderately successful and well known.

Edmund had a special reason to resent Rae. He had
known him in his childhood days. Rae's mother, who was
matron of St. George's Hospital, had been friends with
Aunt Price, and the two boys had often met in Aunt Price's
back parlour. There as playmates they had acted scenes
from Shakespeare's plays together and Edmund had far
outshone his friend. Rae, in fact, had regarded Edmund
almost as a maestro and had been content to listen to his
instructions attentively and to abide by them.

But now that their positions were so completely reversed,
Edmund was morbidly suspicious of Rae and thought that
he was treated by him with scant courtesy—coldly and
condescendingly. No doubt Rae, with the weakness of
human nature, was a little too conscious of his new superiority in the theatre and so adopted towards Edmund
the pompous and cultivated manner of a leading actor.

But Edmund was hypersensitive and apt to imagine
affronts which were never really intended. One day at
rehearsal he failed after several attempts to speak a line as
Rae wanted it spoken. At last Rae remarked in desperation,
"Very well, Sir, we'll try it to-night," and then turned on
his heel. A normal young man would have accepted this
as a mild rebuke and would have determined to do better
next time. But Edmund regarded it as an unpardonable
insult which it was impossible for him to forgive or forget.
He would have liked to have answered Rae back—crush-

ingly, flamboyantly—as Cooke had once replied to a complaint of Kemble. Cooke's retort had been: "I won't have your faults fathered on me, and, hark ye, Black Jack, hang me if I don't make you tremble in your shoes one day yet." But Edmund, however passionately he felt, had no powers of repartee—fierce, cutting, or flippant. That was why he was always on the defensive and why he brooded so wretchedly. He could only make "a peculiar motion of his lips, as if he was chewing or swallowing"—and say nothing.

His tempestuous emotions choked him, but he had no way of expressing them. He was gauche and sullen and painfully shy. Already at the age of seventeen he had lost any of the gaiety of youth which he may at one time have possessed. And he was beginning to be oppressed by a sense of his disadvantages, his lack of education and breeding and poise. He hardly dared to speak for fear of making a fool of himself. In the Green Room he sat silently apart from his fellow actors. Even at rehearsals he was embarrassed, believing that all eyes were fixed on him disparagingly; and he could not show himself off to advantage. He was very lonely, for there was no one in the world in whom he could confide his thoughts, except of course "Aunt" Tid and Aunt Price, and they were of another generation.

Only at the tavern could he recapture a little of what to him was the glamour of his childhood. He did not go to Finche's, which was patronized by the smart London actors and was the social centre of the stage—almost as exclusively Thespian as a certain West End restaurant is to-day. Edmund would have been abashed in the presence of his superiors. He preferred the Harp or the Antelope, where circus men, country managers, unemployed strolling players, and the riff-raff of the profession met together. In such gatherings Edmund felt more at his ease. They drank far into the night and the players sought jobs from the managers and the managers drove hard bargains. At intervals some tipsy actor got up to recite or to sing a comic song or to give imitations. After a glass or two Edmund could conquer all his reserve and become as aggressive and overbearing as his yearnings urged him to be. Except by bombast, how was he to show that he was really great? And would one day, in spite of his present inferiority, be acclaimed? Meanwhile London, where he had been humiliated, was not for him. He must find another job in the provinces—anywhere where they would allow him to play parts worthy of his merit. Perhaps it was either at the Harp or the Antelope that he arranged to become a member of Mrs. Baker's company in Kent.

3

Edmund arrived at Tunbridge Wells to fulfil his new engagement some time in September of 1806, and he opened as Lord Hastings in *Jane Shore*. He was lucky to have got a job with Mrs. Baker, for she was a woman of rare if peculiar qualities. She was neither a wit nor a scholar, nor even an actress. She lacked completely taste and artistic feeling. She had no real love of the drama for its own sake. And she did not care how tatty her shows looked provided they made money.

But like other robust, uneducated women who have, at odd times in the history of the stage, bludgeoned their way into theatrical management, Mrs. Baker had a very capable head for business. Gradually she had built up her Kent circuit into being one of the most extensive of its kind in England. Now she controlled a whole series of playhouses ranging from a converted public-house at Sandwich to a "great, grand theatre" at Canterbury. She saw personally to all the financial arrangements of her concern, acting at one and the same time as her own box-office keeper, accountant, cashier, and banker. In these various capacities she kept a tight hold on outgoings and grasped eagerly at incomings. *Ars gratia pecuniae* was her motto. And Mrs. Baker was, therefore, a rarity in her profession. She was a rich woman.

Under her management there was a certain spice and variety to be got out of life. Her employees visited town after town, where they could generally rely on playing before large and enthusiastic audiences. That was not the usual experience of strolling players. More often they went the dreary round of bedraggled theatres which were poorly patronized; they pranced and leaped and shouted themselves hoarse for the entertainment of a few bored and ribald yokels who lolled about on the half-empty benches; and at the end of the week they could never be certain that their harassed manager would have enough money to pay them their salaries.

Mrs. Baker's business acumen was certainly a great asset. But she had one crowning virtue. In spite of her official rapacity and aesthetic barbarism, she was extremely kind-hearted. Strollers were apt to arrive at a new town without a penny in their pockets, and it was not a pleasant experience to have to go through an arduous evening's bill on an empty stomach and afterwards be faced with the disagreeable task of finding lodgings. But Mrs. Baker, unlike the majority of provincial managers, was at pains to look after the members of her company. She never allowed them to go hungry or homeless, or to suffer rebuffs from landlords who objected on principle to strolling players. She was always ready to lend them a few shillings (in advance of salary) and quite frequently entertained them to meals at her own very well-stocked table. All in all, she treated her actors as members of her family. And that was not really surprising since quite a number of them actually were.

Even Edmund had to admit that there was a great deal to be said for being with Mrs. Baker, and in fact he remained under her management for more than a year. He would have liked to have stayed even longer, but unfortunately he came up against the ill will of Mrs. Baker's stage director, whose name was Long and who was personally distinguished by being very tall and by having ten fingers and no thumbs. According to Edmund, Mr. Long had "an unaccountable objection to small men," and for that reason kept him deliberately in the background. "He frequently gave those characters which undoubtedly were mine to fellows who certainly would have adorned the handles of a plough but were never intended for the stage . . ." Edmund said afterwards. It was the same old story over again. He would not play inferior parts. Comfort and security were, in his view, as nothing compared with the satisfaction of his pride. He would rather starve to death as Hamlet then grow fat as Rosencrantz. And so he left Mrs. Baker's company in a resentful spirit, convinced that he had been the victim of Mr. Long's malice.

Yet, in his heart, he knew quite well that Long was not alone in thinking a small man unsuited to play the heroes of tragedy. It was the view generally held by managers and critics and the public. John Philip Kemble was the model, and Kemble was tall and handsome and statuesque. Edmund realized that it would be impossible for him ever to follow in Kemble's footsteps. He was only five feet four inches in height, his figure was not impressive, and his features, though striking (especially his eyes), were far from classical. If he were to succeed he would have to popularize a new style of acting of his own, just as Garrick had done. But unlike Garrick he would have meanwhile to contend with ridicule and ignorance and stupidity.

From Mrs. Baker's company Edmund went back again to Sheerness. It was a retrograde step, of course. But at least he was given "leads" to his heart's content and his salary was increased to a guinea a week, a rise of five shillings. One night, when he was appearing as Alexander the Great, a rather truculent officer kept shouting at him from a stage box, "Alexander the Little." Suddenly Edmund interrupted his performance, folded his arms and walked up to the box where the officer was sitting. Then "with a vehemence of sarcasm and a glaring look that appalled the interloper," he rejoined, "Yes—with *a great soul*." Off the stage, of course, he would have been speechless. But in the presence of the public he was always without fear. And though his answer was in itself a trifle bombastic, he had given that audience a foretaste of what his acting would be one day. At least he had shown them the psychology behind it.

He remained at Sheerness on this occasion until the beginning of 1808. Besides being the star performer, he made himself additionally helpful to the management by turning stage carpenter. Out of "matches, pins, and paper" he constructed "the models of the tricks" which were used in the pantomime of *Mother Goose*.

Eventually he left the company, not from choice but "in consequence of some misunderstanding with one of the townspeople." Though the details of this dispute are not really known, a gossipy account suggests that Edmund aroused the conjugal jealousy of a local baker. At all events his enemy set a pressgang on his trail and he was forced to make an adventurous getaway "on board the Chatham Boat."

In that spirited, vagabond fashion the second period of his life came to an end. From Sheerness he went to Gloucester. And there he met the woman who was to be his wife.

4

Mary Chambers and her sister Susan were already members of the Gloucester company when Edmund joined it in March of 1808.

They had not been actresses for very long and were still regarded as amateurs, though Mary was given leading parts to play. Neither of them was talented, and it is strange that they ever ventured on the stage. For they belonged to a respectable bourgeois family in Waterford (Ireland), and they must have been brought up to believe that the theatrical profession was next door to perdition.

depths of feeling. In adversity she was not even loyal. She was just dull and woeful.

Edmund would discover all about Mary—in time. But was she also blind when she first determined to win him? Certainly she was fascinated by his earnest enthusiasm. It did not matter to her that he was nine years her junior, for he looked older than his age and mentally, too, he was prematurely developed. Besides, he seemed so sure of himself, so convinced of his own powers. Though she had no critical faculty, she really did believe that he was talented. He would, she thought, assuredly get on in his profession, and be able to give her the things that she wanted—wealth and position. She decided she would never be happy unless she were married to him.

And yet did she not understand what sort of man he was? Did she really suppose that he would win success easily and that without any further effort from her he would remain as buoyant as he was now in the ardour of his young, imagined love? If so, she must have been very stupid and very unintuitive. Even during the four months of their courtship she had at least one warning of the difficulties of his temperament.

It happened at Stroud whither the company had moved from Gloucester. In Gloucester business had been bad enough. Indeed, at a certain performance given for the benefit of Kean and Jack Hughes (who was to be a life-long friend of Edmund), receipts had amounted to the handsome total of 1s. 6d. But at Stroud the average nightly returns were more consistently disastrous, and so the manager decided to import a star attraction for two nights. He chose Master Betty.

Master Betty, the histrionic freak of the early nineteenth century, was now nearing the end of his sensational career as an infant prodigy. In London he was no longer the craze of fashion and could not command the success of four years ago—when the House of Commons had come in a body to see him play and at Covent Garden and Drury Lane all financial records had been broken on the occasion of his first performances. But, at the age of seventeen, he could still excite enough wonderment in the provinces to draw the crowds; and, despite his advancing years, could safely rely on his lasting reputation as a child genius.

In Stroud, Master Betty chose to appear as Hamlet and as Norval in *Douglas*. Edmund, who up to then had been the company's leading actor, was asked on these two special nights to take second place and play as Laertes and Glenalvon.

He did not refuse ostentatiously. He did not shout and scream and swear he would do no such a thing. Indeed, though he may once again "have made a peculiar motion of his lips as if he was chewing or swallowing," he did not demur at all. And accordingly his name was printed on the bills.

But he nursed an unbearable grievance. Why should he, who was a genius, be put in the shade by an infant prodigy whose success was due to luck and not to merit? Betty had gone straight to the top, while he had worked and starved and learned his trade. But Betty could not act, whatever the silly audiences, hypnotized by a name, might think. He would not, no, he would not suffer the degradation of being subordinate to this young impostor.

His feelings were those of a sensitive child who has been "insulted" by a grown-up. And his consequent actions were equally immature. He ran away and hid himself in the wilds. There he remained sleeping on the hard ground and feeding himself on cabbages and turnips, until, after two nights, he knew that Master Betty had left Stroud.

He went straight to Mary's lodgings on his return and told her that in spite of the physical sufferings he had endured he would go away again "as often as he saw himself in such characters." "Damme," he said, "I won't play second to any man living except John Philip Kemble."

Mary neither understood the cause of his upset nor sympathized with his behaviour. But she had believed him gone for ever; and she was now so glad to see her Edmund again that she humoured him and allowed him to remain convinced that she really was his champion in everything he did and felt.

Perhaps, she thought, in her simple way, that as soon as he was married he would place his responsibilities as a husband before the satisfaction of his "stupid" pride. But she was wrong. And she had neglected an opportunity to realize her mistake.

In July 1808, Edmund Kean and Mary and Susan Chambers were acting in a company at Cheltenham. The theatre there belonged to the same circuit as those at Gloucester and Stroud and was controlled by an Irishman named John Watson. Watson was an important provincial manager of more than thirty years' experience and also included in his circuit playhouses at Brecon, Hereford, Cirencester, Warwick, Lichfield and Coventry. He was personally distinguished for his hearty anecdotal humour and for the fact that in days gone by he had been a stroller with the great Kemble.

But whatever regard Watson may have had for Edmund Kean's ability, he only rewarded him with a guinea per week; and from such a salary the most prudent of men could not have saved much. It speaks volumes for the financial stability of Kean's marriage that, in order to pay the fees of the ceremony, he was obliged to borrow half a guinea from Miss Thornton, who was the daughter of Watson's box-office keeper.

That loan enabled him to do the thing in style—just as he wanted to do it. On July 17, 1808, Mary Chambers and Edmund Kean alighted from a postchaise at the parish church of Stroud and were there, in the presence of a Mr. White, a Mr. Howell, and Susan Chambers, joined in holy matrimony. The party returned to Cheltenham for a wedding breakfast provided out of the bounty of Miss Hyett, proprietress of the Dog Tavern.

Thus an unhappy marriage began. They lived together

for years in disharmony and no one cared. But when at last they parted company, it happened that the eyes of a hostile world were fixed on Edmund, so that he was blamed exclusively for the failure of their marriage and was thought to have cruelly victimized his wife. It was not a fair verdict. It was based on contemporary prejudice and misunderstanding. But strangely enough it has never since been challenged, and I must pause here, for a moment, to explain the reasons why.

In the first place, Edmund's side of the story has never been adequately advanced. He was himself, in spite of his gutter-snipe mentality, extremely reticent about his private affairs. Until the end, when he was goaded beyond all bearing, he remained, in his own fashion, steadfastly loyal to his "little Mary." In 1810, for example, he wrote in a letter to a friend: "To give you a description of Mrs. Kean as she ever has and still continues to appear in my eyes is impossible. . . . I soon led her to the altar, by which she made me the happiest of men." Even then those fair words, convincing as they appear, were far from the truth. Yet Edmund, however bitter his real feelings, was infinitely too proud to bleat about them to the world in general.

Mary, on the other hand, had no such fine scruples. She was guided only by her prodigious capacity for self-pity. She could not resist deluging the world with accounts of her wretchedness. She expressed herself typically in a series of letters written to her sister Susan and her great friend Margaret Roberts during the days when Edmund was still a stroller. Some of these have been preserved and we shall happen on them in due course. But a fair extract from one may be quoted now. It is found in a letter addressed to Margaret Roberts on September 5, 1813, a few months before Kean's triumph at Drury Lane. "My first step to misery was going on the Stage. My character I preserved pure and unsullied. I then married my husband—possessed of every talent requisite for his profession, educated to give grace to that talent, and could he have endured patiently a little longer, fortune might have rewarded his very great abilities. To forget sorrow he first took to drinking. Every dissipation followed, of course. His nights were spent with a set of wretches—a disgrace to human nature. One step led to another, till inevitable ruin was the end." A deluge indeed! And, incidentally, it shows how firm was her faith in Edmund. She called him damned, when his fame and success lay all out in front of him.

In the second place, Mary outlived her husband by sixteen years and during that time she had the field entirely to herself. There is no doubt that she supplied Barry Cornwall, who wrote the first full-length biography of Kean, with a good deal of his material. I have seen one of her several letters to Cornwall, and almost everything in it is detrimental to Edmund's memory—parts, indeed, are so prejudiced that Cornwall clearly decided not to use them. Nevertheless, he did incorporate in his book a great number of the stories of which she informed him and these have been repeated, with slight variations, by later biographers. It is likely that they are substantially true, for Mary had not the wit to invent. But up to now they have been told only from her point of view, which is exactly as she intended.

All this is meant to suggest, not that Mary was the culprit, but that she was the recriminator. It would be no fairer to put the exclusive blame on her than on him. But up to now she has always been pitied as a sweet-natured, adoring, and ill-treated wife, while he has been denounced as a callous, inconsiderate, and impossible husband. That is a facile, distorted estimate of the case.

From the beginning they never stood a chance of getting on together, for only a very deep affection and understanding could have justified their marriage. Materially speaking, there was nothing to be said in favour of it. Edmund was not yet twenty, and he had tied himself to a woman nine years his senior, who was blessed with not a penny of private means and had very little earning capacity. More than this, he had alienated the one person to whom he had been able to turn in moments of real distress. "Aunt" Tid disapproved of his marriage. Perhaps, with all her possessiveness, she would have been prejudiced against any woman whom her nephew had chosen to wed. But she had more solid reasons than mere jealousy for hating Mary. And she hated her relentlessly.

Though she never ceased to love Edmund and never lost her interest in him, she would not lift a finger to help him in his capacity as a husband. On the contrary, she was only anxious to break up his marriage. So she, who had once personified his stable background, became just another of the evil influences which eventually brought about his downfall.

Edmund had always found it hard enough to keep his head above water, but now, with a wife to support, he was going to find it infinitely harder. It had been his dream, of course, that they would conquer the world together, and perhaps he had cherished a mistaken idea that Mary was a histrionic genius. If so, he was quickly disillusioned. Even in Watson's company, where they remained for the first few months after their marriage and where Mary had started as a leading lady, she was soon reduced almost to a supernumerary. Her failure was due, not to any caprice of fortune, but simply to the fact that she was, on her own admission, quite unable to "support any line of business." In other words she could not act. From the outset, therefore, she was doomed to be of precious little assistance to the family exchequer.

It did not take them long to realize that their relationship was quite barren of any spiritual accord. Passion thrives badly on a guinea per week, and the harsh circumstances in which their life together began caused their conflicting temperaments to clash violently and soon. In Birmingham, where they arrived, still with Watson's company, in October of 1808 and stayed until September of the following year, things began to go seriously wrong.

Edmund's position in the company was prominent

enough. Though the stock repertoire was not particularly distinguished and he appeared, therefore, infrequently in tragedy, he was given leads in opera, melodrama and farce. He was acknowledged besides to be an unrivalled Harlequin and on that account had his salary raised from one guinea to thirty shillings per week. Admittedly the company was otherwise strong in talent, but he was not called upon to fill really bad parts; and all in all he had as much reason to be thankful as he had so far had in the whole course of his career.

Yet he was not content. Marriage had merely intensified in him all those instincts which before had caused him so much anguish—his impatience, his arrogance, and his passionate desire for recognition. Mary had shown her confidence in him and he would have to succeed now for her sake as well as his own. But he seemed farther away than ever from the achievement of his ambition, which was to go to London and become the greatest tragedian of the British stage. Others, not much older than himself, like Rae, for example, were already established at Drury Lane or Covent Garden; and yet he, after five years on the road, was still unknown, was still being offered second "leads" by tin-pot managers, was still the prey of any Tom, Dick or Harry who cared to insult him. Even when he was given the chance of appearing in tragedy he ran the risk of being ridiculed by some dunderhead critic. During the summer of 1809 the company moved for a short season from Birmingham to Lichfield, and then the following notice appeared in the *Staffordshire Advertiser*:

"Mr. Kean, who has been figuring here as the principal tragic hero, is another instance of the blundering folly of misplacing actors of which we see so many in the country theatres. Without energy, dignity or the advantages of a voice, he dragged through the heroic scenes with a dull monotony oppressive to himself and doubly so to the audience. He appears to understand his author, but the effects of a clear conception are totally lost in the natural defects of his voice and person. This performer's genius is nevertheless of an elevated cast—he is a good Harlequin!"

That last sentence was of the kind which hurt Edmund most. Once he had liked to show off his versatility as Harlequin—and for the matter of that, in comedy and opera and farce. But not now that they had laughed at him in tragedy and thought him only fit to be a measly little contortionist. Could they not understand that he was destined to be a great tragedian? Richard and Othello and Shylock were worthy of his talents. But Harlequin and the like were beneath his dignity. The very life which he was forced to lead seemed to him a cause for misery and dejection.

He needed more than ever the encouragement that once Mary, without knowing it, had been able to give him. Now he turned to her in vain. She could no longer pretend to sympathize with his extravagant restlessness and his insane arrogance. She could not even listen to his troubles with a good grace. Marriage to her meant the assumption of responsibilities. And of these he appeared to have no appreciation. His chance, she argued, would surely come; why, then, did he not await it calmly? And meanwhile think of the comfort and security and, above all, of her who should have been by every right his chief care. As it was, he sacrificed everything to his vanity, and by his impulsive behaviour risked landing them both in complete destitution.

Hers was the common-sense view. But unfortunately she had neither the strength of character to impress it on Edmund nor the bold warmth of heart to abandon it and go his way. She left him hopeless. And her injured attitude bored and irritated him.

Still, he had to find some outlet for his feelings, and if, as Mary said, drink eventually brought him to ruin, then in Birmingham he was already on the downward path. On one occasion he got so intoxicated that "He attacked a mail coach which was stopping to change horses, seized the leaders by their heads and, after a magnificent struggle, was duly lodged in the hands of the 'Guardian of the Night.'"

The night watchman in question generously refrained from taking the delinquent to prison and, instead, conducted him safely back to his lodgings. But even after this escape Edmund was not sufficiently sobered to accept his wife's advice to go quietly to bed. On the contrary he ended an undignified episode as flamboyantly as he had begun it. He would not rest until he had tried—and failed—to throw his landlady out of the window!

There were many repetitions of such scenes, which were not mere youthful pranks, and Mary naturally abominated them. Yet when she supposed that he drank "to forget his sorrow," she only showed her ignorance of his temperament. His sorrow (if we accept the misnomer) was his power, the wild, ungovernable will to greatness without which he would never have triumphed. It tortured him only because it was frustrated. And he yearned, not to obliterate it, but to give it expression. Far from resorting to alcohol as a narcotic, he took it deliberately for what it was—a stimulant—and under its courageous influence he supposed himself already what he longed to be.

But dissipation was not an end in itself. Even Mary would have admitted that. He could no longer share his thoughts with her and she could no longer comfort him. But still they were together and he would go on struggling and hoping for her sake as well as his own. She had not married just a weak, idle, bombastic braggart, but a fierce genius who, in her own words, "studied and slaved beyond any actor I ever knew." "He used to mope for hours, walking miles and miles alone, with his hands in his pockets, thinking intensely on his characters. No one could get a word from him."

Indeed, it was essential for him to work hard and tirelessly for the success which he craved. Even if he had had influence behind him, he could not, by the mere desire, have reached the top. For though there may have been actors born "with every talent requisite for their profession," Edmund was certainly not one of them. And, in his heart, he knew it.

Macready, who in his schoolboy days saw Edmund act at Birmingham, later recalled the experience in these words: "A little, mean-looking man in a shabby green satin dress (I remember him well) appeared as the hero, Alonzo the brave. It was so ridiculous that the only impression I carried away was that the hero and heroine were the worst in the piece. How little did I know, or could guess, that under the shabby green satin dress was hidden one of the most extraordinary theatrical geniuses that have ever illustrated the dramatic poetry of England."

That impression was not exaggerated or inexpert. Macready was the son of a provincial manager and had been brought up to know the stage. He was also a balanced and impartial critic. The truth is that Edmund Kean worked and slaved because, in spite of his heritage and early environment, he was not extraordinarily gifted. All his acting was artifice, acquired through the dynamic force of his nature; and all his innovations of style were the superb devices by which he overcame his initial handicaps—of voice and person and figure.

In Birmingham he was not even a good actor. But after five more years of suffering he would emerge as a genius in the theatre.

CHAPTER III

I

MARY's fears of a financial crisis were soon realized. The Keans left Birmingham owing debts amounting to fifteen pounds, for which Edmund's instability was responsible. Their total assets were a little less than twenty shillings in cash and a promise of an engagement in Andrew Cherry's company at Swansea.

The cash remained from a two-pound loan, which little Cherry, himself once the victim of privations, had sent to Edmund in advance of salary. But it was not enough to pay for any kind of conveyance, and so the Keans set out on foot.

On the journey from Birmingham to Swansea they faced their first experience together of real distress. They might, had they been gay and in love, have found it an adventure, at times hard, at times exciting—even funny. They might have laughed to think of their escape from angry creditors as they walked out of the deserted streets of Birmingham at sunrise on a June morning. But they were a forlorn couple. Edmund always appeared dark and grave, except when he was drunk, and now, dressed from head to foot in blue, with four theatrical swords slung over his shoulders, and attached to these the bundle of all his own and his wife's belongings, "he looked like a penniless naval lieutenant on half-pay." Mary did not smile at this resemblance but was pleased that it would entitle them at least to respect. She followed miserably behind, knowing that in three months' time she would be a mother.

For both of them it was a long, dreary trail. But for Mary it was a physical ordeal made almost unbearable by the anguish of her mind. She had married to share in her husband's success, not to endure his poverty. And now, when most she needed care and comfort, she was forced to trudge along mile after mile, eating too little, getting weaker and more exhausted every day. Years later she could recall many of the nightmare incidents of this journey which signified to her illness, hunger, continual anxiety and fear. She had memories of Edmund bathing in a river while she sat dejectedly on the bank beside, guarding the bundle and the four swords; of arriving penniless in Bristol after a hundred miles tramp; of spending there an agonizing week at a tavern called the "Mulberry Tree" while they awaited a further loan from Cherry; of lying on a coil of ropes on board a small boat which took them to Newport; of being sickened by the smell of the ship's cargo of tar and hemp; of going without breakfast at Cardiff and begging for meals in other towns; of being threatened by a maniac whom Edmund scared away at the point of one of his own property swords; and finally, of being refused a glass of milk by a cottager when she was nearly fainting of fatigue.

Mary was rocketed to the summit of happiness by riches and plunged to the depths of wretchedness by want. She first faced complete destitution at a time when she was least able to bear it. No wonder she never forgot these days of suffering, and for ever after lived in dread of their recurrence.

Had Edmund been of the same mind, she would have had less need to worry. Unfortunately for her, he was not easily made desperate by mere distress. He had been brought up on poverty, and he longed for money only in so far as it was synonymous with power. Such things as weariness and hunger and debt were the least part of his troubles. They aggravated his discontent, because they were symbols of his failure. But in themselves they did not scare him. And as soon as he had reached his destination, he recovered from whatever physical discomforts he had endured—or at least he could think of them with a light heart.

He was now earning twenty-five shillings per week as a

member of Andrew Cherry's company. Though the salary was small, his position was really quite distinguished, for Andrew Cherry, unlike the majority of country managers, was not a parsimonious, illiterate vulgarian who had built up a theatrical circuit for want of something better to do. He was an author with several published plays to his credit and he was an accomplished comedian who had, in his time, once graced the London boards—not without success. He was, besides, educated beyond the immediate needs of his calling, and consequently he commanded an unusual respect both from the patrons of his theatres and from the local Press. His circuit embraced Swansea, Carmarthen and Haverfordwest in South Wales, and in Ireland, Waterford and Clonmel. At each of these towns he could rely on an abnormal measure of support and approbation. For example, the Swansea newspaper *Cambrian*, in whose columns he was a discreet and consistent advertiser, praised him fulsomely; and towards the start of the present season, wrote as follows: "Mr. Cherry has on all similar occasions paid the strictest attention to the preparation of new pieces and placed them before the Public in a style of theatrical correctness and effect never before witnessed in the Principality, but on the present occasion we must declare his taste and liberality have gone hand in hand and he has produced *The Exile* in all that perfection of excellence which scenery, rich characteristic costume, machinery and good acting can display." That, at a time when it was customary to sneer at most country performances, was a glittering notice indeed. But little Cherry was a manager among managers. In Carmarthen he was considered of sufficient eminence to be invited to the Mayor's annual dinner at the King's Arms; and there he raised half the sum of money necessary for the building of a new theatre!

He appointed Edmund the leading actor of his company and the official "getter up" of ballets and pantomimes. Consequently, Edmund came in for a good share of the Cherry prestige. Of his performance of Daran in *The*

Exile the *Cambrian* wrote that "he gave to that mysterious character the full force of his assumed ferocity and the tender breathings of his genuine humanity"; and of his first ballet called *The Savages*, that "it was prepared under the immediate direction of Mr. Kean with an effect highly honourable to that gentleman's pantomimic abilities."

Edmund felt that at last he had made an advance. It was a little humiliating, perhaps, that Mary, after being tried out in a leading role, was again found wanting; and when the company came to Waterford, which was her home town, he asked Cherry to release her from her engagement, so that she should not be seen by her relations in inferior parts. Otherwise he had few complaints. He was now working for a manager who had the wit to humour him, and he was being praised in the Press and applauded by the public.

He is supposed, it is true, to have been partially put in the shade by Bengough, a large, bluff, raucous, unsubtle actor, who arrived at Swansea in September in order to play the leading roles in tragedy. But Bengough did not really do more than divide the honours with him. Though at his benefit performance he appeared as King Lear to Edmund's Edgar, that was testimony to his tact and not to his superior position in the company. On the stage he was "an elephantine simpleton," but off it he was a diplomat; and he flattered Edmund, telling him that his powers were shown to most brilliant advantage in flashy, melodramatic parts like Daran in *The Exile*.

Between the summer of 1809 and the summer of 1810, the Keans went with Cherry from Swansea to Carmarthen, from Carmarthen to Haverfordwest, and from Haverford-west across the Irish Channel to Waterford. On July 21, 1810, they were welcomed back to Swansea by the *Cambrian*, and between then and the summer of 1811 they followed the whole round of Cherry's circuit over again.

Nothing occurred in these two years to injure Edmund's pride, and he was happier earning twenty-five shillings per week than he would ever be afterwards in the days of his great wealth and fame. He was not, of course, completely at peace, because it was his curse, except in moments of rare exhilaration, to live perpetually in the future and to cry continually for things which he had not got. But now in the flush of his new-found prominence he was at least ready to believe in the benignity of Fate; and recognition brought him, by chance, into contact with a number of people, socially and intellectually his superiors, who encouraged him to find other outlets, besides dissipation, for the super-abundance of his impulsive energy.

He was not, in spite of the isolation of his spirit, an impossible man either to know or to influence. But his sensitiveness and consciousness of the disadvantages of his birth and breeding seemed incurable, so that when he was in the society of those whom he considered his betters, he became at once on the defensive and had to be wooed and cajoled and met the whole way before he would converse freely. Unfortunately, he met few, during his life, who would bother to conquer his sense of inferiority for him, and that is why Kean, the celebrated tragedian, eventually "damned all Lords and Gentlemen," and recruited his friends from the tavern and from the lower ranks of his own profession. But Kean, the leading member of Cherry's company, belied his later protestations. Indeed, he attributed a part of his success to the fact that he was noticed by his superiors, "which gave him in Private Life as well as in public an ascending, over his brother professionals."

He met Ann of Swansea. Mrs. Hatton was her real name, and she had something in common with Edmund, for, like him, she was psychologically at variance with the world. She was the fifth child of Roger Kemble, and knew herself as the family failure. Sarah and John Philip were the undisputed leaders of the British stage, while handsome Charles was ready to follow in their footsteps and even fat Stephen did quite well for himself as a manager and a "star" actor in the provinces. But the story of Julia Ann, however adventurous, was lamentable. The victim of a bigamous first marriage, the widow of a second husband with whom she had been driven from America by the yellow fever, and in Swansea had later run an hotel and "house of assembly" at a consistent loss, she was now plain, middle-aged, and poverty-stricken. She poured her soul and her spleen into her writings, and she lived on the precarious generosity of her distinguished relatives.

Locally, of course, she was quite a celebrated, picturesque figure. Frequently she sent to the *Cambrian* her verses, of which the following is a typical example:

> The restless waves that lave the shore,
> Joining the tide's tumultous roar,
> In hollow murmurs seem to say,
> Peace is not found in Swansea Bay.

There was peace nowhere for Ann at Swansea, and there was none for Edmund Kean. That she loved him and wrote a drama for him is a rumour. Certainly she was his friend and influenced him, no doubt, in various ways. He began to express his own thoughts in immature, rather pathetic doggerel and to develop his native, untutored talent for musical composition. Mrs. Hatton had once kept "a school of dancing and deportment" and now Edmund turned to making a little extra money by giving private dancing lessons. There were times both before and afterwards when he rejected such a practical course as being far beneath his dignity. So perhaps Ann of Swansea must be thanked for the "grand fête and dance" which on September 25, 1809, was performed by "Mr. Kean's pupils" during the second act of *The Foundling of the Forest*.

Thomas Colley Grattan first saw Edmund in Waterford. There, one night when *Hamlet* was being performed, he went to the theatre. With that amused, indifferent, rather lackadaisical attitude which English gentlemen affected towards country theatricals, he purposely arrived late—during the fifth act, in fact, when the fencing scene was already in progress. He noticed that Edmund—"the thin,

pale little man"—looked a mere pigmy beside the handsome
and very tall Laertes. All the same he was struck by Hamlet's
"quiet gracefulness of manner while he parried the cut-
and-thrust attacks of his adversary," and also by "his quick
glance of haughty resentment at the uncivil laugh" which
greeted his efforts. And when Hamlet "began to return
the lunges *secundum artem*," Grattan was surprised to see
"the carriage and action of a practised swordsman."

He went round to see Edmund afterwards and tactfully
suggested that Edmund should give him fencing lessons.
There was really no practical point in this, for Grattan did
not need instruction from a master who, off the stage, was
no more accomplished than he was himself. Yet it was
typical of him that he troubled to make the acquaintance
of this small, down-at-heel, and strangely talented provincial
actor. Grattan was then only eighteen years old and a
subaltern in the town garrison. But the boy's outlook was
essentially the same as the man's would be. He was the son
of a Dublin solicitor who had retired to his country seat
in order to devote himself to agricultural pursuits, and he
inherited his father's love of detachment from the world
and also the means to indulge it. He dabbled widely. He
was, at different times, a soldier, a writer, a dramatist, a
politician, a diplomatist, a courtier, a speaker, and a
raconteur. In all this variety of activity he was charming,
capable, and mildly successful—but never conspicuously so.
He was a wanderer, who settled down in France, Belgium,
Holland, Germany and America, and who ended his days
in London. He was the acquaintance of many celebrities,
including actors, statesmen, beaux, poets, authors, and
professional "diners-out." He liked most of them, but was
really intimate with none. He lived, as it were, on the fringe
of life; and because he was more concerned with his fellow
beings than he was with himself, he has left behind him
only the faintest memory of his achievements.

He was, in short, a student of humanity, and in Waterford
he began, in a vague kind of way, his study of Edmund

Kean. At the time, of course, he had more influence on Edmund than Edmund had interest for him. To Grattan, Edmund was just a stage player who was not extraordinarily gifted, but whose personality was somehow compelling and whose manners were agreeably modest and unpresuming. Later, these slight impressions would be supplemented by others and would contribute to perhaps the only faithful and sympathetic portrait of the great tragedian that has ever been painted. But by themselves they were not particularly important.

Edmund, on the other hand, was very much influenced by Grattan. Grattan was an officer—a gentleman—who put him at his ease and whom he regarded almost as a friend. Why should he not be the friend of other gentlemen besides? After all, if he were destined to be famous, fame would inevitably be a passport to the houses of the rich and the distinguished. He would occupy a place in London Society. He would meet and be honoured by men and women of every class. And he would have to impress them with his personal qualities. He would not be content to be hailed as a genius on the stage if he were regarded as a dull, stupid, vulgar dolt off it. He wanted to live as a great man as well as a great actor.

There is something infinitely pathetic about his attempts at self-education. In his copy-books he set down simple phrases and translated them into Latin, Greek, Italian, Welsh, and even Portuguese: he wrote down notes on history, natural history, geography, and details of the lives of Isaac Newton, Cicero, and Plutarch. All these scattered bits of learning he tried to memorize, and often reproduced some of the Latin and Greek phrases in his letters to managers and others. Most touching of all, perhaps, is the inscription which he wrote on the cover of his copy-books—Edmundus Kean, Anno Domini 1810. Edmundus Kean, The Latin Scholar.

In Waterford, too, he turned his attention to play-writing and produced a melodrama, called *The Cottage*

Foundling, or The Robbers of Ancona. It was performed by Cherry's company on his benefit night, and he had hopes that it might be done in London. He wrapped it up in a large parcel and sent it off to "Aunt" Tid. But postal dues were heavy in these days and Miss Tidswell, practical woman that she was, declined to pay them. So *The Cottage Foundling* disappeared.

There were other efforts of the same kind, now no longer extant, and some of them were inspired, perhaps, by the example of Sheridan Knowles, who had come to Waterford to serve in Cherry's company. Knowles was not of the ordinary run of strolling players. Far from it. He was the son of a lexicographer and himself already had academic achievements to his credit. He had thrown up the chance of a prosperous medical practice in order to go in for the theatre, and naturally he had done so in defiance of his family's wishes. But though he was stage-struck, he sought fame as a dramatist and not as an actor.

Knowles was essentially big-hearted and took an immediate liking to Edmund. They had things in common, these two poverty-stricken strollers. Both were ambitious, self-willed, and determined; and both were staunch believers in their own powers. But intellectually, Knowles was far better developed than Edmund, and morally much more stable. Ten years would pass before he would win his first success in London with *Virginius*, and during most of that time he would earn an obscure, if respectable living as a schoolmaster in Belfast and then in Glasgow. He would continue, the while, to write, of course. But he would await his opportunities patiently and well.

Knowles was another who bothered to understand Edmund; and his affection both for the actor and the man, in spite of one severe test, never wavered. At Waterford, he wrote a tragedy specially for him, which was performed by Cherry's company with eminent success. It was not actually a work of much note and did not help to make the author's name. But Knowles never forgot it. In 1833, when he was at the height of his fame, he acknowledged in a speech to the Edinburgh Shakespeare Club how much he owed to the encouragement of "Poor Great Edmund Kean, that noble, enthusiastic fine little fellow."

Objectively speaking, these years which Edmund spent in Cherry's company were the most tragic of his life. They show so clearly what he might have been in contrast to what he became. Perhaps he was not, by nature even, a man of intellect or breeding or culture. But at least he was sensible of his own deficiencies, and he had the inclination to overcome them. He might have done so had his wife been sympathetic enough to encourage him and strong enough to direct his energies wisely. As it was, his efforts to gain knowledge and equipoise were crude and fitful, the results merely of chance influence.

Even now there was no harmony or understanding in his home. He was not Mary's ewe lamb and never would be. She did not recall the times when he sat over his Latin dictionary or wrote his plays or showed her his heart in his poems or music. She only remembered his cryings-out against Fate and his wild, cruel behaviour. She remembered that in Waterford he used to carouse with some low friends whom he had found among the disaffected Irish (called "Croppies") and that he used to protest in his mad, vain way that he would become the champion of the Croppies and lead them to victory; that often he appeared drunk on the stage and shocked and alienated his audiences; that on one dreadful occasion he returned from the theatre, still in his stinking costume of a chimpanzee, and went to bed without undressing, forcing her to spend an uncomfortable night on the sofa rather than be suffocated by the odious smell of his monkey skins.

These were sordid memories. But they remained with Mary because they led to the inevitable conclusion of which she had lived in dread ever since that never-to-be-forgotten journey from Birmingham At the close of the second Waterford season Edmund quarrelled with Cherry. Perhaps he was restless, perhaps he wanted a larger salary, perhaps he felt himself "insulted" in some way. What did the cause matter? Cherry's company returned to South Wales, leaving the Keans stranded, without money, without prospect of another engagement even.

Now they had not only themselves to consider. They were four. In Swansea on the 13th September, 1809, had been born Howard Anthony Kean. He was a beautiful child, whom Edmund loved with a fierce pride. Howard would be given better chances than his father, he would be educated as a gentleman and sent into the Navy, where he would be entitled "to the respect of high and low." Howard would never have to suffer the degradations of the theatre and would never be obliged to battle for a place of honour in the world, for it would be made for him. Howard's future became inseparable from Edmund's own ambition.

He was not so interested in his second son, Charles John Kean, who had been born in Waterford on January 18, 1811. But Mary would have said she adored both her children equally and her concern was with their present. What was to become of them? How were they to be fed or clothed or kept alive at all? Edmund had applied in vain to the managers of the Bath, Liverpool, and Dublin theatres. So now the only course open to them was to make for London, where at least Edmund had relatives and where provincial engagements were more easily found.

Their immediate expedient was to hire an assembly hall and there give a benefit performance. From this they drew just enough money to pay for their passage across the Irish Channel.

2

In July of 1811 they reached Whitehaven. They had a bundle of clothes and books, and a dog called Daran—the only tangible reminder of those days of luxurious security in Cherry's company, which now seemed so far off. And they

had the means to earn a precarious income by giving
"recitations." Otherwise they had nothing. They were
penniless and helpless And thus they set out on their long,
agonizing trek to London.

They moved from town to town, always living on the
verge of starvation, fearful of the future, making a little
money here and no money there, selling clothes in Whitehaven and books in Dumfries and Daran in Penrith, often
being scorned and persecuted, and occasionally being
grateful for chance generosity—vagabonds in truth.

For five months they endured this torture, travelling on
carts and wagons, stopping in squalid public-houses, eating
bad food and too little of it, trying to quieten their two small
children who cried most of the time for want of proper care.
Neither was of the least comfort to the other. Mary, of
course, blamed her husband entirely. Oh, he was resourceful
enough in his way. In the various towns where they found
themselves stranded he set to work to hire a hall, arrange a
programme, write out play-bills in his own hand, scout round
for local patronage, engage the bell-man to announce their
forthcoming performance, and then, with her, act scenes
from well-known comedies and farces, and by himself sing,
dance, and give his imitations. But all this weary effort
generally resulted in so little profit. In any case it would
never have been necessary but for his fault which had
landed them in this desperate plight. Even now he was as
blind as ever to his responsibilities as a husband and a
father. He drank and swore and ran up debts. He seemed to
be quite devoid of conscience or stability.

Yet of what use to Edmund were Mary's reproaches?
They wore him down. It was humiliating enough to be
unemployed and apparently unwanted in the world. But it
was unbearable to live with a woman who wept and wailed
and moaned and prayed for death; who looked at him
accusingly and whose very presence reminded him of his
failure. In York he was driven so frantic by her recriminations that he tried to join the Army. As it happened his

application was turned down. But he was none the less in the mood to sell his destiny for the price of a common soldier's pay.

Mary, of course did not care a rap for her husband's pride or his feelings. Their sufferings were mutual, but in her view they engulfed only herself—herself and her babies. She had no faith left and no courage, and when at last they came to London in December of 1811, she could scarcely have been worse equipped to impress and conciliate the dreaded Miss Tidswell. She said afterwards that "Aunt" Tid peremptorily turned them out of her house and refused them help of any kind, and that they were thus obliged to rely on the exclusive hospitality, rather unwillingly given, of Mrs. Price (Aunt Price). As a matter of fact, she allowed her prejudice to colour her memory a little, and she did not speak the entire truth.

Certainly Miss Tidswell took an instantaneous dislike to Mary and would have nothing to do with her; certainly she refused to lend her nephew money, either because she really had none to spare or because she supposed, in her uncompromising way, that a loan to him would indirectly be of assistance to his wife; certainly she let Mary and the children find shelter where they could—with Mrs. Price, as it happened. But she had Edmund to stay with her. And probably she was instrumental in getting him his next job. It was with Richard Hughes who managed theatres at Weymouth and Exeter on behalf of his father—John Hughes—who was personally in control at Sadler's Wells, London. Miss Tidswell was still living at 12 Tavistock Row, Covent Garden, and from Tavistock Row Edmund wrote a letter to John Hughes, from which the following is an extract.

> DEAR SIR,
>
> Having travelled lately some hundred miles with a large family and very expensive baggage, I am left in London in a situation (which many of our brother professionals are acquainted with) *Non est mihi argentum.* It is my wish, there-

fore, to depart by to-morrow's coach for Weymouth, but I
frankly confess I at present have not the means; if, Sir, you
would oblige me with the sum of ten pounds, Mr. Finch or
Miss Tidswell will become answerable for my immediate
appearance at Weymouth, and Mr. Hughes might proceed to
the reduction of ten shillings per week till the debt is discharged.
As I am fully sensible this is a great obligation from a stranger,
it is my wish to pay interest on the money you may please to
demand, and as Mr. Hughes, jnr., will have the means in his
hands there can be no doubt of the payment, and I shall bear
the recollection of your kindness παῤ ὅλον τὸν βίον . . .

Had "Aunt" Tid had her way, Edmund would have
left London alone. From now on she would conduct a
tireless campaign against Mary, using all her persuasive-
ness and all her feminine opportunism to take her nephew
away from his wife. Eventually she would succeed and
by so doing would contribute in a large measure to the
ruin of him whom she loved. But that would not be for a
long time yet. At the moment, in spite of her protestations
to Edmund that Mary did not care for him and that Mary
was a drag on his career, the Keans travelled to Weymouth
together.

For more than eighteen months they remained under
Hughes' management, moving from Weymouth to Exeter
and from Exeter to Guernsey, with Edmund as the undisputed "star" of the company, earning two guineas per
week, and Mary occasionally being called upon to play
small parts. They were in employment again and richer by
ten shillings than they had ever been before. Yet there was
happiness for neither of them. They were now properly on
each other's nerves.

At the age of twenty-three Edmund was already old in
spirit. Had there ever been days when he was young and
care-free and really hopeful? He could not remember them.
The strollers' life was a hard and a cruel one—enough,
surely to embitter any man—and he had stood it for nearly
eight years. The small glories of being top dog in a country

theatre no longer satisfied him. Good notices in the local Press, applause from local audiences, the patronage of the local bigwigs—what were these compared with the prizes which London offered ? And—more important—how wretchedly they compensated for the worry of living on two guineas per week, now that he was a father ambitious for his children's future and a husband whose wife perpetually nagged him. Would it not be better to go to London even if that meant playing secondary parts?

He wrote to Arnold, manager of Drury Lane, " . . . if the service of so humble a candidate for public favour would be accepted . . . I should be most happy in becoming a member of the new community . . . to be settled in the metropolis in a third or fourth rate situation on a salary sufficient to support my family with respectability would be the summit of my ambition. . . ."

He was crawling at last, and perhaps he knew that he was deceiving himself. But he did not think so when Arnold ignored his application. To be refused even an obscure position in the London Theatre blinded him to his present advantages, and he began to believe that fate was permanently set against him. He became more sensitive than ever to every trifling disappointment and every little irritant. He was miserable when Lord Cork, a reputed connoisseur of the Drama, came to the theatre and took no notice whatever of his efforts to impress. . . . "Whilst I was playing the finest parts of Othello in my best style," he said, "my Lord Cork's children were playing at hot cockles in front of the box and Lord and Lady Cork laughing at them." He was pathetically indignant when Master Betty— now a fully-grown actor whose "speech was very coarse and provincial" and whose voice was "on the higher notes harsh and dissonant and on the lower notes scarcely audible"—again trespassed on his territory. "I must feel deeply, Sir," he told a friend who found him striding up and down outside the theatre, his hands thrust impatiently in his pockets. "He commands overflowing houses;

I play to empty benches. I know my powers are superior
to his."

Even his success, in a world which was far too small for
him, was mostly of the kind which he resented. It was still
the same. He demanded recognition as a tragedian, not as an
acrobat. And yet audiences crowded to see his Harlequin,
while they stayed away from his Hamlet. A local reputation
for pantomimic brilliance, was that to be the limit of his
achievements? It was fearful to realize that it was the chief
cause of his value to Hughes and of his popularity with the
public. He began morbidly to hate Harlequin and to dread
his appearances in the part. He said he never felt so degraded
as when he had "the motley jacket on his back."

Of course, his distaste for the job was not noticeable to
his vociferous admirers. On the stage "he was all life and
vigour—turning somersaults in the most graceful and
astonishing manner, dancing . . . to the delight of the
house, and finally (his great feat) leaping through the face
of a clock." Oh, he deserved his applause all right. But beforehand he had sat in the Green Room "sad and depressed,
awaiting his call, declaring he was stiff, that it was impossible he could go through his part." And afterwards,
"with a great coat flung over his patchwork dress," he would
seek balm for his lacerated feelings in the tavern. There
among his fellow actors and his fellow tipplers he could
rise, at least in his own estimation, far above the status of a
provincial Harlequin. Harlequin! He'd be damned if he
ever played the part again!

Edmund was at the end of his endurance. "If I succeed,"
he said, "I shall go mad." He felt himself alone. He could
cry out his heart to the skies and the sea, or yell and bluster
in public-houses, but there was no one to whom he could
turn for consolation. He was alone in his failure and would
be so in his triumph, which was now painful to contemplate
because he could not persuade his conscious self that it
would ever happen. He had been frustrated too long. In the
provinces his appearances as Richard, Othello, and Hamlet

got him no further, for so few people understood acting. And in London, where perhaps he might have been noticed even as Laertes or Richmond, he was not wanted.

Mary, of course, had lost all confidence in his future. From Exeter she wrote to her friend Margaret Roberts that "he was entirely ruining his health with drink," that she herself had been very ill and that the two boys had nearly died "in measles and whooping cough." She urged her husband to find an engagement, however inglorious, in London, for there she would at least be able to make a home for herself and her children and live in some permanency— even security. But what was there really before her, except misery? How could this man, whose conduct went from bad to worse, ever succeed? Their sufferings had made him not wiser but more impossible. Wantonly he threw away his chances and prejudiced his popularity. Nightly carousals, public brawls, scenes with outraged landladies—these were not enough for him. Quite often he appeared drunk on the stage and sometimes did not appear at all. Then he had to apologize to his audiences, and not very gracefully, for he had neither the art nor the nature to be contrite in public. And poorly attended benefit performances were the consequence.

In Guernsey he said, "Mary, what do you think, I can get brandy here for eightpence a bottle—I can drink it instead of beer." And in Guernsey, as a result of a silly quarrel, his engagement with Hughes came to an end. The quarrel was of his own seeking. He was cast for a part which he disliked—Charles I in *The Royal Oak*, a piece which had been specially requested by some local celebrities. He was so determined not to play in it that he got drunk instead and at the last moment sent a message to say that "King Charles had been beheaded on his way to the theatre." Then he took a seat in the auditorium and began to mock Hughes who was reading King Charles' lines in his stead. "Bravo, Hughes," and "Well done, my boy," he yelled, until he was eventually thrown out at the demand of an infuriated audience who were otherwise enjoying the piece. Hughes fined Edmund a fortnight's salary for this unmannerly display of bad temper, and Edmund, rather than swallow the insult of being punished, resigned his position in the company.

So they faced the same fearful plight from which they had escaped only eighteen months before. As if the memory of those days of penury and uncertainty were not sufficient torture in itself, they were now obliged, through Edmund's cruel fault, to go through the whole agonizing routine again. A farewell benefit performance at the Assembly Hall, Guernsey, which was patronized by the Governor of the Island, recitations which failed in Teignmouth, a one-night stand in Exeter—these were to Mary like the dark incidents of an oft-recurring nightmare. In the early September of 1813 she found herself alone with her two children in Exeter, and from there she addressed her famous "ruin, utter ruin" letter to Margaret Roberts. Edmund, she wrote, had gone to London leaving her "penniless and friendless." What was she to do? She could not act, for "disease on disease" had ruined her health. Would dear Margaret be kind enough to lend her a little money? She hated begging, but she had nothing to boast of save "a heart and character unsullied, nothing to blush for but her misery." Howard was her only means of livelihood—Howard who was "wonderfully clever" and graceful, who had appeared in ballets at the Exeter and Guernsey Theatres and who was called "The Pupil of Nature." Howard, at the age of three, was already beautiful and talented enough "to gain a dinner for his parent." Yet really she wanted to preserve her children off the stage. She hoped eventually to make them "good clerks," and then, perhaps, they might be willing to help her in her old age. Meantime she was desperate. Her tears blinded her. Would dear Margaret please send her a trifle or at least advise her what she should do—return to Ireland, run a school? She was so wretched, she could not think clearly herself.

She planned to desert her husband. But while she did so, Edmund was in London and was suffering, in his own way, no less acutely. He had come in search of a job at one of the minor theatres. That seemed his only chance now, and he knew quite well what it would mean. Once at a minor theatre he would be debarred from appearing in legitimate drama and would find the way to fame at Covent Garden or Drury Lane irrevocably closed to him. But really he could not remain in the provinces any longer, and he had given up hope that he would ever be recognized as a tragedian. Now he was prepared to sacrifice all his dreams for his family's sake—especially for the sake of Howard, who was his pride. By clowning, dancing and singing he would at least earn for Howard the chance to be great, not on the stage, but in a far more honourable profession. There was some consolation in that.

He had not had the money to bring Mary with him to London. Besides, her presence would only have annoyed "Aunt" Tid, whose help he needed at the moment. As it happened Miss Tidswell promised to use her influence on his behalf with Robert William Elliston, who, among numerous other activities, planned, in a few months' time, to reopen the Olympic Theatre in Wych Street.

So his fate seemed settled. Towards the close of September he joined Henry Lee's company in Barnstaple and with him went Mary and the children. But this was only a temporary engagement—to tide over the period while he awaited Elliston's pleasure. A little longer in the provinces, a few more unnoticed appearances in tragedy, and then he would take his family to the metropolis, where he would be doomed to eke out the rest of his life in obscurity, as a member of one of London's minor theatres.

On October 2nd he heard from "Aunt" Tid that her negotiations with Elliston had been successful, and that Elliston was prepared to engage him to "superintend the stage business" and play all the principal parts for a salary of three guineas per week. On the same day Edmund wrote

to Elliston, "The terms I own do not bring my expectations
to a level with the respectability of the establishment, but I
place so firm a confidence in your reputed liberality, that
on the proof of my humble abilities and asiduity [*sic*] towards
the general promotion of the business you will be inclined
to increase it, that I accept your present proposals, simply
requesting you to name the extent of the services expected
from me and what time you expect me in London. . . ."
Thus he concluded a legally binding agreement with the
manager of the Wych Street Theatre, and at the time had
every reason to suppose that he would fulfil it.

Continual disappointments, some imagined, had driven
him to take a step which only a little while before he would
have considered out of the question. Yet even now, had he
been more calculating, more able to regard facts dispassionately, he might have realized that circumstances
were at last moving in his favour. Did he not remember
that in Exeter, despite the vast majority who had worshipped
his Harlequin, there had been a few staunch admirers of his
Richard, his Hamlet, and his Shylock? Did he not remember, in particular, a Mr. Nation, who had been his enthusiastic patron, who had tirelessly "promoted his interests,"
who had delighted to discuss Shakespeare with him, and at
whose house he had often been a guest? In Mr. Nation's
company he had been unassuming, well-behaved, and very
receptive.

At Nation's request, Doctor Joseph Drury came over
from his country house at Gourlay to see Edmund Kean
perform; and the Doctor was considerably impressed.
Drury lived in retirement now and had the leisure to
cultivate his artistic predilections. As headmaster of
Harrow School he had been known as a disciplinarian, a
stickler for scholarship and industry. But he had also been
liked for his sympathy, his kindliness and understanding.
Had he not won his way even to Byron's perverse heart?
Perhaps he looked on Edmund rather in the same fashion
as he would have regarded a difficult pupil. At any rate

he took an almost paternal interest in the queer, untutored little man who worked so hard, who was so determined to get on and who acted with such fire and brilliance.

Drury was an ardent playgoer, an amateur critic of the Drama and a man of some influence in the theatre world. He knew the facts about the London Patent Houses—facts which were widely whispered, and printed in the Press for those who cared to read them. Covent Garden, under the experienced direction of Thomas Harris, with a first-rate team of actors headed by John Philip Kemble, was prospering. But Drury Lane was tottering towards bankruptcy. Its management was muddleheaded and disorganized, being in the hands of a committee of Lords and Gentlemen, whose Chairman, Samuel Whitbread, M.P., though eminently successful in the brewery trade and laudably energetic in the House of Commons, was hopelessly deficient in his knowledge of the stage. The shows at Drury Lane were cheaply and indifferently put on; the plays were ill-chosen; and the actors, except on the comedy side, were unattractive and not extraordinarily talented. The plight of Drury Lane was a favourite topic of conversation at dinner-tables. Suggestions were put forward by theatre-goers who loved to voice their opinions and to think that they had a finger in the pie. After all, as things stood, one man had as good a claim as his neighbour to advise the committee of amateurs who were making such a mess of things. What was needed was this, that and the other thing—most of all the discovery of a new star in Tragedy.

It was an opportune time for any well-connected patron of the drama to go about and talk and push the claims of some wonderful young actor, still languishing in obscurity. So that when Doctor Drury found himself at a dinner-party sitting next to Pascoe Grenfell, who was a member of the Drury Lane Committee, he immediately proceeded to tell him—in glowing terms—all about Edmund Kean. His words did not fall on deaf ears. Pascoe Grenfell began to make investigations and to influence his colleagues and his chairman.

These happenings were unknown to Edmund at Barnstaple on October 2, 1813. He heard about them a few days later from Doctor Drury. But by then he had already accepted Elliston's offer of an engagement at the Olympic Theatre.

3

Meanwhile, Edmund was still a member of Lee's company, and at the beginning of November the company moved from Barnstaple to Dorchester.

Howard was very ill and needed every attention and luxury which his parents could afford. They had only enough money to pay for two of them to go by coach, so Mary took Howard with her, while Edmund followed on foot, carrying baby Charles on his back.

Mary had not liked entrusting her second-born to his father's erratic care, and she was waiting nervously in Dorchester when she saw them approaching from a distance —dusty, dirty and travel-stained. She was glad to see them, but she did not behave as if she were. How could Edmund have neglected Charles so shamefully? His clothes were absolutely ruined and they'd never have the money to buy new ones. Edmund answered wearily that she ought to be very thankful that they had arrived at all. It was just like Mary to complain and to go for him when he was worn out with fatigue.

Yet they were closer now that they had been for a long while—or would ever be again. At last they had an interest in common—anxiety over Howard. Mary nursed him and Edmund stayed with her and gazed silently at his child who was suffering so much. He could scarcely tear himself away to go to the theatre. It was such pain to sing and dance and make them laugh who could not guess his agony of mind or know that he was an adoring father whose son was dying.

His spirits were at their lowest ebb. Of course, he would allow nothing to stand in his way if those negotiations, which

Doctor Drury had mentioned, should really come to anything! But would they? So often he had hoped and as often been disappointed. Why should his cursed fate ever change? He had enough faith to boast to Lee, who was his friend and supporter as well as manager, that he was going to Drury Lane, but not enough to convince himself of the fact. And now he was no longer in the position to gamble with chance. Whatever happened, he could not risk being left stranded again. He needed above all things money—to pay for food and doctors and medicine. He had to save Howard's life.

Days passed without a word from Drury Lane and he grew pessimistic. At last he wrote a final appeal to Doctor Drury, stating his perplexity, and begging, in his muddled, desperate and verbose way, for reassurance. Should he seek an interview with Samuel Whitbread? If something definite were not settled soon, then he would have to go to the Wych Street Theatre.

He did not receive Doctor Drury's reply. And so, on November 11th, he reaffirmed his acceptance of Elliston's offer. Once more he had capitulated, in his view, to relentless ill fortune.

Four nights later he was acting Octavian in *The Mountaineers*. The house was nearly empty, but he noticed a stranger sitting in a private box, who seemed anxious and attentive and unlike an ordinary provincial. After the play was over, while he was changing for the ballet of *The Savages* in his dressing-room below the stage, he overheard a conversation between Lee and the stranger. It concerned himself. "Kean," Lee was saying, "a wonderfully clever actor, he is going to London." "Certainly he is clever," replied the stranger, "but he is very small." "His mind is large," countered Lee, who was loyal to the members of his company, and especially so to his chief player.

Edmund reappeared on the stage. He told the stranger, who congratulated him on his performance, that he would not be much longer in Dorchester, that he had signed an agreement with Samuel Whitbread. Of course it was not true; but he had to keep up an appearance, to make a brave show in public. He could not admit to an intelligent admirer of his work that he was under contract to a minor theatre. But the stranger was not interested in Edmund's pathetic bravado. He wanted to talk business. "My name," he said, "is Arnold. I am the manager of Drury Lane."

Edmund (to use his own words) staggered as if he had been shot. He did not know where he was or what he was doing. He could scarcely get through his part in *The Savages*. But it did not really matter. The business was as good as settled. He was to be given a trial in one of the famous roles of tragedy on the stage of the Theatre Royal Drury Lane. Only the financial details—of trifling concern to him—remained to be discussed over breakfast at Arnold's hotel in the morning.

Now at last he could go home with joy to Mary. He had news for her which would wipe out all the bitterness and all the recriminations of the past few years. She had not believed in him, but he had always known that he would succeed. He had justified himself and she would admit it, just as the world would admit it too. "My fortune is made," he told her, "my fortune is made."

Was it? In his moment of exhilaration he had been lifted above the realities of the present. He had forgotten Howard, or rather had imagined subconsciously that the same change of luck which had brought Arnold to Dorchester had also cured his son. But now that he saw the sick child lying there—in pain—just as he had left him only a few hours before, he wondered whether he would ever know complete peace. Yet surely Fate could not be so cruel as to give with one hand and take with the other. Howard would live—he must—to share in his father's triumph. It had been ordained so.

Edmund did not go to bed that night. He was so overwrought that he would not have slept. He stayed up, thinking of his performance of Octavian, brooding over setbacks in the past, imagining achievements in the future, and talking joyously to Mary, as he had done in the days of their courtship, talking in fact to himself. Now that he was at last one of His Majesty's servants he thought that no one could possibly impede his triumph. The fact that he was technically bound to Elliston of the Olympic Theatre simply did not enter his head.

Next morning he kept his appointment with Arnold.

On November 20th, Arnold attended a meeting of his committee at Drury Lane. He reported "that he had declined the services of (a) Mr. Faucet on the part of the sub-committee, but having learnt that Mr. Kean an actor of great promise was playing at Dorchester, he had at the request of the Chairman (Samuel Whitbread) undertaken a journey for the purpose of seeing that gentleman play and that he had in consequence concluded an engagement with Mr. Kean from the beginning of next month, upon terms which he considered very advantageous to the Theatre"— to wit, £8 per week for the first year, £9 per week for the second year and £10 for the third.

On November 21st, Edmund wrote to Doctor Drury telling him the story of the last few days, and expressing, in a gloriously belaboured mélange of English and Latin, pompous and pathetic, his excitement, his joy, his unbounded and everlasting gratitude. Six days had passed then since his first meeting with Arnold. And on November 22nd Howard died.

How could Edmund and Mary share their grief? Only Howard was gone, but each had lost a different child. Howard had belonged to his father and to his mother, but not to both of them. Perhaps they suffered equally. But at least Mary shed tears which brought her relief; and even if the death of her elder child was her supreme sorrow, she painted it in colours no more and no less vivid than all the rest of her woes. She was a woman who liked to wallow in misery and she said herself she was never happy except in writing or thinking of that Gem who was "cold, cold in the earth." "It changed, his golden locks," she wrote to sister

Susan, "changed very much a few hours before he died . . . as I left Dorchester where he is interred, as I gave a last look at his grave, my heart strings cracked, my soul, my happiness lay entombed there. As it was the last experience I was at with him, I had him carried to his last home as well as I could. . . . His coffin was handsome, an angel bearing an infant, the plate on it—his name and age. I got up to see him carried out. Four girls dressed in white bore his coffin, others all white, strewing flowers; while he, the loveliest flower, was insensible to all. But no mourners had he—no tear wet his grave. I could not see the earth laid on the sweetest child ever mother had. . . . As we took leave of his corpse, his angelic countenance, with that look of his glory and seraphic smile it ever possessed seemed to say, 'Mama I grieve for you—but do not grieve for me—you know not how happy I am.' "

Mary felt painfully but not deeply. And so she expressed herself—with a wealth of luscious detail and graphic morbidity which even to-day is seldom excelled.

Simpler but infinitely more moving is this letter which Edmund wrote to Doctor Drury on November 25th:

> The joy that I felt three days since at my flattering prospects of future prosperity is now obliterated by the unexpected loss of my child.
>
> Howard, Sir, died on Monday morning last. You may conceive my feelings and pardon the brevity of my letter.
>
> This heartrending event must delay me longer in Dorchester than I intended. Immediately I reach London I will again, and I hope with more fortitude, address you. In the midst of my affliction I remember your kindness and with greatest respect sign myself,
>
> Yours, etc.,
> E. KEAN.

Yet his outward show of grief was terrible while it lasted. On the actual night of November 22nd, Mary feared he was going off his head. He looked on his dead child and burst into a flood of wild, uncontrolled, indescribable tears. He rushed madly from the house to drink, and discovered that there was not enough brandy in the world to dull his sorrow. He returned home to rage and swear that it was impossible Howard had gone, and that he would bring him back to life.

But all that was soon over. Next morning he awoke (according to Mary) more composed.

His grief was now personal to himself. He would not have Howard's name mentioned in his presence, for he could not bear to hear it or discuss his loss with anyone— least of all his wife. How could she understand how he felt? For her there was consolation, but for him there was none. She still had Charles—her second son—to whom she transferred all her affection. But, unreasonably perhaps, he believed that Howard had been the only one of his family who understood him and whom he loved in turn. Now he was left quite alone, and it seemed that he was robbed even of the joy of success, for Howard would not be there to share it with him. He imprisoned his sorrow in his own soul—to mingle with those other emotions which he could express vulgarly in the tavern or magnificently on the stage, but nowhere else. The death of his son made him an unhappier man and an even finer actor.

On November 29th he gave his last performance in Dorchester. Next day he left for London, having arranged that Mary and Charles should follow him a little while later. He took with him the good wishes of his fellow actors, and particularly of Lee who had made much on the Dorchester play-bills of Mr. Kean's forthcoming début at Drury Lane. He was twenty-six, though in spirit more than twice that age. He was embittered, heartbroken and physically weakened by want and dissipation. But after eight years of strolling he had at least schooled his passion to serve his trade. He had longed to be great; and he had learned how to be a great player.

His triumph was inevitable, but his last battle was not yet won. Had he remembered the matter of his contract with the Olympic Theatre and had he known what sort of man Mr. Elliston was, he might have guessed that in London still further trouble awaited him.

CHAPTER IV

I

"PRODUCED under the immediate direction of Robert William Elliston."

One cannot help feeling that the most colourful personality of the early nineteenth-century stage was born at least a hundred and fifty years too soon. How gloriously he would have served as the chief of a vast film organization—sitting in a gaudy office surrounded by telephones and secretaries, thinking in millions and paying out thousands to script writers and actors, always being inaccessible—here, there and everywhere! And how he would have revelled in conferences with his publicity manager—contemplating magnificent new stunts, having his name written in huge letters across the sky! Yet he belonged very much to his own generation. He gambled and drank in a big way. (He did all things in a big way.) He was a poseur who loved to mystify his friends and subordinates, and to make long, flowery, absurdly exaggerated or untrue speeches. And he fascinated his contemporaries. Indeed, at the age of forty, he was an eminently successful man. With a salary of thirty pounds a week, he was the highest paid member of the Drury Lane company and played both in tragedy and comedy, though better in comedy. He controlled two of London's minor theatres—the Surrey and the Olympic (which he had rechristened "Little Drury")—and various other theatres in the provinces. He was the enthusiastic proprietor of a circulating library in Bristol which he called "a literary association." He hoped to stand for Parliament one day. And he yearned above everything to be given a knighthood. And after all, why not? He was well born, well educated, lived in a large house in Stratford Place (Mayfair) and knew everyone worth

knowing from the Prince Regent downwards—or up-
wards.

He conducted his many and various negotiations in a
studiously eccentric manner. He was never, by any chance,
ordinary and direct. Even in the trifling matter of Edmund
Kean's engagement at the Olympic he had been typically
vague and indefinite. Though he had received letters of
acceptance from Edmund, he had sent back the most
tantalizing replies, altering the terms of the engagement,
refusing to specify from what date it should begin and
concluding in his best managerial manner "that he would
write again later." Really he did not care two pins whether
the little actor from Dorchester came to the Olympic
Theatre or not. But he liked to treat everyone as puppets—
to be dangled at the end of a string.

Meanwhile he was not going to commit himself.

That was the position until November 19th, and then it
underwent a sudden transformation. Elliston received the
following letter from Edmund:

> SIR,
>
> Since I last wrote to you, I have received a very
> liberal offer from the proprietors of Drury Lane Theatre. It
> gives me unspeakable regret that the proposals did not reach
> me before I had commenced negotiation with you; but I hope,
> sir, you will take a high and liberal view of the question when
> I beg to decline the engagement for Little Drury. Another
> time I shall be happy to treat with you.

Was the great Robert William to be brushed aside so
lightly? Not if he knew anything about it. He replied at
once calling Edmund a deserter and loftily reminding him
of the contract which he (Elliston) intended to enforce. By
nature Elliston was contrary. And now there were special
reasons why he wanted to indulge his whim.

Drury Lane was hard up for tragic talent—no doubt of it.
Though there were competent performers in the permanent
company—Elliston himself, for example, and Alexander

Rae whom we have already met at the Haymarket—none
were sufficiently attractive to draw the town. Various
"discoveries" from the provinces had all failed to create a
good enough impression and had soon returned to the
country again. Things had reached a pretty pass when
Stephen Kemble, who was ludicrously fat and fitted by
nature only for Falstaff, had been specially engaged to
play Shylock. In the circumstances tragedy was proving
increasingly expensive and was avoided as much as possible.
It was found less disastrous to put up comedies and farces in
which the renowned Joseph Munden and William Dowton
could display their gifts, or "grand melodramatic spectacles"
like *Illusion*, in which the magnificence of the scenery and
dresses discounted indifferent acting.

But Arnold had come back from his trip to Dorchester
immensely pleased with himself. He had encouraged the
members of his committee to believe that in Edmund Kean
they had at last got hold of someone really good. They
began to brag and engineer a little preliminary "puffing."
News travelled fast in theatrical circles and Elliston became
aware of the facts considerably before the following
paragraph appeared in the *Morning Chronicle* of December
16, 1813.

"A phenomenon, it seems, has been discovered in a
provincial theatre, who is to be brought out at Drury Lane.
His name is Kain, and he is already by anticipation called
Le Kain, from the great actor of that name in France. The
gentleman who gave information of his wonderful acting
said that he had certainly never seen anything comparable
to him for voice, passion, energy and expression since
Garrick."

Now here was a chance for Elliston infinitely too good to
be missed. He was not naturally malevolent, and even in the
altered circumstances he had no reason to be particularly
attracted to Edmund as a business proposition. After all, a
tragedian, however gifted, would have been of little use at
the Olympic Theatre where legitimate drama was legally

"The Manager of Little Drury"

ROBERT WILLIAM ELLISTON

barred. Besides he was doing remarkably well at the moment with a couple of performing dogs. The dogs were a "sensation" and he had announced that they might be visited during leisure hours by those who cared to write down their names in a large book specially provided for the purpose. The formality was regal.

But Elliston could not resist an opportunity to show off his importance and to exploit a really dramatic situation. Now that he had the power to prevent the newly discovered "phenomenon" from appearing at Drury Lane, he determined to make a grand pretence of doing so. He knew that eventually he would give in gracefully, but in the meantime he set out to promote a terrific Ellistonian shindy.

He succeeded most convincingly. To him, of course, the whole thing was just a game which he could prolong or cut short at his will; and though he played it, in his inimitable way, with determined gravity, he enjoyed himself immensely.

But Arnold saw nothing amusing or "make-believe" in the situation which Elliston brought to his notice. It was perfectly clear that Edmund was under contract to the Wych Street Theatre, and he had behaved very badly in not disclosing this at the beginning. He had been guilty, in fact, of a palpable deceit. Arnold was responsible to a committee whose chairman, more used to dealings in the brewery trade than in the theatre, believed that lack of business rectitude was identical with incompetence. It would be difficult, therefore, to explain matters satisfactorily to Samuel Whitbread, and Arnold thought that the young man, for whose engagement he had been responsible and whom he had been at such pains to boost, had not only let him down badly but had come perilously near to undermining his managerial dignity. For the sake of his own self-importance and for the future prosperity of Drury Lane, he was determined to extricate Edmund from his engagement with Elliston. But he was also excessively annoyed and he did not intend to let the culprit off lightly.

Such was the conflict in which Edmund became involved during the first month of his stay in London—in December of 1813, when it was very cold and the Thames was frozen over. On arrival he had been welcomed by Arnold "with more than common appearance of pleasure" and had been handed his first week's salary of eight pounds. Everything, it had seemed to him, was settled and he had only to await patiently the night of his appearance as Shylock—the part which had been promised him and which he had himself chosen for his début. He had taken "expensive" rooms at No. 21 Cecil Street, and there Mary and Charles had joined him.

But a few days later the storm broke. When he went to the "Treasurers" to collect his second week's salary, he was informed that he had been struck off the Drury Lane pay-roll. He flew to Arnold and was met by him "with cold, repelling looks."

"Young man," said Arnold, "you have acted a strange part in engaging with me, when you were already bound to Mr. Elliston."

What could he do? By Elliston, who was an able and experienced protaganist, he was quite outclassed. His entreaties, threats, violent expostulations were of no avail. On December 6th, he wrote: "The fate of my family is in your hands. Are you determined to crush the object that never injured you?" He went on to misquote Virgil and to conclude rhetorically, " . . . Am I to be cast again into the provinces, the rejected of this great city, which should afford a home to industry of every kind? With my family at my back will I return, for the walls of Wych Street I will never enter."

To this effusion Robert William sent back an Ellistonian masterpiece:

Sir,

To any man with the smallest gift of intellect and the dimmest sense of honour it must appear that on 11th November, and previous to that time, you deemed yourself engaged to me, and that subsequently a more attractive offer having been made, you held it convenient to consider a pledge as idle as words muttered in a dream. To your rodomontade I send nothing in reply, and your Latin Hexameter I beg to present you with again as it may be useful on some future occasion. . . .

All my engagements are made and fulfilled with honour on my part, and I expect an equal punctuality from others!

Edmund was in a helpless position—the wretched victim of one man's caprice and another's anger. He spent his days running after Arnold who "shunned him as something noxious" and chasing Elliston who was "almost inaccessible on account of his various speculations." Even when a tripartite meeting eventually took place, it resulted in no settlement. Elliston, at his very best, talked so volubly that Edmund could not get a word in. Arnold, formal and frigid, explained that though Mr. Kean was undoubtedly under contract to the Wych Street Theatre and would not, therefore, be allowed to perform at Drury Lane, he was also a member of the Drury Lane company and would, therefore, be injuncted from appearing anywhere else. And that was that.

Meanwhile, Edmund was stranded in London without money and without friends. Now that his wife was with him even "Aunt" Tid avoided 21 Cecil Street like the plague. Night after night he returned home—after another weary day of trying to straighten things out—empty-handed: and he dreaded doing so, for Mary, as usual, had abandoned herself to recriminations and despair. But for the generosity of his landlady, Miss Williams, "who somehow believed that he would be a great man," it is likely that Edmund and his family would have died of starvation in the cold, December air.

The dispute dragged on for more than three weeks. And then, as if for no reason, Elliston suddenly made that grand, generous gesture which from the outset he had intended. He agreed to forgo his claim to Edmund's services.

But even so, Edmund's troubles were not at an end.

Though Elliston had had enough fun, Arnold was still very angry. The rest of the dreary story is best told from a letter which Edmund wrote to Doctor Drury at the beginning of January.

"Mr. Arnold told me he could not again mention my name at the Treasury . . . without a written document from Mr. Elliston which that gentleman promised he would give me. I conceived now the affair was settled and flattered myself that next day I should, by receiving my salary, get rid of a part of my difficulties. . . . Friday 24th from ten till three I was employed in running east, north, west and south of this great city after Mr. Elliston. At three I fortunately encountered him at the Surrey Theatre and received from his own hands the required document and hastened overcome by fatigue and anxiety to Mr. Arnold. I could not see him then, therefore sent in my name and *lex scripta*. For nearly one hour I waited in the passage with the rest of the menials of the theatre and had the mortification of seeing them all conducted to his presence before myself, and when summon'd at last to appear, was with the continued brow of severity informed that I had no claim on the Treasury, my engagements had all to begin again."

That was what happened. Edmund spent a cheerless Christmas with no money and no spirit to celebrate. On the following Friday he got his salary, but the New Year's outlook seemed gloomy enough. After a month of being bullied and starved he thought that everyone in London was against him, everyone that is to say except Doctor Drury, to whom he addressed long and desperate appeals. He begged Doctor Drury to intervene on his behalf with the heartless pundits of Drury Lane.

Actually, his future was secure, and he needed no one's help. But how could he understand this? How could he guess that Arnold, in spite of his outward show of bad temper, really valued his services? And that the committee, too, were counting on him to make a hit, were saying so openly among themselves, were preparing the way for him in the Press and elsewhere? He had been too badly treated to calculate. He only knew that on December 29th, Huddart, an actor from Dublin, had made his début at Drury Lane and as Shylock, the very part which had been promised *him*. Was that not evidence enough of the bad faith of those in authority? Did it not show that they were set on humiliating him? Huddart had failed and had been condemned by the *Morning Chronicle* "as loud and vehement but not discriminating." But that was cold comfort to Edmund. The fact remained that he had been thrust callously aside to make room for a rival. And the same thing might happen over and over again.

Of course, he had read the flattering paragraphs which had appeared in the newspapers. But now the memory of them gave him no pleasure. They were mere mockeries which by contrast made his real position seem even more painful. He would fight for his rights, but he could not understand, in view of everything that had happened, why he had been brought to London in the first place. No one wanted him. Whenever he stepped inside the theatre he met with derision—not only from Arnold but from the Drury Lane actors as well. They laughed at him, mocked him, made fun of his small stature and his sad eyes, his lack of push and his dejection, his miserably shabby appearance. They called him "the little man in the capes" because of an unwieldy garment which he wore to keep out the cold and which nearly submerged his diminutive figure.

They hurt him with their insults, but they did not rob him of his courage. On the contrary he was more determined than ever to play Shylock and to succeed. His purpose was now a mania. He did not need the urgent advice of Doctor Drury, "Bear all, bear all, only come out," for in the midst of his anguish, mental and physical, he said himself, "Let me but once set my foot before the floats and I'll let them see what I am." Yes, he would show them. His triumph would be his revenge—on Rae who had deliberately cut him, on another actor who had been offensive to him, on all those who had dubbed him "Arnold's hard bargain" and had foredoomed him to failure.

The day arrived at last—January 26, 1814—when the Drury Lane playbills carried a notice of *The Merchant of Venice* with Mr. Kean in the part of Shylock ("his first appearance"). Who can blame Edmund for thinking that in the outside world he was unheralded and unknown, that by his fellow actors he was actively despised and that by Arnold and the Committee he was merely being shoved on to the stage as a last resort? That was the story which he told afterwards and, though it was not at all accurate, it has never since been challenged. But then Edmund could not regard facts dispassionately, as history must. He could only believe what his heart told him was true. And his heart had been tortured.

2

The Thames was beginning to thaw, but the sun did not shine on January 26, 1814. In the place of the snow of a few days before, a ceaseless drizzle fell on the slush-covered streets. It was dull, bleak, dirty weather. And in the evening, who wanted to go to the theatre? Well, very few ventured to Drury Lane even though the "phenomenon," who had been puffed in the Press, was making his first appearance.

The house, in fact, was less than a third full. Doctor Drury, with a party of friends, was there to applaud his protégé. William Hazlitt had come to represent the *Morning Chronicle* and had instructions from his editor to be as kind as possible to the new actor. He and the emissary of the *Morning Post* were the only professional critics present. Miss Williams was in the pit, having been given a free pass by her lodger. Her lodger had been sent a whole pile of free passes or orders as they were called. He had burnt fifty of them.

On the stage an actor looked through a peephole in the curtain, and saw that the audience was very small.

"What can you expect?" he said. "There will be nothing till half price."

Edmund, overhearing this, interpreted it as a deliberate affront—another indication of the hostility of his fellow players and of the world's indifference to him.

But now at least he was master of his own destiny. Though there might be very few of them sitting in front there—in extreme discomfort on wooden benches—yet each one was, in his own estimation, a connoisseur of the art of acting. Whether in gallery, boxes or pit they had all come, not to see *The Merchant of Venice* which they knew by heart, but to judge a performance of Shylock by Edmund Kean. And that performance was exclusively the actor's work and would, according to the practice of the times, be recognized as such. Every inflection in it, every gesture, every step were the result of Edmund's own inventiveness. For no one had stood over him to supervise his speaking of the lines and to direct his movements. The producer was an unknown figure in the theatre of the early nineteenth century, and the player was not subsidiary to the play. On the night of January 26, 1814, Edmund Kean was responsible to his audience alone.

He had had years to think out and perfect his interpretation of Shylock and he had had one rehearsal—that same morning at twelve—to familiarize the Drury Lane actors with its bare routine. Raymond, the stage-manager, whose duty it was to marshal the crowds and to ensure that the small-part actors played up properly to their star, objected to at least one piece of Edmund's stage business.

"It is an innovation," he said. "Depend upon it, it will not do."

"I wish it to be so," Edmund replied. "If I am wrong the Public will set me right."

His whole conception was a brilliant innovation. Yet how could Raymond have guessed this? At the rehearsal, Edmund mumbled through his part, and he did so deliberately. Now that his opportunity had come at last, he was self-sufficient, and did not want the encouragement and advice of those who had tried to down him. In his heart he had not a doubt that he would succeed, but he could not bring himself to make a show of his confidence. He was still oppressed by a sense of grievance and he thought that the more unexpected his triumph, the sweeter would be his revenge.

He kept away from his fellow actors, chose to share a dressing-room with some of the supernumeraries, and remained lonely, silent, and doleful.

"Last Music" was called and Edmund already stood in the wings, awaiting his first entrance. Naturally, they had not much confidence in him behind the footlights. The strange, morose little man did not resemble a tragedian. He looked so pathetically insignificant. Besides, for Shylock he was quite wrongly made up. Instead of being the dirty, repulsive stage Jew who always wore a red Judas wig, he appeared almost Christian-like in an ordinary black wig— and with his face clean and his costume tidy. Had he dressed himself thus through ignorance or with deliberate intent to flout tradition? In either case he was courting disaster.

But in front they saw him for the first time when he stepped on to the stage, and then he was miraculously transformed. He was no longer the insignificant little man, the miserably incongruous "candidate for public honours." He was the histrionic mesmerist and the complete master of the scene.

Most of them in the audience had been led to expect "something" from the good reports they had read in the Press, but soon they realized that he was infinitely better than they had ever dared to hope. He came forward and bowed gracefully and they were impressed. He took up his position, leaned on his cane, gazed at Antonio, and Doctor Drury, anxious, knew that he was safe. The black eyes, which were to be famous, had already begun to work their magic. Before he spoke a word, Edmund Kean had captured his audience.

He had done well to choose Shylock for his début. It was a part which hid his physical disadvantages, and yet it gave him boundless scope to exploit those brilliant artifices by which he had overcome them. It was unnecessary, in any case, to be an Adonis to act the Jew. But he showed them a Shylock such as they had never seen before—not just a stage "prop." but a man who felt and hated passionately; who inspired pity as well as loathing and fear as well as contempt. He brought all his art into play in order to produce these effects—his energy, force, and agility; his impassioned yet disciplined use of speech and gesture and movement. He acted not only with his voice but with his whole body, especially with those eyes which, fierce or tragic, frightful or melting, could express as much in a few moments as most actors could describe in a night.

Particularly Shylock suited his present purpose to perfection. Any young actor, intent on scoring a sensation overnight, would have done well to choose it. But especially Edmund who had the power, according to Coleridge, to reveal Shakespeare "by flashes of lightning." While the part is neither long nor requisite of much sustaining, it gave him every opportunity to rise, suddenly, amazingly to greater and greater heights. And that was his *forte*. The very way in which the story of Shylock is developed, boldly, swiftly, dramatically, enabled Edmund's lightning to flash with increasing frequency and each time with more brilliance.

So his progress through the play was triumphant. In the first scene he cast his spell upon the audience and they applauded. By the end of the trial scene they were shouting themselves hoarse. Outside the drizzle was still falling and inside the house was less than a third full, but judging from the noise, the excitement, the tension, it seemed that the evening was a most glorious occasion and that, to do it honour, Drury Lane was packed from floor to ceiling. And the gallant few who had created this illusion knew that they were privileged to be present at the birth of a new genius in the theatre, the first reformer, perhaps, since the great days of David Garrick, one who would revivify the histrionic art.

They were used to the cold, formal, declamatory style of acting—the classical school as it was called—practised by John Philip Kemble and his satellites. Kemble was dignified and spoke his lines beautifully and looked fine and impressive, but he played according to rule and consequently made one part appear very like another. This Edmund Kean was dexterous, impulsive, passionate and magnificently scornful of stage conventions, so that the familiar lines seemed to be coming not from his mouth but from the mouth of the actual character; so that he appeared not to be acting the part of Shylock, but to be representing on the stage Shylock in person.

That was how his performance appealed to William Hazlitt who, in deference to truth and not to his editor's instructions, wrote glowingly of it in the *Morning Chronicle*. Hazlitt had criticism to make of Kean's interpretation of Shylock (it did not entirely coincide with his own), but he concluded that "no actor had come out for many years at all equal to him," and in sum he welcomed him as a "naturalist," a throwback to David Garrick, and the long-wanted challenger to the domination of Kemble's artificiality.

Was Kean really a naturalistic actor, for through the influence of Hazlitt and others he became known as such? In the modern sense he was nothing of the kind. Nowadays, naturalistic acting is a result, not of the will of the player, but of the fashion of the play, and if applied to classical tragedy is merely a facile excuse for lack of histrionic power. Whereas Kean rose to the greatness of Shakespeare's characters, the so-called naturalistic actors of the present time bring down Shakespeare's characters to their own level. In other words they attempt to turn tragedy into realistic drama, which is now supposed to be the beginning and end of naturalism.

Was Kean, then, the stage representative of the Romantics? It is certain that he was not influenced by the romantic movement in literature, even though his first London appearance happened to coincide with it. He revolted from the Kemble school, a little because he disliked it, but chiefly because he was cute enough to realize that he could not have succeeded as a "classical" actor even if he had been so inclined. He lacked the necessary accomplishments, both mental and physical, and he was forced, therefore, to evolve a style of acting which was individual and suitable to himself. But he played according to rule, just as surely as Kemble did, even if the rules were of his own making.

In private life, of course, Kean was a Romantic *par excellence*—eccentric, wild, excessively emotional. But it is absurd to suggest that he carried his feelings on to the stage and there allowed them to pour out from him, unregulated and unchecked. There is no acting without method and Kean was extraordinarily methodical. He never made a gesture or a movement which had not been previously thought out, and, according to Vandenhoff, his steps were measured and his inflections and intonations might almost have been read from a musical score. In his histrionic capacity he simulated passion—at his best so convincingly that the artifice was not apparent, at his worst so blatantly that he was accused of resorting to "trick." But a player should, in any case, not give performances that can be dissected and analysed by laymen. He is the exponent of "make-believe" and he should use his art not to show what he is but to persuade his hearers to think him what he is not. On the night of January 26, 1814, a small audience hailed the achievement of a young man who had brought Shylock to life on the stage of Drury Lane and, at that moment, the triumph of Edmund Kean was complete.

Or at least it should have been. From the beginning he had set out to conquer the Public—that fickle, adoring, masterful, sycophantic being in whose presence he became quite fearless. Now the Public in London had recognized him as a great actor, and their example would be followed slavishly by playgoers throughout the rest of the British

Isles. Was that not enough? Had he not reached the summit of his ambition?

In his moment of exultation that night perhaps he thought so. Perhaps he realized then that he was a player whose business was exclusively with those in front. In the first interval he did not go to the Green Room but prowled behind the scenes, outwardly the same silent, gauche, doleful little man as before, inwardly impatient for his next entrance, knowing that he had only showed his audience a fraction of what he could be. During the scene with Tubal, which was the high-light of his performance, his astonished fellow actors crowded in the wings to watch him, while Raymond hovered at the back ready with a glass of hot wine in case he should have exhausted himself. But Edmund ignored all this sudden tribute to his power from those who had previously despised him: and at the end of the play he deliberately avoided their attentions. To them it must have seemed that he was strangely modest and unmoved. He behaved as one who was content to have done his work finely and wanted no fuss.

When Doctor Drury went behind the scenes to congratulate his protégé he found him in his dressing-room alone with the supernumeraries, hurriedly changing back into his shabby day-clothes and preparing to leave the theatre as unobtrusively as possible. For him the evening was over.

No one knew what was really going on in his mind, for he had determined to say nothing until he reached 21 Cecil Street, where Mary would be waiting up for him. He was wildly excited, but refused to show it. His thoughts were in a turmoil, but, as always, he kept them to himself.

That was the way he wanted it. His success had come just two months after Howard's death, and there was really no one now with whom he could share it wholeheartedly. So that, in a sense, he could not think of the future except in terms of the past. Other men in days of ease and luxury and recognition might look back on the hardships that had

gone before as if they had never happened. But not he.
Nothing would obliterate from his memory the sufferings
he had endured, the insults to which he had been subjected
and the occasional kindnesses for which he was grateful. He
would repay them all. He would give Mary the things she
had always wanted—wealth and finery and position. He
would have Charles educated as a gentleman. He himself
would assume in the world at large a position of power and
eminence. And all that would be a kind of vengeance on
the past.

He rushed into the living-room at 21 Cecil Street.

"Mary," he said, "you shall ride in your carriage and
Charley shall go to Eton."

He might have added, "And I shall be a great man as well
as a great actor."

CHAPTER V

I

IN 1814, when Edmund Kean made his début at Drury Lane, London was still a cultural capital; and it was governed, socially at least, by a leisured class who had the time not only to get drunk and to risk their fortunes at the gambling tables, but to converse brilliantly and to patronize the Arts. Though England was engaged in a death-struggle with France, that meant, among other matters, a reprieve for the old order of things. The Napoleonic War had temporarily stemmed the tide of industrial revolution, and had allowed the eighteenth century, with all its paraphernalia of wit and snobbery, dissoluteness and formality, dirt and culture, to encroach on the nineteenth. Soon London would be rid of its ill-lit, cobble-stone streets, its smells and its lack of sanitation, its gambling clubs and its brothels. Soon the plutocracy would rise up and submerge that gilded Society which had once dictated the spirit of the times. Soon there would be no room for those who understood the art of doing nothing utilitarian. Soon beaux and poets and pamphleteers would be shown their proper place in the national scheme.

But the period of the Regency (and a little while afterwards) was the lull before the avalanche of progress, when those few who lived in elegant houses—the men of taste and fashion—had their last, big, magnificent fling.

As a whole, they did not help much in the cause of humanity. They were debauched and selfish and dilettante. But at least they kept alive that interest in aesthetics which had given England the reputation of being a civilized country in spite of the fact that two-thirds of her population could not read or write.

While they remained in command, the theatre was

regarded, not as an idle relaxation for the tired masses, but as a particular hobby of literate connoisseurs. It was "National" in the highest sense of the word—as it has never been since and probably never will be again. That is why the measure of Edmund Kean's success cannot be interpreted in terms of the modern stage.

During his first season at Drury Lane he played Shylock, Richard III, Hamlet, Othello, Iago and Luke in *Riches*. His performances were received with an almost hysterical enthusiasm. He began to earn for himself a vast amount of money. Those admittedly are stock facts which could be told of many actors of the past and the present. But they do not show how completely Edmund Kean captured the Town. Within a month of his début, he had become not only a popular favourite of the moment but an established institution.

In the first place, he saved Drury Lane from financial collapse. On February 26th, Arnold told a meeting of the sub-committee that "Mr. Kean had performed the characters of Shylock and Richard III and had succeeded beyond the capacity of any actor within his recollection." Arnold did not overestimate the case. The money was rolling in. No orders were allowed and no free seats given away. At the second performance of *Richard*, crowds literally stormed the doors of the theatre and the official box-office return approached £600. A figure like that had not been dreamed of since the opening of the new building three years before. And so it would continue throughout the remainder of the season—for Hamlet, Othello, Iago, whenever Edmund Kean appeared in fact. He had done what no one else had been able to do. He had put Drury Lane back on the map: and that in itself was sufficient to secure his position.

But more important than his value as an investment to the older of the Patent Houses was his significance in the English Theatre. The romantic movement was at its height, and a great personality was needed on the stage who would be a representative of the times and who would do the same for the histrionic art as Byron and Shelley and Keats were doing for literature. Edmund Kean seemed completely equipped to fill that bill. He supplied a demand.

As an actor, perhaps, he had faults—faults which would later become apparent and which even his staunchest admirers would be ready to admit. He was not good at sustaining a long part; he was apt to be careless, hurried, inaudible sometimes in the quiet, explanatory passages. Restraint was alien to him, and he could not simulate unaffected happiness. Essentially he was "flashy," "all energy and passion," and he could not show off his real powers until the chance came to let himself go. And then, apart from his physical defects, he was handicapped by a voice which was not naturally melodious. Though he could command it as he pleased, it was often hoarse and grating—"somewhat between an apoplexy and a cold." Leigh Hunt compared it "with a Hackney Coachman's at one in the morning."

But for the moment none of these things mattered. As Shylock he proved himself not only a fine player but an *original* interpreter of Shakespeare's character. And that was the secret of his success. It would be time enough later for audiences to decide whether they preferred his Richard to his Hamlet, his Othello to his Iago, to judge him, in other words, dispassionately. Now they rushed to see him in whatever famous part he chose to play, for they knew that he would at least re-create it, and they were agog to find out in what way. He was the embodiment of a new style of performance—romantic, naturalistic, call it what you will; but certainly representative of the spirit of the times which called for truth and feeling.

He embodied a new style of performance in its fullest sense. He was the actor, the producer, one might almost say the play. Many of his brilliant innovations which disarmed contemporary criticisms were what we should label production. For example, in the tent scene of *Richard III*, he stood for a while as if in a reverie, drawing lines on the ground with the point of his sword before suddenly recovering himself "with a good-night to his lords." And in *Hamlet* he did not make the usual definite exit after bidding Ophelia "To a Nunnery, go," but returned impulsively to kiss her hand, and then hurried off the stage. Hazlitt selected that as "the finest commentary that was ever made on Shakespeare," and quite rightly he gave Kean the credit for it. But were it to be repeated in the theatre of the present, your modern critic would call it business and correctly presume that the producer had invented it.

Kean produced himself, and in a way which delighted his contemporaries. After his first appearance as Othello, the following letter from an anonymous correspondent was published in the *Examiner:*

"I am convinced that Mr. Kean's deficiency of dignity does not in the slightest degree disqualify him as a representative of Shakespeare's *Othello.* There is a delicacy about the taste and feelings of this extraordinary young actor which must be instinctive. His genius in this, as in some other of its characteristics, appears to me to bear a striking resemblance to that of Shakespeare himself. Had they lived in the same day Shakespeare would have stretched out his human hand to him and have welcomed him with delight as at least a kindred spirit."

That is a perfect summing-up of what was the general trend of opinion. Edmund Kean was the new representative of Shakespeare. He gave expression to the overwhelming desire for a break with artificiality. He did not have to fight for recognition of his methods, for the victory was won as soon as he appeared on the stage of Drury Lane. Inevitably he became the great personality of the Regency Theatre.

Kemble, of course, was still at Covent Garden: but Kemble belonged to another generation and was nearing the end of "his long reign at the head of a fine school of art"—already moribund. In himself he was a habit, and playgoers would remain loyal to him—more or less—for the brief remainder of his career. But the tradition which he

represented was clearly doomed, "the electric flashes of
Edmund Kean's genius having swept through it, like
lightning withering, without actually prostrating a stately
grove."

If Kemble was still the King of the British Stage, Kean
was the heir apparent and already enjoying many of the
privileges of sovereignty. When Charles Mayne Young—
second only to Kemble as an exponent of the classical style
of acting—played Richard III at Covent Garden in an
attempt to rival Kean, he was ridiculed. Young, with his
good looks and his melodious voice, had deservedly reached
the top of his profession; and he would remain a popular
actor for a long while yet. But he would have to readjust his
values: and for the moment, certainly, refrain from challeng-
ing the new star of Drury Lane on his own ground.

All this is not meant to suggest that Edmund Kean was
universally acclaimed. The diehards—still devoutly attached
to the classical tradition—denounced him as a cheap impostor; and though they were far outnumbered, they
managed to make their voices heard above the general
chorus of praise. They became not merely his detractors but
his "enemies." For the stage was regarded almost as a
prize-fight ring in which the leading players of the day
battled for supremacy—and with the minimum amount of
good feeling. Consequently partisanship was apt to be fierce,
even violent.

And yet it is surprising how little the diehard antagonism
to Kean was reflected in the newspapers. Essentially, of
course, he was the favourite of what one might call the
Left-wing Press. Hazlitt of the *Morning Chronicle* and the
critic of Leigh Hunt's *Examiner* (Leigh Hunt himself was in
prison) welcomed him with an almost political fervour,
if only because of his challenge to the artificial school of
acting. Both these passionate apostles of truth showed their
hand from the beginning. Hazlitt, who considered Kemble
"an icicle on the bust of Tragedy," naturally revelled in the
performances of an actor of whose death scene in *Richard III*

he could write: "He fought like one drunk with wounds, and the attitude in which he stands with his hands stretched out after his sword had been taken from him had a preternatural and terrific grandeur as if his will couldn't be disarmed, and the very phantom of his despair had the power to kill." The critic of the *Examiner* was even more whole-hearted in his enthusiasm than Hazlitt. He summed up the feelings expressed in all his previous euolgies of Kean, when he wrote, " . . . his Iago, is, we think, the most perfect piece of acting on the stage; it is the most complete absorption of the man in the character."

Certainly the *Morning Chronicle* and the *Examiner* led the huzzas. But the *Morning Post* did not lag far behind when it described Kean's speaking of the soliloquies in *Hamlet* "as the workings of nature itself." And even *The Times*, steadfastly conservative as always, had to admit that, in spite of his many faults and his marked inferiority to Kemble, he was "evidently a player of no ordinary cast."

That, perhaps, was the weakness of his opponents' position. He could not be ignored or dismissed in a sentence. He had, of course, to suffer the shafts of criticism even from his staunchest admirers, for now that Leigh Hunt had set the fashion for incorruptibility and impartiality, no critic worth his salt was content to record empty gush or meaningless generalization. (In our own polite, gentle days, Hazlitt's most eulogistic reviews read suspiciously like bad notices.) They examined Kean's every performance in the minutest detail, and since each had his pet prejudice, it was natural that what appealed to one appalled another: what the *Examiner* called "animation," *The Times* condemned as "lack of dignity." But however much he was praised or blamed and however greatly opinion differed as to his particular merits, he was at least the centre of the controversy. And that only showed the measure of his attraction. There was common sense as well as flippancy in the following letter which appeared in the *Examiner* on March 1, 1814.

SIR,

I am afraid you may consider a newspaper an odd channel for the advice which I wish to give you which is not to mind what the newspapers say:—A morning paper says—"The frequent smile Mr. Kean wore in Richard destroyed the dignity that belongs to the character." Says the Evening Editor:—"Mr. Kean forgot to diversify the sullenness he wore by the spirit of coarse merriment with which Richard contemplates the success of his projects." A weekly publication states that "Mr. Kean's extreme decrepitude in Shylock cast an air of imbecility over the malice of the character"; but a lively wag in a magazine writes—"Mr. Kean should not make old Shylock trip across the stage with a step light enough for Gratiano." . . . If you will just allow me to remark that your tone and manner in the third scene of the fourth act of . . . but why should I make remarks which I have just advised you not to attend to . . .? "

Nothing could really stem the floodtide of Edmund Kean's success. He did not, it is true, break box-office records with his five repeat performances of Shylock during the early days of February. But that was not very surprising. For, although his début had been sensational, only two critics reported it and the most the Drury Lane management could do in the way of capitalizing it by advertisement (the science of "puffing" was still in its infancy) was to print, in small type, at the foot of their play-bills, "Mr. Kean . . . was greeted throughout with the most flattering testimonies."

But it was only a matter of waiting for the news to get round and that did not take long. On Saturday, February 12th, he appeared for the first time as Richard, and then, although the house was not full, every critic in London was present and there was a general atmosphere of excitement and expectancy. It was the occasion, not for an unknown actor to prove his worth, but for a young player already recognized as remarkable to show what he could do with the famous character which had made George Frederick Cooke's name a generation ago.

Edmund was nervous, however. As Shylock, he had had complete confidence in himself, but now he was suffering from a bad cold, and he was fearful that his voice would let him down altogether. He might disappoint and then it would mean starting all over again. He realized that an actor's position could never be secure. It was so hard to reach the top, but so painfully easy to slip back. He would risk his reputation almost every time he set foot on the stage

He might fail as Richard just as surely as he had triumphed as Shylock. He was so apprehensive that he insisted on a "public apology" being made for him. Wroughton, one of the Drury Lane actors, came forward to explain that Mr. Kean "was very much indisposed."

But there was no real need for anxiety or fuss. Edmund spoke with a hoarser voice than usual, but he brought Richard III to life. It was one of his finest parts, offering him opportunities to display the whole range of his virtuosity—his violent passions, his panther-like gaiety. The audience knew that he was physically handicapped, but that only accentuated their appreciation of his new brilliance and made his power and violent energy seem to them even more astounding.

They applauded him throughout. And at the end they stood up and waved and shouted. Their enthusiasm was boundless. With Shylock he had unlocked the gates to recognition: with Richard he banged them wide open. From now on he would be regarded by the Public almost as a national treasure, and their attitude was at once reflected in the Press. On February 18th, the *Morning Post* printed the following news item:

"Mr. Kean has been extremely ill since last Saturday's performance. The great exertions requisite to sustain the part of Richard so much increased his disorder as to produce an expectoration of blood. Dr. Pearson has in consequence been called in, and we are assured his report is favourable to a speedy recovery. It is even said he will be sufficiently well to appear again to-morrow in the arduous character of Richard. We trust he will not, unless he is fully recovered. The Public are unusually interested in the success and recovery of this promising actor."

He did appear, and he did not disappoint the vast audience who had come to see him. But it was obvious, all the same, that he was still far from well, so that at the end there was as much anxiety as applause. "The best compliment was paid him when Rae came forward to announce a repeat performance of *Richard* for Monday. Contrary to the usual practice when a play goes off well, hisses and cries of 'No, no, shame,' etc., burst from all parts of the house. In the evident puny state of his health everyone felt that Mr. Kean's strength was not sufficient to enable him to repeat the character so soon, and the conduct of the audience on this occasion, highly flattering to Mr. Kean, was equally creditable to their own humanity and discrimination."

He reappeared as Richard on February 24th, and the *Morning Post* reported that "his attraction was unprecedented in the annals of theatricals," and that "it was generally admitted that he was honoured with more approbation than ever was experienced by the oldest actor on the stage."

But audiences were still dissatisfied about his health. A report gained currency that their "favourite" was being heartlessly exploited, for purposes of profit, by the Drury Lane management; and they began to express their resentment so markedly that Arnold was at length obliged to ask Edmund for an official denial of the rumour. Edmund set the public mind at rest with the following letter to Arnold which was printed both in *The Times* and the *Morning Post:*

"I have great pleasure in authorizing you to contradict in the most unequivocal terms the report to which you allude. You have never pressed me to appear upon the stage one day earlier than was perfectly agreeable to my own feelings, and you are aware that I have wanted no other spur to exertion than the gratification of appearing before a public who have conferred upon my humble efforts the distinction of so much flattering approbation. I am happy to say that I am in perfect health, and at the service of the theatre whenever and as often as you think proper to call upon me."

Actually, his employers treated him with a considerable show of liberality. At their meeting on February 26th, the sub-committee empowered their chairman to send Mr. Kean a bonus of one hundred guineas and also to conclude a fresh agreement with him whereby he should be paid £16 per week for the remainder of the present season, £18 per week for the next season and £20 per week for the three seasons following. On March 12th, in recognition of his success as Hamlet, they decided to raise his salary immediately to £20 per week. And on July 16th they voted him five subscription shares in the theatre.

Of course, in their view, they were guided more by hard common sense than by impulsive generosity. They could not possibly afford to be mean to the little man who, by his efforts alone, was heading Drury Lane towards unbelievable prosperity. They had got him under contract now for five years and they would have to keep him at any cost. They would have given him the earth, had he demanded it.

To Edmund, who had never before earned anything like a double-figure salary, £20 per week was already a fortune. But it represented only a fraction of what his total income would be. There was his Drury Lane benefit performance which would bring him in several hundred pounds at least. There were provincial engagements which he would be free to fulfil during the summer vacation, and for these he would be paid, as a star among stars, fifty guineas an appearance together with the receipts from a clear benefit night. And there were the lucrative gifts which arrived almost daily from his wealthy and distinguished patrons— for example, one hundred guineas from the Prince Regent, one hundred pounds from Lord Jersey, thirty guineas and a gold watch chain, seals, etc., from Mr. Coutts, the banker, in testimony of "his admiration of the talents which Mr. Kean had displayed and the pleasure which his performance had afforded."

According to newspaper comment, Edmund had particular reason to be gratified by the last-named gift because Mr. Coutts was a well-known admirer of Garrick, "insomuch that Arthur Murphy dedicated to him his life of that unrivalled luminary of the stage."

But as a matter of fact, Edmund was being fêted by an even stauncher admirer of Garrick than Mr. Coutts. To quote the *Morning Post* of March 1st: "The venerable Mrs. Garrick, relict of the celebrated actor, has constantly witnessed the performances of Mr. Kean; and she was heard to declare that since the days of her husband she has never seen an actor who, throughout the part, so strongly impressed her with the recollection of his performance of Richard."

Mrs. Garrick was approaching her ninetieth birthday, and she was old enough to consider the Kemble tradition newfangled or perhaps reactionary even! But she was still an inveterate playgoer, a familiar figure in the private box, near the Prince Regent's, which the Drury Lane management kept permanently at her disposal. She did not give Edmund very tangible proof of her admiration for him, for she guarded pretty carefully the hundred and twenty thousand pounds which her distinguished husband had bequeathed her. But she "took him up," invited him to her house, made him sit in Garrick's favourite chair and then proceeded to tell him, in her kindly, direct way, in just what "points" he was inferior to her "David."

Garrick had been an epoch in the theatre: and now Edmund could be the same. The future belonged to him—undoubtedly. It was only a question of how he would behave, caught up as he was in a sudden, almighty turmoil of wealth and fame and adulation.

To those who worshipped him, of course, his past had not existed at all, or if it had, was simply a romantic background which served to heighten the colour of his present eminence. But to him his past was a reality which, even if he wanted to, he could not forget. There were too many reminders of it.

To begin with, that "expectoration of blood" which the *Morning Post* reported after his performance of Richard was not the result of a common cold. Though he recovered from it with apparent ease, the cure was impermanent. He would be ill again in April, "suffering under severe indisposition," and so it would go on. There was no use disguising the fact that he was already, at the age of twenty-five, a sick man. Perhaps, with care and comfort, he might eventually rebuild his constitution. But he could not wipe out the effects of years of malnutrition in a month or even in a year.

He was bound, too, by old, dangerous attachments. All manner of unworthy acquaintances whom he had met in taverns and elsewhere came to fawn on him now, to cash in on his success, to drink and be fitted out at his expense. He was not the man to ignore them. He was not the man even to disown Ann Carey, who turned up soon enough, as if from nowhere, complete with a grown-up son and daughter-in-law and a grown-up daughter. Perhaps he did not welcome her with open arms but at least he agreed to give her an allowance of £50 per year, and he made some efforts to help her in her desultory stage career. In September of 1814 the whole Carey family would be basking in Edmund's reflected glory at the Peckham Theatre, with Ann Carey calling herself Mrs. Kean and Phoebe Carey calling herself Miss Kean and Mr. and Mrs. Darnley content to use their own names.

And then there was "Aunt" Tid, whom Edmund felt bound to reward, in a material way, for her previous kindnesses to him. That is why—some time in March—he asked permission of the Drury Lane sub-committee, which they refused as it happened, to perform at Miss Tidswell's benefit. "Aunt" Tid had once served his interests devotedly after her own fashion; so perhaps she did merit his affection and loyalty and respect and all the tangible proofs of his

gratitude which he would show her. It was just unfortunate
that she had better opportunities than ever now to make
trouble between him and his wife.

No one cared about his past. But everyone was curious
about his future. What would happen to the slum child who
had grown into a rich and famous man? How would he
stand up to success? Would he live wisely and serve the
public faithfully? Or would he succumb "to the temptations
which beset an actor?"

Both those who wished him well and those who wished
him ill were anxious to know the answer to these questions.

2

Mary, of course, was completely transformed.

Marriage with a starving genius whom she did not understand had been no fun at all, but she adored being the wife
of a man of means and position. Her triumph was really as
great as his. She had stuck to him through all the years of
misery and illness and poverty, in spite of that one occasion
when she had nearly run back to Ireland; and now, at last,
she had got what she wanted. In the living-room at No. 21
Cecil Street bank-notes were piled high on the mantelpiece
and Charles played with golden guineas on the floor.
"Riches (unlooked for riches) pour in on them daily," wrote
Susan. "She will be as rich as a Jew!"

Susan had every reason to be excited. For Sister Mary
obviously did not intend to be selfish with Edmund's money.
The whole Chambers family were to share in the spoil. All
their debts were to be paid. Old Mrs. Chambers, living in
Waterford, was to be given a new house, a new wardrobe,
and anything else she fancied. Susan was to buy herself, for
a start, "thirty or forty pounds worth of clothes—the richest
and best"—all from the inevitable Margaret Roberts, who
was apparently a costumier. "Send me," wrote Susan,
"patterns of what muslin you have, both worked and plain.

You can put them in the letter. I should like clothes of the same coloured satten as the bonnet you sent me."

Meanwhile, in London, Mary—dressed up to kill—had plenty of opportunity to try out her social gifts. Every day—morning and afternoon—distinguished callers alighted from their carriages at No. 21 Cecil Street. There were those who wished to pay their respects to the great actor; there were those who simply had a curiosity to see what he looked like off the stage; and there were the individual members of the Drury Lane sub-committee—Samuel Whitbread, Pascoe Grenfell, the Hon. Douglas Kinnaird and Lord Essex—who came, under the guise of flattery, to give him their advice.

Mary was the hostess who received her husband's grand friends, and she seemed to them a sweet little suburban Irishwoman—not brilliantly intelligent, but touchingly proud to be the adoring wife of a celebrity. She lived for Edmund. She would talk of him as if he were a god. She would listen delightedly to all the flattering remarks about his genius. She would assure inquirers, as in fact she once told Whitbread, that "he was the best man in the world." And she would recall wistfully her devotion to him in those bleak days immediately before his London début. "Ah," she would say, "the Drury Lane actors only looked at his little body. They did not know what he could do with his eye." Grattan, when he called to renew his acquaintance with the Keans some years later, was particularly impressed by Mary's "warm-hearted and overflowing recognizance of ever so trivial a kindness, or tribute of admiration offered to 'Edmund,' before he became a great man."

Everyone liked her for what they called her naïveté. Lady Elizabeth Whitbread and Mrs. Pascoe Grenfell ("who was daughter to Lord Doneraile") took particular notice of her. In fact, Susan was able to write boastfully to Margaret Roberts: "She has as many great friends as he has—which I consider a greater compliment."

Mary had forgotten the past, for the present was so intoxicating. Her letters to Susan (who was still in Ireland) read more "like enchantement than reality." She had wealth and position and a baby whom she would spoil with her lavish fondness. What did it matter that Edmund had once caused her so much misery and had been so impossible to live with? The trappings surely made the man. Already she was enjoying the fruits of his success, and she could look forward to a lifetime of buying and spending, of rubbing shoulders with Lord this and Lady that, of dining out here and there, of entertaining "the best people" at her own table, of being, in fact, the wife of a famous tragedian. In her shallow way she was blissfully happy.

Mary had made her plans for the future without doubting that Edmund would fall in with them. And though she might have known better, it did seem at first as if he were trying hard to keep a level head. Certainly success had had none of the effects which it usually has on men of his kind. It had not spoiled him or made him difficult and temperamental and overbearing.

He showed no inclination to challenge the authority of his employers or to disregard their instruction. Far from *demanding* an increase in salary, "he was very grateful" to the sub-committee for their liberality. On February 26th, after his performance as Richard, Arnold was able to report that "he had conducted himself with the greatest propriety."

Inside Dury Lane, of course, he was a king, occupying the best dressing-room and receiving homage from most of the actors who, only a short while ago, had affected to despise him. Pope, a well-known tragedian of the second rank, was particularly unstinted in his subservience. He followed Edmund about everywhere, regaling him, in public and in private, with his pompous, effusive praises. A curious man, Pope; he maintained his position on the stage, in spite of having been flayed alive by Leigh Hunt and generally labelled "bombastic and ridiculous." He was a gifted painter "who exhibited at the Royal Academy fifty-nine miniatures." He was also a snob among actors, a gourmand "who had to be in Plymouth for the mullet season," and who refused to sit with Madame Catalani "because she cut a fricandeau with a knife." It was typical of him that he clung as closely as possible to the new star of Drury Lane, who was after all the man of the moment.

But though Edmund did not avoid Pope, "he endured his fulsome flatteries with indifference." He seemed, in fact, impervious to any amount of adulation. Even the wild enthusiasm of his audiences left him comparatively unmoved. He meant it when he said to Douglas Kinnaird, "I have often acted the third act of *Othello* in the same manner as now calls down such thunders, when the whole house laughed. After that can you think that I care much for public taste?"

Outside the theatre, in spite of all the fuss that was made of him, he remained modest and appeared anxious to avoid saying or doing anything indecorous. "He is a simple man," said Douglas Kinnaird, "he sent his wife to Pascoe Grenfell, his patron, to ask him if he thought it would be any presumption or impropriety in his keeping a horse. Grenfell said no, and his partner Williams sent him one that cost eighty guineas."

The Grenfells asked him and Mary to spend Passion Week with them at their house in the country. Mary arrived decked out in all her new, rather flamboyant fineries. But Edmund's manner was quiet and subdued: and Grenfell remembered "that he drank but sparingly of wine."

Everyone who met him remarked on his reserve. On May 19th, John Cam Hobhouse—then in the springtime of his intellectual and political ambition—saw his Othello with Byron and Thomas Moore. Afterwards they all went round to the Green Room to offer their congratulations, and Hobhouse records: "Miss Smith who had been acting Desdemona, came in. She said that Kean affected her very much in his Othello. She couldn't help crying. She said also that he is a very kind and encouraging actor to play with . . . Kean came in a pepper and salt suit, a very short man, but strongly made and wide-shouldered, hollow sallow face and thick black hair. Lord Byron was introduced to him and on some compliment from him, said he was proud of his lordship's approbation. Douglas Kinnaird introduced me. I asked him after his health, which, he said, was tolerable, but that he sometimes found his voice fail him. He has a sweet accent and manner. He soon withdrew."

Not a very productive interview. But Edmund seemed content to leave it to others to be illuminating about him, to describe his habits and to tell anecdotes of his past. He was, of course, a topic of conversation at every fashionable table; and well-known *raconteurs*, with a reputation to keep up, naturally had a fund of "authentic" Kean stories at their disposal.

Sheridan, dining with Lord Tavistock, remembered that back in 1800 when he was in control at Drury Lane, someone had urged him to bring out young Kean as a rival to Master Betty. But he had turned this down with the sage observation: "No! one bubble at a time is enough, if you have two they will knock against each other and burst." The company laughed, and Sheridan remembered that only the other day Kean had been seen prancing along the Strand on the "fine" horse which Grenfell's partner had given him. "Take care," said a friend, "you are a good actor but——" "But what?" asked Kean. "You don't know that I was paid thirty pounds for breaking in three horses last year at Brighton."

At another party, young Lord John Russell had "certain knowledge" that "Kean was going to drown himself when he had been in London a short time and had been refused by manager Harris [of Covent Garden!] who told him that he was too short for any character. He thought, however, of his wife and child and fortunately had a kindly landlady."

Then there were those in the theatre world itself who claimed, mysteriously enough, to have known him since his birth, and who kept the *raconteurs* well supplied with titbits. For example, Michael Kelly, the singer and composer, had been asked by Edmund (at the time of his row with Elliston) for a loan of two pounds "so that he might take a place in the stage coach and quit London forever." Kelly had refused. He would lend him two pounds or twenty pounds, "but not to enable him to quit London. He ought to try his hand again."

Michael Kelly was particularly inventive. He told, with a shameful disregard for truth, that when his operatic version of *Cymon* was produced at Drury Lane in 1791, he gave the boy Edmund Kean his first job. He engaged him to play the part of Cupid. He chose him from a whole bunch of child actors because of his fine black eyes!

But while these stories were being bandied about and while the wits attempted to invest him with a personality, Edmund remained extremely unforthcoming. He was often invited to the "mansions of the Great," but he hardly spoke at all except in answer to direct questions and he looked constrained and ill at ease. In June he attended a dinner-party at Holland House, which was perhaps the social pinnacle of London, the foremost of "those arenas where the collision of learning, taste and talent brought forth a galaxy of brilliant things not to be met with elsewhere." Here Henry Fox and his beautiful and dominating wife gathered together lions from every jungle; here came authors and poets and painters to talk of many things; here came statesmen and Whig politicians to discuss the burning topics of the hour—Penal Reform, Catholic Emancipation, the Abolition of Slavery, and so on; and here, as a modish embellishment, came the Regency beaux—George Brummel, Scrope Davis, "Poodle Byng," "Kangaroo" Cooke, "King" Allen and the rest—the graceful *flâneurs* to whom a witty retort or a featherlight sarcasm was worth more than all Wellington's victories put together.

On this occasion, Edmund was supposedly the attraction of the evening, and the guests who had been invited to meet him were distinguished enough. Lord Byron had for some reason declined, but Hobhouse was there, and also Grattan and Martin Archer Shee, the poet and painter, and Major

Stanhope and Lord Ebrington, who both came in rather late. The conversation drifted away from Edmund: and Hobhouse noticed that he "ate most pertinaciously with his knife" and "knitted his brows . . . when he could not exactly make out what was said."

At length, Lady Holland turned her attention to him. She asked in her commanding, somewhat tactless way (did not Talleyrand say of her, "Elle est tout assertion"?) "why all the actors said 'Give me the hand' as if 'thy' were 'thee.'" Edmund replied that he never said "thee" instead of "thy." He was particularly sensitive about this question of pronunciation. After his first performance of *Hamlet*, the critics had reprimanded him for saying "contŭmĕly" and "ăbsĕnt yourself." He did not want it thought that he had made these errors through ignorance, so he had hastened to explain to Kinnaird that they were slips caused by his "alarm" at having received an anonymous and abusive letter just before going on the stage.

In short, the man who acted so passionately in the theatre was a little disappointing to meet socially. His eyes were certainly brilliant and his fine "Italian" features were impressive, so that one could not help being struck by his appearance. But though his manner was agreeably unassuming, he was rather too nervous of committing himself, rather too set on being gentlemanly, rather "too frequent with ladyships and lordships, as was natural to him." One would have appreciated a trifle more boldness, a trifle more vigour, a trifle more vulgarity even. In modern parlance, he was a bit "dumb."

But did it really matter? Even if one's curiosity were completely satiated after a few minutes' converse with him at a dinner-table, one would nevertheless go again and again to see him at Drury Lane. On the stage he was the master; his personality was dazzling and supreme. To be sure, there were the disgruntled traditionalists who resented his success and, like a certain Mr. Taylor, said that "he was a humbug . . . a pot-house actor." But who were they

EDMUND KEAN AS OTHELLO

compared with the brilliant throng which flooded the vast
Drury Lane auditorium whenever he appeared—the professional men jammed uncomfortably together on wooden
benches in the pit, the aristocrats in the boxes craning
forward to get a better view of the stage, and far above in the
gallery the gentlemen's servants and the ladies of the town
ogling, perhaps, for more advantageous places in the tiers
below? They sat in suffocating airlessness, with the stink of
burning candle-wax in their nostrils (a little later it would
be gas fumes), but Edmund could still them into silence or
melt them into tears or rouse them to frenzies of applause
almost at his will.

Throughout the season his hold on the public showed no
signs of weakening. On the contrary, some of those who
had at first been a trifle backward in admitting his genius
went to see him again and became increasingly enthusiastic.
Hobhouse noted in his journal on June 4th that Lord Grey
"was one of the last to be converted to his style but at last
was one of the warmest of his admirers"—and that within
five months of his début!

Crabb Robinson, who also kept a diary, saw Edmund for
the first time as Richard III, and though he admitted that
"he played the part better than any other man I ever saw,"
he harped a good deal on his defects. "His most flagrant
defect is want of dignity . . . he projects his lower lip
ungracefully . . . his declamation is very unpleasant. He
gratified my eye more than my ear. His speech is not fluent,
and his words and syllables are too distinctly separated."
But a few weeks later Crabb Robinson was completely
swept off his feet by Edmund's Othello. "It is the character
for which he is least qualified but one in which he has most
delighted me . . . I could hardly keep from crying . . . it
was pure feeling."

That is what impressed his admirers most—his ability to
make them forget that he was really an undersized little
man with an unmelodious voice. Perhaps he was particularly
suited to be Richard or Shylock or Iago: perhaps there

needed to be something warped or deformed or monstrous in a character to hide his physical defects completely and to give his powers full scope; perhaps his greatest performance of all was as Richard, which allowed him to show off "that tempest and whirlwind of the soul, that life and spirit and dazzling rapidity of motion, which filled the stage, and burned in every part of it." Yet as Hamlet, in spite of his essential lack of nobility, he revealed beauties before undreamed of. And as Othello, especially in the scenes of pagan passion and heartrending pathos, he seemed, as it were, to rise up out of himself and to become, in truth, the Noble Moor of Venice.

"By God he is a Soul," said Byron. And Byron, unlike the majority of his class, tried patiently to discover the soul of the actor in the man. But at least the majority worshipped him as a player and after they had seen him in a part, treasured the memory of each separate expression of his face and each separate inflection of his voice. At least Lady Caroline Lamb "presented her compliments to Mr. Kean and wished to know whether so great an admirer as she was of his talents might venture to suggest one question: why, when his Othello was perfect, had he altered his manner of saying two things, 'Is she honest?' and 'A fool! a fool!' "

3

The season moved towards a glorious close.

On May 25th, Edmund took his benefit, "which was boasted a bumper." He appeared then for the first time in *Riches*, a melodramatic concoction of no great literary value based on Massinger's *City Madam*, a kind of forewarning of what would eventually become the nineteenth century's taste in Drama. The play, in fact, is banal and tedious and was considered so—at least by the leading critics who either gave it a very cursory notice or, like Hazlitt, ignored it completely. But the part of the hypocritical villain, Luke, who at first smarms, and then triumphs wickedly, and finally meets with just retribution, provides stuff, however artificial, for a histrionic *tour de force*. Edmund made magnificent use of his chances. His acting (in this case, how could it conceivably have been naturalistic?) was sufficiently a show in itself to electrify his audience and to send them into raptures.

On June 16th he performed Othello before the King of Prussia and the Emperor of all the Russias. Their Majesties were conducted to the Prince Regent's private box by Messrs. Arnold, Raymond, and Ward, acting as candle-bearers, and were received there by Mr. Samuel Whit-bread, M.P.

On June 29th the sub-committee met to consider the unfortunate case of Mr. Elliston who, though still the highest paid member of the Drury Lane company, had failed to appear a few nights ago owing to intoxication. It was decided to fine him £10. The sub-committee were having no such trouble with Edmund Kean, and even if they had been, would not have dared to punish him. He was now giving his farewell round of performances before the summer vacation—"his last appearance but three, his last appearance but two, his last appearance but one, his last appearance!" in Shylock, Richard, Hamlet, Othello and Iago.

On June 16th the season ended. Samuel Whitbread wrote Edmund a letter, full of affectionate regard and gratitude, but finishing on rather an anxious note. "If it be true that you are to play at Cheltenham and Gloucester on the same day—morning and afternoon—I wish it had been other-wise. Spare yourself for the sake of your health . . . Lady Elizabeth desires her best regards to you and Mrs. Kean."

Edmund, so it was said later, received Whitbread's advice without rancour—"as a man." But he did not follow it. In the days when he had found it hard enough to keep alive at all, he had not been encouraged—or allowed even— "to spare himself." So why should he begin now, when he was assured of money and acclamation galore wherever he chose to go in the provinces? Country managers were clamouring for his services and were willing to pay him any price he cared to name. It would always be the same of course; for London set the fashion in actors, which was followed, virtually without question, in every other important playgoing town of the United Kingdom.

But Edmund was not prepared to bide his time and to pick and choose his provincial engagements. He wanted to capitalize his success at once—while the going was good. He had suffered too much in the past to be confident that his luck would last for ever or that he would hold his present position indefinitely. No matter what the physical strain, he was, in his own words, determined "to make hay while the sun shone."

And so he went into the country, accompanied by Mary and his faithful flatterer Pope, immediately the Drury Lane season was over.

On July 24th, the *Champion* was able to report the following happening, presumably a few days old. "Mr. Kean was announced to play Richard at the unusual hour of twelve o'clock noon! at the Cheltenham theatre on his way to Dublin, his engagement at the latter place not admitting any delay on the road."

He opened at the Theatre Royal, Dublin, on July 25th—again as Richard. Pope, who was with him as a kind of histrionic *aide-de-camp*, played Richmond, and the resident company were "new clothed by the management as a mark of respect to Mr. Kean." It was altogether a glamorous occasion, and the fact that Edmund "laboured under the effects of a cold" did not detract from it in the least. The critics were content to dwell on "his magic eye" and his "originality." For the rest, it was the usual success story—an overflowing house, wild applause, adulation.

Edmund felt like a conqueror returned to his native land. He was proud of his Irish blood and had always supposed that there was a bond of sympathy between him and his lost compatriots. (Had he not once fancied himself as the leader of a rebellion?) Now he was the biggest draw for years at a theatre whose doors only a little while ago had been closed to him, and he was being slapped on the back and abundantly fêted by hard-drinking, vociferous, and warm-hearted Dublin playgoers.

He was being prodigiousy well paid, too. As the *Monthly Museum* periodical put it, "It is not long since his application for an engagement at Belfast on a salary of two guineas a week was declined, and a similar thing happened in Dublin. He might have been engaged at two guineas a week, instead of at the sacrifice of half the night's profits."

He remained more than a month in Dublin, appearing in all his Drury Lane parts, and adding to these Macbeth, Reuben Glenroy in *Town and Country*, and Jaffier in Ottway's *Venice Preserved*. The *Monthly Museum* decided that his Jaffier was bad and added what was a significant comment in the light of after events. "We felt the loss of Miss O'Neill in Belvidera. Miss Walstein *plays* the character but can't look it."

Eliza O'Neill was a member of the resident company, and though a great favourite with local playgoers, was not, of course, so popular as to vie seriously with the sensational star from Drury Lane. But in a few weeks' time she would be playing leading parts at Covent Garden; and then Hazlitt would consider her Belvidera to be "as near perfection as anything he had ever seen." She would be the first to trespass on Edmund's domain.

But for the moment he was unchallenged, and he left Dublin with his colours flying and his pockets full. At the beginning of September he returned to Cheltenham, where his reception is best described in the words of the *Cheltenham Chronicle*.

"The all powerful attractions of Edmund Kean were on Tuesday last fully shown by the throng which attended our theatre to witness his unrivalled performance of Richard III. At the early part of the week all the boxes were taken; and such was the desire to see him that even the gallery became the resort of respectability. The musicians relinquished their seats in the orchestra, taking their station behind the scenes."

Six years ago he had been in Cheltenham—an unknown actor playing to empty benches: and the local gossips harped romantically on the contrast between then and now. They did not recall, of course, that particular day when he had set out in a hired postchaise, with half a borrowed guinea in his pocket, to get married to a woman with whom he had vainly supposed himself in love. But Edmund was rather drearily reminded of it by the presence not only of his wife but of his sister-in-law as well. For in Ireland, Mary had taken the opportunity to persuade Susan to come and live with her permanently. There would be plenty of room for both of them at No. 21 Cecil Street.

On September 2nd, Samuel Whitbread addressed the annual meeting of the Drury Lane shareholders held at the Crown and Anchor Inn. He concluded a lengthy peroration in praise of Mr. Kean with these stirring words. "It is to him that, after one hundred and thirty five nights of continued loss and disappointment, the subscribers are indebted for the success of the season; and it is to him that the public are indebted for the high treat which they have received by the variety of characters he has represented."

Edmund returned to London with Mary and Susan. On October 3rd he began his second Drury Lane season with a performance of *Richard III*. In the past eight months he had earned just over £4,000.

CHAPTER VI

I

WILLIAM HAZLITT had been sacked from the *Morning Chronicle* on account of his neglect (among other such trivial matters) "to get a new velvet collar to an old-fashioned great-coat." He was now dramatic critic of a weekly periodical called the *Champion*, and in his professional capacity he was among the crowded audience which welcomed Edmund Kean's return to Drury Lane in *Richard* on October 3rd. There was general enthusiasm that night. But Hazlitt did not share in it. He was disappointed, and he expressed his feelings in a very forthright and uncompromising notice which appeared in the *Champion* on October 4th.

"We do not think Mr. Kean at all improved by his Irish expedition . . ." he wrote, " . . . his pauses are twice as long as they were and the rapidity with which he hurries over other parts of the dialogue is twice as great as it was. In both these points his style of acting always bordered on the very verge of extravagance; and we suspect it has at present passed the line. . . . The quickness of familiar utterance with which he pronounced the anticipated doom of Stanley, 'Chop off his head,' was quite ludicrous. Again the manner in which, after his nephew said, 'I fear no uncles dead,' he suddenly turned round and answered, 'And I hope none living, Sir,' was, we thought, quite out of character. . . . He frequently varied the execution of many of his most striking conceptions, and the attempt in general failed, as it naturally must do. . . . We object particularly to his varying the original action in the dying scene. He at first held out his hands in a way which can only be conceived by those who saw him—in motionless despair— or as if there was some preternatural power in the mere manifestation of his will; he now actually fights with his doubled fists, after his sword is taken from him, like some helpless infant. . . . We really think that Mr. Kean was in a great many instances either too familiar, too emphatic, or too energetic. In the latter scenes, perhaps, his energy could not be too great; but he gave the energy of action alone. He merely gesticulated, or at best vociferated the part. His articulation totally failed him. We doubt if a single person in the house, not acquainted with the play, understood a single sentence that he uttered. It was 'inexplicable dumb show and noise.' . . . We wish to throw the fault of most of our objections on the managers. Their conduct has been marked by one uniform character, a paltry attention to their own immediate interest, a distrust of Mr. Kean's abilities to perform more than the characters he has succeeded in, and a contempt for the wishes of the public. They have spun him tediously out in every character, and have forced him to display the variety of his talents in the same instead of in different characters. . . . Why tantalize the public? Why extort from them their last shilling for the twentieth repetition of the same part, instead of letting them make their election for themselves, or of what they like best? It is really very pitiful.

"Ill as we conceive the London managers have treated him, the London audiences have treated him well; and we wish Mr. Kean, for some years at least, to stick to them. . . . After he has got through the season here well we see no reason why he should make himself hoarse with performing Hamlet at twelve o'clock and Richard at six, at Kidderminster. . . . To a man of genius, leisure is the first of benefits as well as of luxuries.

"It was our first duty to point out Mr. Kean's excellences to the public, and we did so with no sparing hand; it is our second duty to him, to ourselves, and the public to distinguish between his excellences and defects, and to prevent, if possible, his excellences from degenerating into defects."

That notice was full of forebodings. Superficially, of
course, it merely meant that Edmund was tired and ill after
his exertions in the provinces, and had had to resort to a
measure of "trick" acting in order to conceal his fatigue.
But one may read between the lines that Hazlitt's first
excitement at discovering the stage representative of "truth
and feeling" had mellowed. He was now calm enough to
regard the actor dispassionately—in fact, to judge him
strictly on his own merits.

Hazlitt's attitude inevitably became the general one. For
it was obvious that the crusade against artificiality was
victorious and that the new naturalism had come to stay.
Nothing proved this better than the policy which Covent
Garden decided to pursue at the very beginning of the new
season. Though Kemble still had his personal following, it
was the duty of his manager to keep in touch with the trends
of public opinion. Thomas Harris realized quite well that
Kemble unaided was not a good enough financial investment; and that it would be madness to allow Covent Garden
to remain exclusively the home of classical acting. That is
why, on October 6th, he brought out Eliza O'Neill as
Juliet.

She captured the town at once, not because she happened
to be a young and rather beautiful woman with a deep,
powerful voice, but because—in Hazlitt's words—"she
perfectly conceived what would be generally felt by the
female mind in the extraordinary and overpowering situa-
tions in which she was placed." She did not drape herself
in statuesque poses, but allowed the emotions of tenderness
and pity, fear and anguish to play about her features. She
did not declaim, sing-song like, in measured, monotonous
tones, but varied her pitch and tempo continually so as to
create the illusion that she spoke from her very heart. She
wept real tears and laughed with the gaiety of young love.
She was, in short, the impersonator of "faultless nature."

She drew the crowds to Covent Garden, not because she
was better than Edmund Kean but because she was com-

parable with him. That, in a sense, was a tribute to his power, for it proved that he had accomplished his purpose in the theatre. But it was also a challenge which meant that his days of real security were over. He had risen suddenly to the pinnacle of fame, and now was reminded of the difficulty of staying there. In his first season he had introduced and popularized a new style of performance. The rest of his career would be taken up in a desperate struggle to remain the undisputed head of his own school of acting.

He did not have to regard Eliza O'Neill as a very dangerous rival, for his qualities were distinct from hers and in the main more exciting. He could electrify, while she could only charm or harrow. He was the impersonator of fierce passions, while she was a "hugging actress" who excelled in the portrayal of grief and fondness. Hazlitt summed up their respective merits in these words: "Her acting is undoubtedly more correct, equable, and faultless throughout than Mr. Kean's, and it is quite as affecting at the time, in the more impassioned parts. But it does not leave the same impression on the mind afterwards. It adds little to the stock of our ideas, or to our materials for reflection, but passes away with the momentary illusion of the scene."

There was room in London for both of them. But she had robbed him of a part of his prerogative. Though she did not actually imitate his methods, she was clearly of the same *genre* as he. And for his part he had to avoid encroaching on her territory. Gone were the days when audiences would flock to see him automatically, for he was no longer the personification of "naturalism," but merely one of its exponents. Now he would have to contrive to keep public interest alive in him by continually showing off his versatility in new characters. And his success or failure would depend largely on how much scope those characters gave for the display of his peculiar talents. He would never cease to be in the limelight. But he would never again be worshipped blindly. Henceforth the box-office would be a rising and falling barometer of his popularity.

Certainly his hold on the public did not seem to have slackened in the least when, on November 9th, he appeared for the first time in *Macbeth* which, according to the play-bills, had been in preparation all the summer. The house was packed out; and excitement was so much at fever pitch that when he made his entrance "amidst his troops on the bridge . . . the pit composed almost exclusively of gentlemen, stood on the benches and gave several hearty and distinct cheers; while the fair tenants of the boxes waved their handkerchiefs in token of a correspondent feeling." Everyone wanted to see him in this part, not only because it was one of the most famous and the most difficult in Shakespeare, but because Kemble's acting of it had served as the model in recent years. They were looking for a new interpretation which would be vigorous and individual and provocative. And they knew that Edmund Kean would not disappoint them.

His performance was by no means perfect. In many scenes it was dull and colourless. Hazlitt described it as sketchy. But there were the usual high-lights, including his acting after the murder of Duncan, which all the critics praised and which Hazlitt considered one of the two finest things he had so far done. "The hesitation, the bewildered look, the coming to himself when he sees his hands bloody, the manner in which his voice clung to his throat and choked his utterance, his agony and tears, the force of nature overcome by passion—beggared description. It was a scene which no one who saw it can ever efface from his memory."

One thing is certain. His Macbeth was strong and powerful—so much so that he dominated the play: and that does not often happen even when Lady Macbeth is given to an actress of inferior quality. Edmund stole her thunder; and one may guess in what manner by the following extract from an anonymous letter which appeared in the

Champion: " . . . Let me here remark a most important difference between the acting of Mr. Kemble and Mr. Kean. To Lady Macbeth's question, 'When does Duncan go hence?' Mr. Kemble replies indifferently, 'To-morrow as he purposes.' With Mr. Kean it assumes a very different aspect. In an emphatic tone, and with a hesitating look . . . he half divulges the secret of his breast—'To-morrow as he . . . *purposes*! . . .' " In other words, by means of a pause and a stress, he gave the impression that the idea of murdering Duncan had already occurred to him. From then on he appeared not the pawn of his wife's ambition but the master of his own destiny.

Perhaps his performance had aesthetic weaknesses which the professional critics were not slow to point out. But at least it seemed worthy of a great star. He was always in command of the stage and always head and shoulders above the rest of the cast. That was how audiences liked to see him. And so *Macbeth* proved as big a box-office success as *Richard* and the rest had done last season. He repeated it twenty-three times and before houses so large and enthusiastic that it seemed he would inevitably follow the same triumphant course as always. He did not have to think about playing another character until the New Year.

But then he made a bad mistake—or rather the mistake was forced upon him by the Drury Lane committee. On January 2, 1815, he appeared as Romeo.

A few months ago, perhaps, he might have got away with it, even though he had none of the right qualifications for the part. But now he invited comparison with Eliza O'Neill, whose Juliet was considered a masterpiece. Inevitably he came off badly. He could neither look like a boy nor could he simulate the ardour of young love. In years he was youthful, but in spirit he was mature. He did not understand how to woo and he had no sympathy with Romeo's calf-like devotion. He acted as if he were forcing himself to speak lines with a show of conviction which really made him blush; so that his performance, far from revealing nature, was essentially anti-nature. According to the critic of the *Sun*, " . . . He exaggerated every passion and tore them to tatters. . . . A rotatory movement of the hand, as if describing the revolution of a spinning jenny; multiplied slaps upon his forehead, and manual elevation of his fell of hair; repeated knocking upon his own breast, and occasional rapping at the chests of others; the opening of his ruffles, like a schoolboy run riot from the playground, and a strange indistinct groping inside of his shirt, as if in search of something uncommonly minute, filled up the round of his action, while a voice most unmusical, exerted to a harsh and painful screech, afforded the finishing touch to a Romeo decidedly the worst we ever witnessed on the London boards."

Not all the critics were so harsh. Indeed, a few expressed themselves enraptured; and even Hazlitt, who was very critical of the performance in general, wrote glowingly of it in two particulars: " . . . In the midst of the extravagant and irresistible expression of Romeo's grief, at being banished from the object of his love, his voice suddenly stops and falters, and is choked with sobs of tenderness when he comes to Juliet's name. Those persons must be made of sterner stuff than ourselves, who are proof against Mr. Kean's acting, both in this scene and in his dying convulsion at the close of the play."

There were undoubtedly great flashes. But according to general opinion his Romeo fell far short of Miss O'Neill's Juliet, and that fact was sufficiently damning in itself to convince the public that his performance was uninteresting and scarcely worth a visit. On the night that he opened in the part the house was crowded. But he only repeated it eight times, and even so drew very little money to the box-office.

Romeo was his initial failure on the London stage; and it marked the end of the peak period of his career. He would go on, of course, to many more triumphs. But he would never be able to *float* on the crest of public enthusiasm as he had done during those first few months after his sensational début. Now he would have to swim to the top of the wave and swim again. His future would be bound up with all the inscrutable factors which determine success or failure in the theatre.

In fact he remained, through the ups and downs of the next eighteen years, the head of his profession. And that was a remarkable tribute to his histrionic power. For he did so in spite of the many blunders committed by the managers whom he served and in spite of the fact that he was, in himself, a tragically dangerous enemy to his own interests.

2

His personal tragedy was already beginning to unfold. Some time in January of 1815 a certain Mr. J. H. Merivale, who was a fervent amateur of the drama and a playwright in his spare time, addressed the following letter to Doctor Drury:

"I hoped to have had some instructions from you to regulate my conduct with respect to poor Kean, having few objects more at heart than to contribute all in my power towards the good work of rescuing him from the imminent dangers which beset him. Evil reports have been crowding in upon us from day to day almost ever since our return to town in November. It was long before I would give anything like implicit credit to the tales with which every indifferent visitor came charged; and when at last, circumstances crowded upon each other so as to leave no room for scepticism, it occupied my thoughts for many an hour how I could in the best way . . . present myself before him in the quality of an adviser, with any probability of a beneficial result. At last I took the occasion of our having seen him in *Romeo*, to write him a few lines . . . hinting, in a manner as adroitly combined of flattery and remonstrance as I could well imagine, at the want of proper confidence in his own genius, and ambition of better things, which gave a handle to his enemies and paralysed his own exertions. This note . . . produced (as we have since found) a suitable effect and he insisted upon being himself the immediate bearer of a message respecting places that we had desired Mrs. Kean to procure for us at *Macbeth*.

" . . . Having in some measure . . . tried my ground . . . I at last devoted a whole morning at Chambers to the composition of a long letter in which I told him . . . that the worst of his enemies beyond all comparison were those who, for the invidious purpose of degrading him to their own level, made him sacrifice his time and health, talents and reputation, to them, and then went about the town publishing his disgrace to *their* glory. This I sent off not without hopes that he would have answered me either by letter or in person. Neither of these, however, being the case . . . on Friday last I called and found Mrs. Kean at home, who received me with a hearty shake of the hand, but with a great deal of dejection and apparent embarrassment in her manner. 'I have wished much to see you,' she said, 'and thank you for your letter,' and upon my inquiring how Kean himself took it, she assured me that he was extremely sensible of my friendship, and that nothing but shame could have prevented him from answering it; but that when he received it . . . he was evidently much hurt, would not show her the contents, but merely exclaimed, 'This is all my fault, d——d fool that I am! etc.'

"But she added this had been . . . a fortnight . . . of severe trial and even agony to her. Beset as he is by these infamous scoundrels who swindle him out of his money and keep him for days together at the alehouse . . . he had never gone so completely and, it seems, hopelessly astray as about a fortnight since when he went off from town unknown to her, and wrote from Woolwich saying that it was his resolution never to see her or his child again—that she may take all their money but he would find freedom in a foreign country. . . . Upon receiving this letter she instantly set off for Woolwich, accompanied by her sister, found him there surrounded by all his most pernicious associates, and after in vain remonstrating with him, was forced to return to town as she came but in a state of fever which had nearly made an end of her miseries. A day or two later he came back—the fit over—and in a state of contrition at least equal to his former madness. Then came my letter, the next day *yours*, and with it calls from Whitbread, Grenfell, and Lord Essex, all directed to the same end, and which, she said, had the more confounded him, as he had deceived himself into a previous opinion that his eccentricities were known only to himself and those immediately about him.

" . . . From all I could collect it seemed to me very evident that if the poor fellow is to be saved from his friends, now is the time. . . . As one important step to his restoration, I have since proposed to him to devote a morning to calling upon those of our mutual acquaintances who have reason to think he has neglected them, and called there again yesterday to fix a time for the purpose. I found him at home and never did I see the gentleman and man of genius more fully combined in his reception of me.

" . . . Much as our poor Roscius is indebted to you for bringing him forward, his present obligation is nothing to what he would owe you for showing him where he ought to stand.

" . . . He is but an infant in experience, and till you taught him, he never learned to stand upright. No wonder his foot slipped; and oppressed as he is . . . he requires every possible assistance to recover his former footing."

There were others, besides Doctor Drury and Mr. Merivale, who were anxious to rescue Edmund "from the dangers which beset him." There were the members of the Drury Lane sub-committee (Whitbread, Lord Essex, and the rest) who realized that it was as much to their theatre's interests as his own that he should be prevented from debauching his success in the same way as the disreputable George Frederick Cooke had done. And there was Mary who feared that he was coming perilously near to ruining her own plans for the future. They were all of them, after their own fashion, passionately concerned for his welfare.

But they were none of them in a position to help him, for they did not understand what was at the back of his mad behaviour. They knew that he spent his time with tavern riff-raff, and got drunk and brawled and threw his money away. But they did not guess why. They only supposed that he was, by nature, foolish, perverse, unstable, and "under the influence of no principle more regular and steady than the moon." So they embarked on the hopeless task of curing him by good advice.

He could not have explained himself. He had always looked forward to the day when he would have the *entrée* to London society: but now that it was his, he protested that he hated lords and gentlemen and that he preferred the bars round Covent Garden to the houses of his distinguished patrons. It seemed a curious change of front.

And yet from the beginning it was inevitable. He was not a snob, immeasurably flattered at the mere chance to "sit down at a lord's table." He was a megalomaniac who was obsessed with a childish desire to be the centre of attraction wherever he went and who always revolted against any milieu where he was frustrated. How could he possibly shine—or even hold his own—in the company of men of fashion? He had none of the right qualities. He could not appear knowledgeable or witty or charmingly gay. Socially he was a pothouse entertainer, not a drawing-room conversationalist.

There were a few, like Byron and Kinnaird, who worked deliberately to draw him out and allowed him to steal a little of the limelight. They would ask him to their small, informal dinner parties where they would encourage him to tell anecdotes of his strolling player days and would persuade him towards the end of the evening, after the bottle had been passed round freely, to give his imitations of Kemble, of Incledon, of Master Betty, and the rest. But though he held their attention and won their applause, he was no more than a professional funny man. On level terms, what chance had he against the brilliant arrogance of Byron, who sat up all night with Hobhouse enumerating a thousand rules for a club of which the two of them were to be the only members? A style and an affectation were the necessary equipment of a man of fashion. And Edmund had neither. Off the stage he was himself and could not play a part. If he had even able to talk of his "art" in a self-conscious, high-falutin manner, it would have gone down well. But when Kinnaird asked him if he felt his characters on the stage, he replied that he never did except when he was acting with a pretty woman. And that was the bald, simple truth.

The nobility continued to invite him to their dinner parties and the like. But he was sensitive enough to realize that "they meant him no honour by these distinctions, which were so many negative tributes offered to their own importance." Their manner towards him was condescending and class conscious. He complained that they did not treat him as an equal but as a kind of wild beast on parade. They hardly addressed a word to him except on the subject of his acting, and even then they seemed more concerned to express their own opinions, which he considered unmitigated nonsense, than to listen to his. Invariably he was left unnoticed after they had done with praising or criticizing his latest performance, for they went on to discuss politics and painting and endless other topics of which he knew nothing. He listened to their talk in moody silence, and began to feel that though he had worked hard all his life he had learned nothing, and that though he had travelled all his life he had been nowhere.

Naturally he turned away from those who made him so acutely conscious of his own shortcomings. It was not a privilege to consort with them. It was an intolerable humiliation. Why should he, Edmund Kean, the famous tragedian, be a nobody in society, when he could be the hero of every pothouse in London? At the tavern they were low and vulgar and fleeced him of his money and his reputation. But at least they healed his pride by accepting him as their leader and by encouraging him to suppose that he had the qualities of a great gentleman.

Drink was a habit. He would get drunk with any man —even with a lord. Benjamin Heath Drury (son of Doctor Drury) and his friend, Knapp, who were both schoolmasters at Eton, often used to sup with him at the Hummums Hotel in Covent Garden. On one occasion they brought with them Lord Eldon's son, who was their pupil. "After supper the party were 'run in' by the night watchman, and had to be bailed out at Bow Street next morning by the Lord Chancellor's (Eldon's) secretary."

But disgrace in such exalted circumstances was a rare occurrence. More often it was a street fight or a tavern brawl which put an end to his night's enjoyment.

Edmund was not proud of his behaviour, and he listened courteously, even shamefacedly, to men like Doctor Drury and Mr. Merivale, who had earned his gratitude. But with their lengthy, rather pompous moralizings they had only a passing influence upon him. He did not want to be patronized and preached at. He asked to be respected and admired.

The members of the Drury Lane sub-committee could not even command his respect, for he knew that it was from motives of self-interest that they were so anxious to keep him in good society. Though they went out of their way to make a fuss of him in order to win his confidence, he liked their flattery no better than he liked their criticisms. As an actor he despised them because they were amateurs. Already he was beginning to assert himself in the theatre and to challenge their authority. He had formulated his petition of rights. Why was he not the highest paid member of the company? (Elliston received £30 per week, while he received only £20 per week.) Why was he not made responsible for the stage-management of his own plays? Why, in particular, was he not allowed to choose his own parts? He had been forced to act Romeo against his will, and it proved a disastrous mistake.

He had legitimate grievances. But he demanded their redress at the point of the pistol, and himself did as he pleased. He was now fulfilling provincial engagements while the London season was still in progress, and as this was contrary to the terms of his contract with Drury Lane, it led to disputes with the sub-committee which were serious enough to arouse comment in the Press. For example, on December 14th, the *Sun* contained the following story: "Mr. Whitbread a few days ago sent a letter to Mr. Kean reproaching him with having performed two nights at Brighton without permission from the managers. The letter was couched in the severest terms, and, among other passages, the writer says he hopes that Mr. Kean will not give him occasion to regret that he drew him from obscurity." And on February 12th the *Champion* reported: "Another misunderstanding has taken place between Mr. Kean and the Drury Lane committee in consequence of his having performed two evenings last week at the Woolwich theatre. Mr. K. admits the fact . . . but plainly tells the board of management that he is determined 'to make hay while the sun shines.'"

Edmund could plainly tell the board of management anything he wanted and in the end he would get away with it. The sub-committee might protest, procrastinate, but they had not the strength of mind to stand firm, for they were convinced that Kean was the theatre's one valuable security. They could not even contemplate the possibility of losing his services to Covent Garden. They would always capitulate to his demands after a feeble attempt at resistance, and the result of their present dispute with him is best told in this paragraph which appeared in the *Sun* on March 15th: "We understand that in generous acknowledgement of the extraordinary services rendered to Drury Lane Theatre by

Mr. Kean, the committee of management have raised his salary to £25 per week and have presented him with the sum of £500. Mr. Kean will set off after the play to-morrow night for Glasgow, where he is engaged to perform every night next week (Passion Week) at a salary of £100 a night; and having obtained a week's leave of absence from Drury Lane, he will play four nights in the evening at Newcastle at the same salary."

Edmund held the whip-hand, and the members of the sub-committee were as powerless to control his conduct as they were to deny him his "rights" in the theatre. Whitbread tried to persuade him "not to get drunk," and Lord Essex warned him against consorting publicly with his low friends, but they could neither of them compel him to follow their advice. They had no sanction which they dared apply.

Ultimately they were obliged, regretfully, to let him follow his own way of life—and what a pathetically inconsistent way it was! His ceaseless scrambling after money, his demand that he should be his own stage-director, his determination that the Drury Lane management should not be allowed, through incompetence, to prejudice his career were all evidence of his will to safeguard the future. But what of his orgies, his reckless extravagance, his gradual undermining of his health and strength? It seemed that with one hand he grasped success desperately and with the other threw it wantonly away.

But then his whole character was apparently made up of conflicting impulses. He was arrogant and humble, cowardly and brave, small-minded and generous. In the tavern he could scarcely have cut a more despicable figure. He sat, like some exalted gutter-snipe, drinking and cursing and laying down the law, ready to hurl a glass of brandy in any man's face who belittled him or caused amusement at his expense. Between him and his boozing companions there did not exist even the crudest bond of affection. William Oxberry was typical of them. He was a well-known Drury

Lane comedian who edited a number of theatrical journals, and who had a passion for alcohol and pugilism. He retired from the stage in 1821 in order to run Craven's Chop House, "where they vocalized on Friday, conversationalized on Sunday, and chopized every day." He died in his chop house on June 9, 1824, from an attack—so it was rumoured —of delirium tremens.

Oxberry was a vulgar, jovial eccentric, with perhaps a few endearing qualities. But Edmund's liking for him was very superficial. Though it stood the test of many bar crawls and wild escapades "into the night," it vanished irrevocably when Oxberry gave an unflattering imitation of one of Edmund's performances.

It was vanity and weakness which made him waste his time in low company. Yet his loyalty to his own class was deep-rooted and unshakable. Though his desire for vengeance on those who had humiliated him was petty, he practised what he preached. He was never unmindful of a favour and he was never too grand to remember those whom he had liked in his strolling player days. His kindness and consideration to the more unfortunate members of his profession was proverbial.

He had vices which earned him the contempt even of his parasites, but he had qualities which won him the affection of those who owed him their gratitude. Little is known about the few who were his real friends—Jack Hughes, William Chippendale, and the rest—for he chose them without regard to their worldly standing. But quite evidently they served his interests faithfully and he was not undeserving of their devotion.

In the whole conflict of his thoughts and actions he was really the slave of the past. He was bound by shackles which had been too well forged to be easily unfettered. If he had been married to a woman with the power to humour him and to make his home a refuge from himself, his story might have ended very differently. But unfortunately Mary was as incompetent to help him now as she had always been.

She was, of course, miserably worried by his conduct, and she poured forth her tales of woe to Lady Elizabeth Whitbread and Lord Essex and anyone else who would come to her assistance. She besought them to advise Edmund and to impress him with their good counsels. In the words of Mr. Merivale, she talked "with all the air of an unwilling witness" of his eccentricities, and she was prepared to go to any lengths to cure him. There was, after all, so much at stake now. It would be as much her tragedy as his if he dissipated his genius and squandered his fortune and alienated all his grand friends whom she liked so much.

She had to stick to him for her own sake. But she had no real sympathy with or understandings of his behaviour. She put a good deal of the blame on Miss Tidswell, who she believed was deliberately exerting an evil influence on Edmund in order indirectly to injure her. She wrote to Lord Essex complaining of Miss Tidswell's machinations and Lord Essex sent back the following very guarded reply:

"When you have lived as long as I have, you will find out, my dear madam, that half the world is made up of envy, hatred, and malice. . . . I do not know anything of Miss Tidswell myself, and am sorry she should wish to be an enemy to those who, I am sure, will always act with gratitude towards her. Kean cannot do better than follow the advice, *upon all occasions*, of two such excellent men as Mr. Whitbread and Mr. Grenfell; and I am also sure that your mind and heart has the right bias, which ought to regulate it. . . . I wish you both happiness and comfort, which, I am sure, is in store for you, and which it is impossible either of you should be so unwise as to sacrifice. Say everything kind from me to Kean. I go to Oxford, otherwise would have called on him."

Had Mary's heart really the right bias towards Edmund? It is impossible to suppose so. No woman can love and cherish him whom she does not respect, and though she was desperately anxious to safeguard the actor's success, she despised the man. She thought him weak, vicious, almost demented. She saw in him none of those qualities which excused his faults and which might well, under proper guidance, have dispelled them.

Mary had all the intolerance and all the snobbish instincts of an exalted surburban. She worshipped the trappings of gentility. And now that she had the chance to move in the best circles she did not intend to let it go. She loved to ride out in her carriage and four and she made valiant, rather conscious efforts to run her home exactly as. a real lady should. Everything was very properly done—trained servants, high-class cooking, refined conversation, and polite, formal dinner parties attended by as many nice and celebrated people as possible. She never for a moment considered the advisability of adjusting her own values to suit Edmund's prejudices. On the contrary, she expected him to conform to her own rigorous social rules, to sit at the head of his table, and to entertain his distinguished guests in a modest, genteel fashion.

The breach between them grew wider. But though there were violent quarrels and times "when he went off his head," he had still too much family loyalty to break away completely. He was always contrite in the end, and so Mary pursued her way relentlessly, without regard to him, only pausing to wonder plaintively why he was so impossible and why he seemed so set on ruining her happiness.

She had grown too grand for Cecil Street. Though it was in the heart of theatreland and within convenient walking distance of Drury Lane, it was too far east of the world of fashion for her liking. London between Charing Cross and the City, once made beautiful by the graceful, timbered manors of the Elizabethan aristocracy, set amidst trees and gardens, was now almost a slum neighbourhood, containing the drab abodes of tradesmen, who owned their little shops in the Strand, and the haunts of the riff-raff. According to a favourite anecdote which, though probably apocryphal, is none the less illustrative, Beau Brummel was excessively confused when espied by Sheridan somewhere near Charing Cross. He went to the trouble of explaining himself at length.

"Sherry, my dear boy," he drawled, "don't mention that you saw me in this filthy part of the town; but perhaps I am rather severe, for his Grace of Northumberland resides somewhere about this spot, if I don't mistake. The fact is, my dear boy, I have been in the d——d city—to the Bank. I wish they would remove it to the West End, for really it is quite a bore to go to such a place; more particularly as one cannot be seen in one's own equipage beyond Somerset House, and the Hackney coaches are not fit for a chimney sweeper to ride in. Yes, my dear Sherry, you may note the circumstance down in your memorandum book, as a very remarkable one, that on the twentieth day of March . . . you descried me travelling from the East End of the town like a common citizen who had left his country house for the day in order to dine with his upstart wife and daughters at their vulgar residence in Brunswick Square."

Brummel's house was in Chesterfield Street, and the smart clubs, the elegant mansions, the spacious parks so typical of fashionable Regency London were all centred west of Charing Cross. The beaux risked their fortunes at a gambling house in Bolton Street (off Piccadilly), where the *cuisine* and management were in the experienced hands of M. Watier, one-time *chef* to the Prince Regent. In King Street (near Pall Mall) stood Almacks, where the waltz and the quadrille were both danced for the first time in England, and where a ball was given each week. Almacks was London's most exclusive club, and its controllers—Lady Castlereagh, Princess Esterhazy, Lady Cowper, Lady Jersey, Mrs. Drummond-Barrel, Lady Sefton, and the Princess Lieven—maintained its exclusiveness with their fierce, aristocratic intolerance. Three-fourths of the nobility knocked at its doors in vain. Even the Duke of Wellington at the height of his success was twice turned away—on the first occasion for wearing trousers instead of knee-breeches, and on the second for daring to attempt a belated entry.

In short, the West End was the hub of the beau-monde. And it was there that Mary wanted to live so that she could entertain her guests, not in a slum as it were, but in their own rarefied setting.

She had her way soon enough. Though it was considered presumptuous for a mere play actor to reside in such an exalted quarter—even Elliston, with his social graces and connections, had been warned against it—she persuaded Edmund to rent a large, handsome house in Clarges Street, Piccadilly. In October of 1815 they took up their new abode.

Mary was completely satisfied. With Susan to help her, she settled down to receive callers, to give musical evenings, to issue instructions to her liveried servants, and to imagine herself a full-blown lady.

But Edmund was nearer to Almacks and Watier's, which he could not have entered even if he had wished (the knowledge of that was bitter to him), and further away from the Harp and the Antelope and the Coal Hole in Fountain Court and the rest of Covent Garden taverns over which he presided. He was surrounded by all the people whose manner towards him he resented and whom he hated with the hatred of a wounded pride. At his own table he was made to feel as insignificant and as uncomfortable as he felt at a Lord's table. His house was alien to him and he came to regard Mary and Susan, not as his allies, but as his enemies. They were two against one. They would be three against one when Charles grew up, for Charles was his mother's son and she was turning him into a proper little prig.

There was no place for Edmund's friends at Clarges Street. But although Mary had her way in most things, she could not persuade him to desert them. On the contrary, he clung to them more fiercely than before, and in their company found freedom from the genteel atmosphere of

his home which stifled him. It was wonderfully refreshing
to carouse with his own kind after playing the part of the
West End host under compulsion.

Gradually he came to look upon himself as an outlaw
from society and was consumed with a longing to get his
own back on a world which had no use for him or for his
companions. He would be violently anti-social. He would
show those who despised him that, though he could not
shine as a conversationalist, he was none the less a man of
no ordinary cast. In short, he would force them to take
notice of him.

In his efforts to build up his personality he degenerated
into what we should now call a ravenous publicity hound.
He was no longer at pains to hide his eccentricities, but
was eager to make a display of all his peculiar deeds, habits,
and tastes, however trivial or inglorious, in order to attract
attention to himself.

That is why so much is known about them.

He kept a pet lion, given to him by Sir Edward Tucker,
which he controlled with his eye, just as he hypnotized
audiences when he was on the stage. His lion became as
notorious as his Richard III was famous. "I can boast of
seven events," wrote a certain J. T. Smith, "*some of which
great men* would be proud of. I received a kiss *when a boy*
from the beautiful Mrs. Robinson, was patted on the head
by Doctor Johnson, have frequently held Sir Joshua Reynolds's spectacles, partook of a pot of porter with an
elephant, saved Lady Hamilton from falling when the
melancholy news arrived of Lord Nelson's death, three
times conversed with King George III, and was shut up
in a room with Mr. Kean's lion."

After his performance at the theatre he often used to
ride furiously into the country, without caring where he
went, not returning home until the early hours of the
morning, and sometimes staying out all night. Once at
Hounslow Heath—to quote the *Champion*—"two fellows on
the pathway attempted to stop him. One presented a pistol

and demanded his money. Mr. Kean struck his spurs into his horse, which set forward immediately with such force as to knock the fellow down and strike the pistol out of his hand. The other fired after Mr. Kean but happily missed."

He was an ardent amateur of boxing. He used to have private sparring matches in his back parlour with Mendoza and other celebrated pugilists; and he knew how to use his fists in an emergency. He was also a regular attendant at professional prize-fights and no doubt was present at the pitched battle between Dutch Sam and Molesworth the Baker, when, according to the *Sun*, "the road up Piccadilly through Hyde Park Corner, and along Brompton, was one endless train of vehicles of every description; coaches and four, chariots, chaises, tilburys, gigs, dogcarts and common carts, filled with the strangest medley of persons that London could disgorge, were pressing on with their best speed to the place of action. Nor were multitudes of pedestrians wanting to fill up the bustle of this disreputable scene. The latter were running along the footpaths. While the former occupied the breadth of the road, and such a mass of thieves and ruffians and amateurs has rarely been exhibited to the disgust of common sense and decency. It was impossible to refrain from thinking what a benefit it would be to the country could the entire assembly have been swept out of it at one fell swoop."

That was a memorable occasion which Edmund would not have missed. In spite of the fact that Dutch Sam was forty-two years old and had trained more or less on gin (he has been known to guzzle down ten or a dozen glasses in a morning), he did not yield the palm of victory to the sturdy young baker until after the fortieth round had been fought.

Edmund was very fond of the river. He was often seen on the Thames in one of several wherries which he owned. He instituted an annual boatmen's race and the day on which it was rowed was an important one for him, as one may gather from this letter which he wrote in answer to a request for a business interview. "To-morrow I give away my annual wherry, consequently for business it is a *dies non*, but if you take pleasure in aquatic scenes I shall be most happy to see you between the heats, to a good dinner and a hearty welcome. We dine at the Red House, Battersea, and adjourn business till next day."

He retained the services of a private secretary—a certain R. Phillips, who was otherwise a small-part actor at Drury Lane. Phillips looked after his arrangements with the managers, communicated on his behalf to the Press, accompanied him on his provincial trips, and attended him at the tavern, rather as one may see working-class children awaiting their parents, prepared to get him away unmolested when he was drunk or underneath the table. He was a devoted follower whom Edmund rewarded handsomely and whom he treated more as a friend than as a servant. But for a stage player to employ a secretary, whatever the real nature of his standing, was quite unheard of.

He founded various fancifully named "communities" such as "The Screaming Lunatics," which met at the Harp and the Wolves Club, and he presided over them in the fashion of a gentleman (he would say, for example, that he was the son of the Duke of Norfolk and had been educated at Eton College) who detested class distinctions and damned the nobility. He lived up to his part, for he did not scruple to avoid an engagement with a Lord in order to fulfil his obligations in the tavern. According to Thomas Moore, "Byron was offended at Kean's leaving a dinner which had been chiefly made for him, at which were Byron himself, Lord Kinnaird, and Douglas Kinnaird. Kean pretended illness and went away early; but Byron found out afterwards that he had gone to take the chair at a pugilistic supper."

These organized gatherings gave a purpose to his carousals and made the tavern more surely his kingdom. Though, seemingly, they provided him with the excuse to finish many bacchanalian nights under the table, he regarded them, in his sober moments, with monarchical gravity.

"Worthy Secretary," he wrote from Cork to Thomas Henneley, Secretary of the Wolves Club at the O.P. and P.S. Tavern, "I cannot sufficiently commend your diligence nor admire the great improvements added to our regulations. I hope our worthy Brothers, by punctual observation, will make their effects as salutary as the decrees are wise. I shall not be among you til [*sic*] the beginning of October. I sincerely lament your accident but hope you are perfectly recovered. You flatter me by printing the humble effort . . . but as it was written *pro tempore* only, I scarcely think it serviceable. I have corrected and sent it to you, however, to use your own discretion. (Signed) Edmund Kean, Captain of the Wolves."

"The Wolves Club" was the most notorious of Edmund's communities, and perhaps the "humble effort" refers to his opening speech which did, in fact, appear in print a little while later and which reads as follows: " . . . Gentlemen, there is one sentiment I am more sorry to see too much neglected in this world of more false pride than talent, which I cannot express better than in the language of Terence: 'Homo sum; nihil a me alienum puto.' . . . It is my wish to instil these sentiments into the minds of our little community, that no insignificant distinctions shall have weight when we can (with personal convenience) serve a fellow creature; or worldly exaltation prevent us from mixing with worthy men, whom I must conceive the great Author of all being intended for equality. . . . Courage, the only distinction our ancestors were acquainted with, must be one of the first principles of our body, and to what better end can we employ that magnificent ingredient than in defence of our friends against the foes of a general cause. It is my hope that every Wolf oppressed with worldly grievance, unmerited contumely or unjust persecution, with a heart glowing with defiance, may exclaim, 'I'll to my brother'; there I shall find ears attentive to my tales of sorrow, hands open to relieve and closed for my defence."

He spoke that speech from his heart. But it came curiously

"The Wolves Club"

A CARICATURE OF KEAN PUBLISHED AT THE TIME OF HIS DISPUTE WITH BUCKE

from a man who was the most successful actor in England and who was earning an average income of £10,000 per annum. What "unmerited contumely" or "unjust persecution" had he to fear? He understood what he meant himself, but no one else did—certainly not the collection of "drunks" who were his listeners and who would have applauded anything he had had to say rapturously and without restraint. In the outside world the Wolves Club acquired a nasty reputation. It was alleged that Edmund had founded it for his personal protection and that its members were sworn to boo every rival tragedian off the stage.

Edmund's foibles were not affectations, but in his insensate desire to appear important he allowed himself to be identified with them so that he merely became known as a notorious, rather absurd figure—vain and conceited and overbearing. He could not help his grievance against society, but he chose to vent it in such an undisciplined way that he earned the scorn of most men and the pity of those few who were discerning enough to detect his real qualities.

"I was sorry to see him drop off from his more respectable connections," wrote Grattan. "The 'evil days' on which he fell I was soon out of the way of knowing the details of; but I heard much of his extravagance, his feats of horsemanship and boatmanship, wonderful journeys and rowing matches, freaks of unseemly presumption with regard to authors, affairs of gallantry, a tame lion, and a secretary."

The end, though distant, was already in sight: and seemingly Edmund was hurtling towards it under his own power, for he closed his ears to the voice of balanced judgment.

Yet, in his heart, he knew his own weaknesses and tried to curb them. He was by no means the unspeakable vulgarian that he chose to paint himself. During his strolling player days he had wasted many hours in the tavern, but he had also worked hard and he had had to do so in order to reach his present eminence. His genius was not a gift from the gods, nor were his "flashes" the inspirations of the moment. He was able proudly to show Douglas Kinnaird five hundred pages of comments which he had made on Shakespeare.

Even now, between his orgies and his ravings against a social order, he set out to employ his leisure wisely. He practised his piano playing, cultivated his love of music, enlarged his knowledge of the classics, and learned how to phrase a letter. He had the same appetite for education, the same inquisitive mind, the same longing to be a man of culture as always.

But though he possessed qualities in plenty, he failed abysmally to make proper use of them. His most violent detractors did not deny that he had the merits of being brave and generous. But often his courage (of which we shall have evidence later) was misplaced and his generosity was too impulsive to earn him the respect for it which he deserved. His guineas were lavished on the poor without discrimination and his decisions to take no money from a country manager who had helped him in the past, or to perform free of charge for the benefit of a needy friend, were suddenly made. There was no care or method in his charity, so that he never won for himself the halo which is placed by public opinion round the head of a well-organized philanthropist.

In the fierce, poetic words of Theodore Norton, one of his few apologists:

> And low he was, and low did he descend,
> He stooped to prove himself the orphan's friend,
> To take the helpless by the hand and give
> The starving wretch the future means to live;
> The dungeon he explored and burst the chain
> Of prisoned captives,—here was low again!
> His cloak upon a winter's piercing night,
> (To shield a crippled beggar from its bite)
> He flung; and this, when rumoured in the west,
> Was voted low again, as may be guessed.

It was Edmund's real tragedy that he had a soul which belied his coarse behaviour. He suffered deep mortification. Years later, when he could look back on what was then a misspent life, he tried to express his tortured feelings in this cry of despair:

> What is this happiness of man?
> Its shadow, catch it if you can,
> Is it in wealth and gay parade?
> Proud nature tells you, all must fade;
> She holds the key to human hearts
> Open to vice, and limpid darts,
> Carries her victim, in false pleasures' train,
> Raises to hope but soon to fall again.
> So drear, so desolate an abyss,
> You know not in the vortex that from this
> You feel the shock, but inward know no pain.
> But drinking largely sets you right again.

3

For twelve months after his failure as Romeo, Edmund's career at Drury Lane remained comparatively unspectacular. He was still the most discussed actor in London, still "food for the critics," and still a popular favourite. The Green Room, with its full-length mirror before which performers strutted and grimaced and examined the effects of their costumes before going on the stage, was thronged with celebrities every night that he appeared. But the auditorium was quite frequently less than half full. He was no longer the inordinate box-office attraction that he once had been. The sub-committee were chiefly to blame. Perhaps, drugged into a state of apathy by his previous success, they still supposed that they had only to print his name on their play-bills in order to draw the crowds. Certainly they showed precious little imagination or business acumen in selecting characters for him to add to his repertoire. He played Richard II, it is true; and though he was essentially miscast and in fact misinterpreted the part, he created a mild sensation in it and won the unbounded approval of the majority of the critics. But apart from that he was forced to impersonate heroes in a succession of indifferent dramas which have long since passed into oblivion and are not regretted.

On April 8, 1815, he paid Mrs. Wilmot the compliment of creating the part of Egbert in *Ina*, a tragedy which she had written in blank verse. The occasion was remarkable because it was the first time he had appeared in a new play, and the house was accordingly packed out. But the piece proved so ineffective and so artificial that it was damned out of hand; and when, at the end, Edmund came forward to announce its repetition, he was shouted down. The boos were intended for the author, not for him. "From the commencement to the close," wrote Peter Finnerty in the *Morning Chronicle*, "Mr. Kean in Egbert had not a single occasion to display those powerful workings of the soul, with which he knows so well how to harrow up the feelings of the auditor."

Not all the parts in which he appeared were quite so barren of opportunities as Egbert: but at a time when the player was really of more consequence than the play, the popular taste in drama was undistinguished, and the heroes of contemporary tragedy were more suited to Kemble's style than to Kean's.

The stage was not considered the proper place for the display of works of art, and that is why the great literary figures of the age, with a few exceptions, never bothered to write for the theatre. Hazlitt contended that, in the main, it was more satisfactory to read Shakespeare's plays than to see them performed. "Shakespeare has embodied his characters so very distinctly," he wrote, "that he stands in no need of the actor's assistance to make them more distinct; and the representation of the character on the stage almost uniformly interferes with our conception of the character itself. The only exceptions we can recollect to this observation are Mrs. Siddons and Mr. Kean—the former of whom in one or two characters, and the latter, not certainly in any one character, but in very many passages, have raised our imagination of the part they acted."

Edmund was placed by his contemporaries on an exalted plane, and he would have done well, therefore, to have confined his attention to classical tragedy and to have neglected such "property" characters as Reuben Glenroy in *Town and Country* and Zanga in *The Revenge*. He should have left it to others to express synthetic emotions and to speak false, artificial lines. For he was revered as an impersonator of humanity.

He continued, of course, to appear periodically in the great Shakespearian parts which had made him famous. But naturally enough the novelty of his interpretations had begun to pall a little both with the critics and the public. And he himself, without the encouragement of frenzied applause to set his genius really ablaze, had become rather lazy and careless, rather apt to rely on mere "trick."

In February of 1915 Leigh Hunt went to Drury Lane "for the first time since his imprisonment." He saw Edmund as Richard III and on the whole he was disappointed. "Mr. Kean appeared during the greater part of his performance to be nothing but a first-rate actor of the ordinary stagy class and to start only occasionally into passages of truth and originality. We expected no declamation, no common rant, etc., but something genuine and unconscious. . . . He is much further gone in stage trickery than we supposed him to be, particularly in the old violent contrasts when delivering an equivoque, dropping his voice too consciously from a serious line to a sly one, and fairly putting it to the house as a good joke."

That, of course, was only a first impression and, as a matter of fact, Leigh Hunt retracted it later *in toto*. Perhaps, as Hazlitt believed, he had sat too far away from the stage to form a just opinion, for after "a nearer and more frequent view of him," he did come to realize that Mr. Kean "was

a perfectly original and sometimes a perfectly natural actor."
But, in any case, critical and even hostile notices of Edmund's
performances were now quite usual and too often they were
deserved.

Edmund fared better in the country than in London,
especially in those towns which he had not visited before
and where playgoers had so far not had the chance to
applaud his Shylock, his Hamlet, and the rest. The receipts
of his first two performances in Glasgow during Passion
Week amounted to £2,000. In Newcastle he was welcomed
by the local critics with an almost fanatical enthusiasm
which provoked the derision of the more sophisticated
London Press. "Grand Hyperbole," wrote the *Sun*, on
April 15, 1815. "A provincial journal, after discovering
that the *defects* of Mr. Kean are actually *beauties*, observes
'that had Shakespeare seen him, he might have had a *better*
idea of some of the characters whose names he has
immortalized!!!!'"

To escape from Drury Lane into the provinces was at
this time as pleasing to Edmund's vanity as it was to his
desire to coin money as fast as he could.

The sub-committee did not appear in the least perturbed
by the fact that his popularity was waning. At a meeting
of the shareholders on May 4th, Samuel Whitbread "took
occasion to pass a just eulogium upon Mr. Kean and
declared his opinion to be, that Mr. Kean had greatly
improved in his old characters this season and had greatly
added to his stock of reputation by those new ones in
which he had been produced." But the discovery of Edmund
Kean was the one profitable move which the committee of
amateurs could claim to have made since they had come
into being, and they never tired of boasting about it. One
shareholder suggested the advisability of letting the theatre
to a professional manager, but Douglas Kinnaird success-
fully opposed this on the grounds that Drury Lane ought
never to be allowed to fall "into the grasp of pecuniary
speculators." "The present plan," he said, "is material to

the upholding of the real drama—to the interest of the profession which has been so materially served by the rebuilding since it has brought forward the splendid talents of Mr. Kean."

On July 5th Samuel Whitbread died. "He was," wrote Byron, "surely a great and very good man." Byron was thinking, of course, of his work in the House of Commons, where he was a radical, and an ardent reformer. But as a servant of the drama, in spite of what has previously been written in these pages, he was not altogether undeserving of praise. It was chiefly due to his initiative that Drury Lane was rebuilt after it had been destroyed by fire in 1809. And he had a thankless task trying to extricate the theatre from the complicated financial tangle which Sheridan's improvidence had wound round it.

He had very little sense of the stage, for that is given only to those who devote their lives to acquiring it. He was, judged by any ordinary standard, an excessively incompetent manager. But at least he was a man of business rectitude, and he left Drury Lane worse off without him because he was the ablest of the gentlemen who controlled its destiny.

After his death a new sub-committee, consisting of Lord Essex, Lord Byron, George Lamb, Douglas Kinnaird, and Peter Moore, M.P., was formed to exercise jointly and severally the powers which had previously belonged to Whitbread as chairman. It was a hopeless arrangement which inevitably led to muddles and rows and endless discussions and very little useful action. Not one of the committee members had the faintest conception of how to run a theatre. But each had his pet little scheme to foster and his own little axe to grind.

Byron was the least harmful of them, for he did not take his duties very seriously. He was amusing and frivolous at meetings, and occasionally he tried to push the claims of some playwright whose work was known to him. Otherwise he was content to be an adornment. During performances, "he sat in his private box, near the stage, and, raising the blind, drank his madeira and cracked his walnuts."

Douglas Kinnaird, George Lamb, and Peter Moore were the three really active members of the new committee. Kinnaird spent his time "ransacking the works of old dramatists for revivals." George Lamb, "a polite gentleman," arranged with the sub-managers, Rae and Dibdin (Arnold had retired shortly after Whitbread's death), the general business of the theatre. Peter Moore, who had a passion for economy, amused himself cutting down salaries and bullying the underlings. He was particularly unpopular both with the Drury Lane employees and with the Press. Finnerty of the *Morning Chronicle* expressed a popular feeling when he published these lines:

> "What," said Dick, with some surprise,
> "Have they sent Peter from the door?
> "From Drury's scene if they were wise
> "They'd send one Pater *More*!"

Kinnaird, Lamb, and Moore apparently made division of their duties, but they all of them attended rehearsals and they all interfered with the goings-on behind the scenes, in that damaging and futile way which is irresistible to amateurs. "Kinnaird introduced upon the stage, as a singer, a lady who resided under his protection and had been known in *another* part of the theatre!" She was nicknamed the Duck on account of her waddling gait.

For the next four years the story of Drury Lane would have been a miserable record of indecisiveness, vacillation, and impending collapse, but near the beginning of their disastrous management the new sub-committee had a stroke of luck. On January 12, 1816, they produced Philip Massinger's *A New Way to Pay Old Debts*, with Edmund Kean as Sir Giles Overreach.

A New Way to Pay Old Debts is best described as a literary melodrama. It is powerful and gripping and contains many of those fine poetic passages which have

persuaded some critics to rank Massinger as second only to
Shakespeare among Elizabethan dramatists. But its success
on the stage depends entirely on the interpretation of the
remorseless villain, Overreach, who, ruthless and vulgar
and ambitious, without one spark of human feeling, robs
the poor, persecutes his relations, schemes for his own
aggrandizement, and finally runs headlong into a catas-
trophic downfall. It is a part in a million. But it is a part
which only an actor of extraordinary force can make credible
or even interesting.

The character of Sir Giles Overreach belonged exclusively
to Edmund Kean from the moment he first played it: and
to him it still belongs. His performance was of a terrible
kind, to-day unknown and, perhaps, unimaginable. That
is why it can no longer be described adequately.

There are those who contend glibly enough, "If Edmund
Kean were to come back, he would be laughed off the
stage." Would he? His audiences understood better than
we do how to jeer and hiss; and it would have been fatally
easy for him, because he was a little man, to have appeared
comic as Sir Giles Overreach, especially at the end of the
play when, cornered by his enemies, he yelled:

> . . . Say there were a squadron
> Of pikes, lined through with shot, when I am mounted
> Upon my injuries, shall I fear to charge them?
> No: I'll fall to execution—Ha! I am feeble:
> Some undone widow sits upon mine arm,
> And takes away the use of it; and my sword,
> Glued to my scabbard with wronged orphans' tears,
> Will not be drawn . . .
> . . . Shall I then fall
> Ingloriously and yield? No: spite of Fate,
> I will be forced to hell like to myself,
> Though you were legions of accursed spirits,
> Thus would I fly among you.

And it would have been still more easy for him to have

seemed ridiculous when, after that speech, he fell to the ground in a fit, foaming at the mouth.

But his audience did not laugh. They were, for a moment, speechless with real terror. Lord Byron was convulsed and several ladies in the boxes fainted. Even the actors on the stage—hard-boiled professionals, jealous of their own rights —showed clearly enough that they, too, were frightened. And then the pit rose up in a body and cheered and went on cheering. Next morning Hazlitt, for once robbed of his critical faculty, wrote in the *Examiner*: "There is something in a good play well acted, a peculiar charm, that makes us forget ourselves and all the world. . . . We cannot conceive of anyone doing Mr. Kean's part of Sir Giles Overreach so well as himself. We have seen others in the part, superior in the look and costume, in hardened, clownish, rustic insensibility; but in the soul and spirit, no one equal to him. . . . He was not at a single fault. . . . The conclusion was quite overwhelming."

Kean's audiences were made up of men like Hazlitt and Byron and Coleridge and Leigh Hunt. No one can seriously believe that they were so unsophisticated and so barren of taste as to be swept off their feet by acting which would make modern playgoers merely feel uncomfortable. On the contrary.

With Overreach, Edmund reached the pinnacle of his histrionic achievement. It was his greatest part: and it was his *coup de grâce* to the classical school of acting. Even Kemble, who by right of the dignity of long standing should have been immune from partisan ferocity, came an almighty cropper when he was rash enough to appear as a rival Sir Giles. "We have hardly ever experienced a more painful feeling," wrote Hazlitt, "than when, after the close of the play, the sanguine plaudits of Mr. Kemble's friends, and the circular discharge of hisses from the back of the pit, that 'came full volley home'—the music struck up, the ropes were fixed, and Madame Sachi ran up from the stage to the two shilling gallery, and then ran down again, as fast as her legs could carry her, amidst the shouts of pit, boxes and gallery!" Hazlitt himself did not mince his words. He tore this Sir Giles, so decorous, so devoid of passion, and so "shy of nature," to tattered ribbons. But he ended his notice on rather a sad note. "With all his faults, Mr. Kemble has powers and faculties which no one else on the stage has; why then does he not avail himself of them, instead of throwing himself upon the charity of criticism? He has given the public great, incalculable pleasure; and does he know so little of the gratitude of the world as to trust to their generosity?"

Kemble, after a long and, in its way, distinguished reign at the head of his profession, was at last booed and booed lustily. It was a grievous error for him to attempt Over-reach in opposition to his young rival, and it hastened his decision to withdraw from the scene where he had already played his part and where he was no longer wanted. In a year's time he would make his last bow to a London audience, having earned enough money in the theatre to spend the remainder of his life in comfortable retirement.

One day Edmund would learn to envy him. But now he had brought the crowds back to Drury Lane and he had revived for himself all the glories of his first season. Lord Byron gave him a "handsome Turkish sword, with a Damascus blade," and sent him fifty pounds at his benefit. The Drury Lane actors collected £300 and presented him with a gold cup, especially made by Hamlet, the jeweller, "at the end of Leicester Square." Mrs. Garrick said he was greater than ever and was a frequent visitor at Clarges Street. Susan wrote off to Margaret Roberts so excitedly that she forgot all about her spelling and her grammar: " . . . I wish you were here to see the numerous letters of congratulation and visits on the same that is pouring in every day. The house is quite a fair! . . . To see him in the last act I think you would never get over it. Mrs. Glover [the actress] got into strong histerics and many ladies fainted. It has brought 2 thousand pounds to the House tho' but three nights played. He dines to-day at Mr. Renard's to meet the Duke of Sussex, and to-morrow we all dine at Mrs. Bushes in the City. . . . We got a present of a hare and two pheasants from Lady Elizabeth Whitbread yesterday and to-day Mr. Maxwell send us a Hare and Brace of partridge, which we keep for tuesday when Mr. and Mrs. Grenfell, Mr. and Mrs. Utterson, Mr. and Mrs. Bush and Miss Brown, Mrs. Blackman, Mr. Dinman, Mrs. Plumptre & a Miss Maxwell dine here. . . ."

Edmund was at the top of the wave again, and naturally Susan and Mary were there too, trying to hold him up. But he would have to swim on: and stormy waters were ahead of him.

His next play, a revival of Massinger's *The Duke of Milan*, specially vamped up for the occasion, would be a comparative failure. During the course of its run he would get involved in his first contretemps with a London audience.

4

An actor—especially a favourite actor—was in the fullest sense of the word a servant of the public: and the public were punctilious masters, easily offended, sensitive to disrespect, and very jealous of their rights. That is why apologies were so frequently offered from the stage. A hundred years ago it was an almost nightly occurrence.

On Tuesday, March 26, 1816, Edmund aroused the public's displeasure for the first time since his London début. He did not turn up to play his part in *The Duke of Milan*. According to a graphic report of the incident published next day in the *Morning Chronicle*, " . . . Mrs. Bartley had even delivered the prefatory address when it was discovered that Mr. Kean was not come to the theatre. After waiting with the utmost anxiety 'till seven o'clock Mr. Rae informed the audience of the fact and prayed for their indulgence.

"In a short time information was brought to the house

that he had rode out in his one-horse chaise in the morning; and at half past twelve o'clock had left it in East Smithfield, saying he would take a boat to Greenwich and that he would return in a post chaise in time to perform at the theatre. Up to a late hour last night no tidings had been received of him, which gave rise to the most serious apprehensions for his safety. We sincerely hope that no fatal accident has happened to this incomparable artist."

Meanwhile the audience, who had paid their good money to see Edmund Kean in *The Duke of Milan*, agreed reluctantly to accept *Fortune's Frolic* and *Ways and Means* in place of the advertised programme. The plays were very indifferently acted, and the audience went away dissatisfied, not knowing whether to be anxious or angry. It might be that their "favourite" had met with some unforeseen disaster. But it might equally well be that he had allowed his pleasure to interfere with his duty. In any case they were entitled to an explanation.

It was not forthcoming until the following day, when Edmund wrote this letter, dated Wednesday, to Alexander Rae:

> DEAR MR. RAE,
>   I shall be quite unable to play in *The Duke of Milan* this evening. I met with a damned accident yesterday, being thrown out of a gig, and besides being stunned and bruis'd, have dislocated an arm. Hoping soon to recover and with apologies to Public,
>   I am yours in pain,
>   EDMUND KEAN.
> N.B.—Perhaps the great W.C.M. may be got.

That was his excuse, rather tardily given and rather brazenly put, for disappointing his audience on the previous evening. And in due course he supported it with a doctor's certificate which stated that he would have to rest in bed for a few days and that he would not be fit to play again until Monday, the 1st of April.

But the majority of the Press, while expressing their relief that he was safe, received the news of his accident very sceptically. They took the opportunity to invoke memories of George Frederick Cooke, who had often been found lying senseless in a tavern when he should have been on the stage: and without actually contradicting Edmund's story, they made thinly veiled suggestions that he had really gone off on one of his celebrated carousals and had got so drunk that he had been physically incapable of returning to London.

In supplying a detailed account on March 28th, the *Morning Post* wrote: " . . . He dined with a few friends at Woolwich on Tuesday, from whence he set out in due time to be at the theatre by 5 o'clock. He reached Deptford about 4.0, and here he experienced the same kind of untoward accident, to which his brethren of the sock and buskin appear so long to have been unfortunately fated . . . he was completely stunned . . . nor had he become sufficiently sensible of his situation to send off the necessary instructions of his accident to the theatre. . . ."

In a follow-up paragraph next day the *Morning Post* made its meaning doubly clear: "Mr. Kean is returned to London from Deptford. . . . We have heard that on Tuesday some very SPIRITED scenes were exhibited by this great actor at Deptford!"

It was lucky for Edmund that Hazlitt, writing in the *Examiner*, came to his rescue. Hazlitt launched a spirited attack on the groundless insinuations which had been made against Mr. Kean in certain newspapers and also advanced a general defence, from which the following is an extract:

"With respect to the extravagance of actors as a traditional character it is not to be wondered at; they live from hand to mouth; they plunge from want into luxury; they have no means of making money *breed*, and all professions that do not live by turning money into money or have not the certainty of accumulating it in the end by parsimony, spend it. Uncertain of the future they make sure of the present moment. This is not unwise. . . ."

Hazlitt's voice prevailed. When Edmund made his reappearance at Drury Lane he was greeted with a few determined hisses but with three times as many cheers. He walked towards the floats. "For the first time in my life," he said, "I have disappointed the expectations of a London audience; for the first time in this theatre, out of two hundred and sixty-nine nights, as the public will acknowledge and the managers will attest. To your favour I am indebted for the reputation I enjoy, and I throw myself on your candour as a shield against unworthy prejudices."

That speech, spoken unflinchingly, aroused a tumult of clapping and completely quelled the booers.

Edmund resumed his part, and *The Duke of Milan* incident, which now seemed like a storm in a teacup, was closed.

But it was not forgotten. Whether he lied or told the truth (and Mary testified years afterwards that he lied), his word would never have been assailed had he not already done so much damage to his reputation and prejudice to his popularity. On this occasion he won the day. But there were many waiting to pounce on him the moment he took another false step. Unfortunately they would not have to wait very long.

CHAPTER VII

I

SOMETIME, during the summer of 1816, Thomas
Colley Grattan called on the Keans at their house in
Clarges Street. He had not met them since their Waterford
days, for he lived now in the South of France and had only
come to London for a two months' stay.

He was surprised and rather touched by the warmth of
his reception. "I had no sooner sent up my card," he
wrote, "than the servant came quickly to the parlour,
requesting that I would walk up to the drawing-room; and
before I could reach the stairs, Kean himself had sprung
half-way down them to greet me in the most cordial
fashion. (He was in his dressing-gown, having just been
under the hands of the *friseur*, one side of his head showing
several regular layers of curls, the other a profusion of rich
brown hair in tangled masses.)"

Edmund did not receive the majority of his fashionable
visitors in such an abandoned, open-hearted fashion. But he
remembered Grattan as a friend from the past who had
shown kindness when he had really needed it, so that, true
to his nature, he liked him now and went out of his way to be
attentive to him. He frequently invited him to Clarges
Street, where Grattan met "persons of high respectability"
and found that the "dinners were excellent" and that the
evening parties "were extremely pleasant with a great deal
of good music." It must have been fun for Mary to entertain
her husband's former patron and to show him in what a
grand style she now lived. The contrast was remarkable.

But Edmund, from motives of gratitude, not of ostentation, gave Grattan a few privileged glimpses of the life which
he led outside his home. On one occasion he took him to a
prize-fight, and as Grattan had never been to a prize-fight

before, he treasured the most vivid memories of the experience which he later described in these words:

"The battle was fought close to a village about ten miles from town on the Western road. We rode there together, I being mounted on one of Kean's handsome and spirited horses. Great honours were paid to him on the field, of which I, as his friend, partook. We were admitted within the ring, close to the combatants, before the fight began; and I was presented in form to Mister Jackson, to Cribb Oliver, Scroggins, and others.

"I do not mean to describe the battle. Suffice it to say, it greatly excited me, and I by no means felt the disgust I had anticipated. I was neither assaulted; nor was my pocket picked; nor did I encounter any of the mishaps commonly incidental to so blackguard a combination. I returned to town well satisfied with this midsummer day's entertainment, but have never repeated the experiment."

On another occasion, Grattan was introduced to the Wolves Club. It happened that he had invited Edmund to a small bachelors' dinner party—there were four of them in all—at the Sablonnière Hotel in Leicester Square. Edmund drove up in his carriage punctually at six o'clock, and stepped out of it wearing full evening attire—a silk-lined coat, white breeches, and buckled shoes. He apologized to Grattan for being so overdressed, but explained that he had made a previous promise to attend an evening party which he could not possibly break.

But the wine flowed, the conversation ran easily and the dinner was a great success, so that it was not until midnight that Edmund remembered his later engagement, and decided that he really had to be going. He then invited Grattan and his two fellow guests to accompany him; and they, being by this time fairly mellow, readily agreed, and thoughtlessly, too.

"We all squeezed as well as we could into Kean's chariot," Grattan remembered, " . . . and away we went, not knowing or caring in what direction. After a short time, and a furious drive, the carriage stopped at the head of a very narrow passage. We got out without any order of precedence, and followed our leader, with considerable assistance from the walls of the passage.

"We arrived at an open door, evidently that of a tavern . . . from the bustling welcome awarded to Roscius and to us . . . by the self-announcing landlord and half a score of waiters, women and attendant gazers. He staggered rapidly upstairs, we three after him; and he, to the apparent horror of several waiters and others, dashed at once at the large folding doors of the first floor apartment, and we entered into a room where there were assembled full sixty persons at a long supper table. A shout of applause hailed Kean; but when we popped in after him, a loud murmur of disapproval was raised. An explanation ensued; which terminated in our being obliged to withdraw, along with Kean and four or five of the party, into an adjoining room where we were made to comprehend the outrageous violation committed by this Grand Master against the rigid law, of which he was the founder, that no stranger could be admitted without a formal introduction, and a regular accordance to its social regulations.

"In short we each entered our name in an expansive register, got a printed card in return, paid £2 or £3 for fees, took a mock oath blindfolded and were announced as members . . . of the notorious association called collectively the Wolves."

Among the sixty members of the Wolves Club, Grattan only recognized the face of Oxberry. "I had no notion," he wrote, "of what sort of company I was in; and no clear conception of anything but lights, looking-glasses, bottles and decanters. I remember that Kean, from the head of the table which had been reserved for him, stammered a speech in return for his health being drunk; and that I and my two brother novices . . . laughed in such immoderate ill-breeding at the whole adventure, that we soon became ashamed of ourselves and by a simultaneous movement left the room."

It was typical of Edmund that he never afterwards referred, in Grattan's presence, to this impulsive excursion to the Wolves Club. He was sensitive enough to realize that Grattan, a man of some fastidiousness, would not care to be reminded of it; and for his part, behind the bluster and the elaborate dressing-up and all the glorified paraphernalia by which he sought to justify himself, he was secretly ashamed of his vanity and weakness. It did him credit that he was tacitly honest with those few, like Grattan, who had won his confidence, even though he failed to profit by their example.

But no one could stop him from weaving his own tragedy, and now Fate was about to present him with the final thread.

During the summer vacation, he fulfilled a variety of provincial engagements, travelling west to Bath, and South to Plymouth and Exeter, and North to Liverpool and Edinburgh in search of more wealth and fame. It was really in consequence of an act of kindness that he went to Taunton at the beginning of September, for Taunton was by no means among the first flight of provincial playgoing towns. Its theatre, however, was controlled by Henry Lee in whose Dorchester company Edmund had served immediately before his Drury Lane début, and he liked to play for managers who had befriended him in the past. On July 10th he wrote to Lee . . .

> If I go three weeks to Exeter, I shall be *very happy to see* you—the Book you have got of *A New Way to Pay Old Debts* is as it is acted. I shall cut at rehearsal whatever is out in London —but they *must be perfect* or I can't get thro'—no matter how *bad* they are—but make them for God's sake perfect or I shall not play; if they ruin me on the first night I shall not play the second. I shall feel most happy in seeing you and serving you if I can.
>
> Yours truly,
> EDMUND KEAN.
>
> P.S.—I am just preparing for Liverpool and as I shan't have time to write from there I address you now.

He wrote that letter hastily and uncertainly. But it led indirectly to the most fateful meeting of his life.

On the night that he acted Othello in the Taunton theatre, a lady, sitting in one of the private boxes, was apparently so overcome by his performance that she fainted. At his suggestion she was carried across the stage to his dressing-room, where she rested until she was sufficiently revived to be taken home.

Next day her husband called on Edmund at his lodgings. He introduced himself as Robert Cox, thanked Edmund profusely for his kindness and consideration and suggested that they should renew their acquaintanceship in London.

Robert Albion Cox was a native of Dorchester, where he had once been a banker and where he still owned a family estate. He was now middle-aged, and as a Londoner he was a man of some standing, though of no great fortune. He was a City Alderman and one among the numerous celebrities who served on the Drury Lane general committee. In May of 1818 he would be appointed auditor of the theatre. And in June of the same year he would be elected to the sub-committee in place of Lord Yarmouth (the sub-committee was continually subject to reshuffles).

His wife, whose maiden name was Charlotte Newman, was twelve years younger than himself. She came from a good bourgeois family, and she had pretensions to a place in Society. She was not particularly good-looking or cultured or even gracefully mannered. She was, in fact, averagely unattractive and certainly made no impression on men of taste and breeding. But she was emotional, oversexed and flamboyantly vivacious, so that she was incapable of being the respectable wife of a middle-aged husband. She was the kind of woman who would have gladly have gone to bed with her manservant.

Yet Edmund succumbed completely to her charms.

He was, of course, an easy victim, for she had only to let him know that she attracted her, in order to appeal irresistibly to his vanity. Though he had won the hearts of small-part actresses and tavern wenches, he had never before fascinated someone whom the world would acknowledge as a lady. That was enough to intoxicate him. In his eyes, Charlotte Cox was not a vulgar, promiscuous, rather *passée* temptress, but a goddess whom—unbelievably—he had captured by the impelling force of his personality. In time he supposed himself madly in love with her, just as he had once supposed himself madly in love with his wife.

But unlike Mary, Charlotte Cox had the power to hold him for as long as she willed. With the sure instincts of the harlot *manquée* she understood her man. She flattered him in the subtlest way. She took pains to remind him of her own social standing, while at the same time she treated him as her adored one. She played up to all his whims and fancies, allowing him to imagine that she was, in truth, his counterpart. And physically she tantalized him. She made him desire her passionately.

In fact, her feelings for him were carnal and selfish; and his attachment to her was merely the result of a lust for conquest. But while *she* never regarded their affair as anything more than a sordid intrigue, he at least dramatized it into something spiritual and romantic. He fooled himself, of course. But it was only after she had left him, years later, that he understood how hollow his love for her had been. It was only then that he was able to write to his lawyer with savage untruth, " . . . I imagine Mrs. Cox's age to be about forty-five when she first flapped her ferret-eyed affection upon me."

There is no proof—and little likelihood—that their affair actually began before the year 1820. But from the beginning she pursued him relentlessly and things were made exceptionally easy for her.

Her husband—the Alderman—seemed almost as interested in Edmund as she was herself. He used to take her to a private box at Drury Lane on every occasion that Edmund performed: and at the end of the play they would go round together to his dressing-room and have tea with him. Sometimes they would ask him to come back to supper with them at their house in Little Britain, and occasionally they would persuade him to stay the night.

They often used to entertain Mary as well. She naturally liked them because of their social connections. Ironically enough, they were among Edmund's few personal friends whom she used to invite regularly to her select dinner parties. Indeed, for several years, the two couples were on terms of mutual esteem and exchanged frequent cordialities.

For the present, therefore, Charlotte Cox merely lurked menacingly in the background, and the Keans continued to lead their own conflicting ways of life. When Grattan came to London on another visit, in the summer of 1817, he found that Edmund "was going on in the same apparent round of home respectability . . . and tavern dissipation." He again met much good company at Clarges Street—the people of *ton* and of title with whom Mary liked to fill her house—and he noticed that Alderman and Mrs. Cox were invariably among them. But, as before, he formed the impression that Edmund "endured" rather than "took pride" in the society of his guests. "He always behaved," wrote Grattan, "with great decorum and good manners. But when the company took leave, and he was free, his hours of enjoyment began. And I fancy he often slept from home."

Grattan remembered one pathetically revealing incident. He spent his last night in London, on this occasion, at Drury Lane, where he saw Edmund's Othello. After the play was over he went round to Edmund's dressing-room to bid him good-bye. He discovered him "stretched on a sofa, retching violently, and throwing up blood. His face half washed: one side deadly pale and the other a deep copper colour."

This was the state of physical exhaustion to which Edmund was usually reduced after the performance of an arduous part. Yet he would not spare himself. In failure, he had heedlessly sacrificed his health to his ambition: and now, in success, he subjected it to the unbearable strain, not only of tavern orgies and of wild racketing about, but of ceaseless hard work.

He never let up for a moment. Though it is true that in the summer of 1818 he did take a holiday, it was the first in his life and it was far from being a peaceful one. "He went," Mary told Barry Cornwall (Kean's biographer), "to Paris and Switzerland—went to Mount St. Bernard—delighted all the monks singing and reciting—wrote in their book some nonsense I forget what—Jack Hughes whom he took with him to take care of his money can tell you more about it than I can. I was not with him."

It is a sad reflection that even on his holiday Edmund trusted himself so little as to need a purse-bearer (Jack Hughes was a minor Drury Lane comedian with whom he had first made friends during his strolling player days at Gloucester). And even abroad he could not—or would not—keep out of the news. For example, every paper reported that he had narrowly escaped injury when his carriage "was hurled to pieces on the Jura mountains." And because it made good "copy," he returned to England boasting untruthfully that he had climbed Mont Blanc.

Although he was in desperate need of a long, complete rest, he would neither recognize that fact himself nor allow the public to suspect it. Sometimes he was kept from the stage by "indisposition," and occasionally stories crept into the Press that he was dangerously ill. But he always came back soon enough to allay popular anxiety.

During the next few years he would have to fight harder than ever to maintain his position. Yet he would not even contemplate retreat. In spite of failing health, he would continue to coin his £10,000 per annum: and in spite of several serious onslaughts against him, he would remain on his pedestal. It would seem as if his passion for applause had given him the power to triumph over all obstacles.

But he was really like a fine, luxurious building whose foundations are crumbling—apparently imposing but essentially insecure. He was heading directly for a fall, but when that fall occurred at last its suddenness and magnitude would take the world dramatically by surprise and would be to him an unbearable shock.

Charlotte Cox would be the immediate cause of it. But his illicit association with her would begin as the consequence of many events which were all part of his tragedy. She might, had she had the mind to do so, have used her influence over him to his own good. But she was a woman without quality. And he sinned not so much in loving her as in loving her vainly.

2

In October, 1816, Edmund was for some reason prevented from fulfilling an engagement to appear as Sir Giles Overreach at the Brighton Theatre; and in consequence an unknown actor from Worthing named Junius Brutus Booth was called in at the last moment to play the part in his stead.

The audience were disappointed, and they were prepared, uncharitably, to vent their annoyance on Booth of whom they had never heard before and whom they did not wish to see now. But the power of his performance took them completely by surprise and they ended up by applauding him vociferously. They went away convinced that he was every bit as good as Kean himself. In fact, in voice, appearance, manner and method he was exactly like Kean. There was nothing to choose between the two of them.

The news soon reached London. A second Edmund Kean had been discovered in the provinces. At last a tragedian had arisen who would challenge the star of Drury Lane on his own ground, and there was the prospect of a really good fight.

Both the rival Patent Houses were naturally anxious to make capital out of Booth; and on November 1st, Douglas Kinnaird wrote to him:

"I shall be much obliged if you will inform me by return of post where you perform, and what characters on Monday, Tuesday and Wednesday next. . . . I should like to see you play the part of a villain if possible.

"If my name be unknown to you, I beg to say that I am connected with Drury Lane theatre, and have heard Madame Storace speak in your praise."

But Douglas Kinnaird worked with the slowness of a committee member. Thomas Harris acted with the promptitude of a dictator: and he got in first. On February 12, 1817, Junius Brutus Booth made his début in *Richard III* at Covent Garden.

His success was instantaneous. All the critics remarked on his remarkable resemblance to Mr. Kean, though a few of them, it is true, suggested he was merely a mimic. (Thus the *Morning Chronicle* wrote rather scathingly: "He succeeds best, where he imitates his original most. . . . So accurately has he studied the readings of Mr. Kean that he imitates him even in passages where the most judicious critics have decided that that actor was wrong. . . . He traverses more extent of stage than any actor we ever beheld, he accompanies every expression with a gesture that may give an emblem of the words, according to the old story of the Actor, who, in delivering the sentence of 'thro' a long series of ten revolving years,' exemplified the text by pointing to his ten fingers and two ears.")

But the *Morning Post* thought "that many of Mr. Booth's efforts were so happy as to be considered . . . eminently transcendent." And the *Sun* voiced the general opinion when it wrote: "We cannot, in justice, say that Mr. Booth is a wilful, far less a servile imitator."

The public, at any rate, were delighted with him and they were excited as well. Booth was the hero of the moment. At his second performance of Richard on February 13th, the house was packed to suffocation, and the applause was hysterical. It seemed certain that Covent Garden had at last got hold of a really dangerous rival to Edmund Kean.

But there was a hitch—a quarrel over money. Though Booth insisted on a three-years' contract at a salary of £15 per week, Harris refused to foot the bill. He was resolute. Last year he had engaged Booth, at two guineas per week, to play small parts, and now he declined to pay him more than £5 per week until such time as he was firmly established in popular favour. Booth was annoyed; and, with the wilfulness which often comes from sudden success, he walked out.

On February 14th, when he was billed to act Richard for the third time at Covent Garden, he failed to appear. Fawcett, the stage-manager, came forward to offer some kind of explanation. But he was shouted down. The audience were beside themselves with rage. "You've sent him to Drury Lane," they yelled. "You've sent him to Drury Lane."

They were right. Kean and Booth under the same roof! It was too good an opportunity to be missed by the Drury Lane sub-committee. They approached Booth with a tempting offer of a three-years' contract at £10 per week; and he jumped up and swallowed the bait. On February 20th he made his début at Drury Lane—as Iago to the Othello of Edmund Kean.

The greatest histrionic battle of the century was arranged.

That night the Drury Lane stage became a kind of prize-fight ring; and the auditorium was filled to overflowing with excited, wildly cheering spectators. Booth was the challenger with everything to gain. Kean was the champion whose title was in jeopardy. Booth was the sentimental favourite. The odds were about even!

Or so the spectators thought. But the contest eventually proved a very one-sided affair. "On entering, Mr. Booth was welcomed by thunders of applause," wrote the *Morning Post*. "He commenced his performance with great success. But as the play advanced he lost the high ground on which he had stood; and the comparison which the audience were increasingly called upon to make was not very favourable to him. His Iago was . . . nothing like what a too sanguine public had fondly anticipated. . . . In some of the most interesting scenes his labours were witnessed with the most perfect serenity, and a most appalling calm prevailed where heretofore we have been accustomed to look for a storm of approbation. . . . With another actor in Othello, the Iago of the evening might have been thought great, but by the side of Kean we could discover in him nothing strikingly original in thought, vivid in conception, or brilliant in execution . . ."

Booth had done his best. But Edmund had been by far too good for him, had made him look puny. He had risen to the importance of the occasion in a manner that was terrific, frightening, and quite unforgettable. He had suspected that there were many in the audience who would like to see him vanquished. He had believed that his whole future was at stake. So he had come on to the stage possessed of a determination not only to eclipse Booth but to prove to the public, for good and all, that he was the one and only Edmund Kean, and that there was not another actor in the world to touch him.

He fought with a great show of sportsmanship. At the end of each scene, he bowed and smiled and took Booth by the hand and affected to suppose that the audience's applause was meant for both of them. But while the play was on, he fought in deadly earnest. He gave no quarter. He never allowed his opponent a chance. " . . . Up and down, to and fro he went, pacing about like a chafed lion, who had received his fatal hurt, but whose strength is still undiminished. The fury and whirlwind of the passions seemed to have endowed him with supernatural strength. His eye was glittering and bloodshot, his veins were swollen, and his whole figure restless and violent. It seemed dangerous to cross his path and death to assault him. He was excited in a most extraordinary degree as much as though he had been maddened by wine."

Edmund acted that night as he had never acted in his

life before. His Othello was a gigantically selfish performance. But its effect was overwhelming. It swept all the
other players—including Iago—clean off the stage. "Even
the actors, hardened in their art—were moved." One
comedian—"a veteran of forty years' experience"—said
afterwards: "When Kean rushed off the stage in the
third act, I felt my face deluged with tears—a thing
that has never happened to me since I was a crack, this
high!"

Next morning the Press reported Edmund's triumph
with varying emphasis. A few of the critics tried to make out
that Booth had only lost on points, and that he had gone
down gallantly to defeat. But the majority of them stated
what was true—that he had been well and mercilessly
slaughtered

At any rate he did not come back for more. Though
Othello was announced for repetition on Saturday, February
22nd, Booth failed to turn up and Rae played the part of
Iago in his stead. On Wednesday, February 26th, the following explanation was printed in the *Morning Post:*

"The affidavit of a professional gentleman, Mr. Salter of
Norton Falgate. . . . Mr. Salter . . . did see Junius
Booth . . . on Saturday morning last when he complained to Mr. Salter of severe indisposition, owing to the
anxiety of his mind, and fatigue during the last week, and
appeared to be so seriously indisposed as to be totally
incapable of performing that evening. He expressed a wish
to leave Town immediately and wrote a letter to Mr. Rae
of Drury Lane Theatre . . . after waiting in vain to see
Mr. Rae, Mr. Salter immediately proceeded with Mr.
Booth to the house of a friend at Tottenham, where they
both remained until the next day. Mr. Salter further
deposed that the said Junius Booth appeared to be extremely
ill during the whole of the said time."

There was an unpleasant aftermath of battle.

Booth eventually crawled back, with his tail between
his legs, to Covent Garden, claiming peevishly that he had

been fouled. He complained that the Drury Lane management had intended to ruin him by presenting him exclusively in second-rate parts: and that, at Kean's instigation,
they had trapped him into signing an unfair agreement.
He even hinted that Kean had been the first to tempt him
to leave Covent Garden.

Meanwhile, he became involved in a fierce dispute
between the two Patent Houses, for both claimed the right
to his services. Drury Lane threatened to injunct him from
appearing at Covent Garden, and Covent Garden accused
Drury Lane of procuring a breach of contract. The case was
actually set down for hearing in the Court of Chancery, but
before it came on it was settled privately in Covent Garden's
favour.

As a badgered, rather pathetic loser, Booth naturally won
many sympathizers. It was thought that he had been the
victim of a conspiracy, and it was even suggested, in one
newspaper, that the members of the Wolves Club had
pledged themselves to drive him from the stage. But
Edmund answered this charge in a letter which temporarily
silenced his accusers. "The Wolf Club," he wrote, "is no
longer in existence, has not been for the last nine months,
and, when it was, the principles of the institution were
founded in integrity and *universal philanthropy*. The mis-
representations, with regard to this society, laid before the
Public, rendered it, unjustly, an object of reprobation, and in
acknowledgement of my duty to the public, I resigned it."

In spite of repercussions, recriminations, and suspicions,
the fact remained that Edmund, by one superhuman effort,
had paralysed his would-be rival. The Booth bubble was
pricked.

It is true that while Booth remained in the news, he
continued to arouse mass hysteria whenever he performed at
Covent Garden. But that was only for a few weeks, and
inevitably he ceased to attract the public as soon as the
excitement over him had died down. He was no longer
comparable with Kean. He would continue to earn fairly

good money and to play fairly good parts. But he would have to wait a long while yet before he would again meet with real success. And then he would find it, not in England, but in the United States of America.

3

Edmund had won a signal victory, and he was again securely on his throne. But he had by no means placed himself above reproach. There were many who resented the ruthless lengths to which he had gone in order to suppress the pretensions of his rival. While they admired his histrionic strength, they deplored the human weakness which had forced him to bare his teeth. They began to suspect that he was self-enamoured, tyrannic, and incurably jealous of his fellow actors. And, unfortunately, during the coming years, he would give them several clear indications that their suspicions were well founded.

His contemporaries judged him severely on this account. But there is no reason why posterity should follow too slavishly in their footsteps. For though it may be impossible to respect the cruel and ungenerous way in which Edmund waged his battle with Booth, it is none the less easy, knowing his background, to understand and to forgive it. From his earliest days he had learned to fend for himself, and he had been brought up to the idea of rigorous self-preservation. He had fought hard and painfully and single-handed for his success. He had hewn his way through years of misery and squalor and frustrated hopes. Now that he had reached the top he lived in continual terror of his memories. He regarded a threat to his prestige as a menace to his very existence. In his heart he knew that he could not survive without the limelight.

He worshipped the public because they applauded him. But he did not trust them. He was already sufficiently disillusioned to realize that they were fickle and ungrateful, and that, if ever he were eclipsed by another, they would

desert him without a qualm. He believed, quite rightly, that
they were loyal to him only because he was irreplaceable.

He never for one instant felt secure. He was continually
in the same state of mind as a dictator who rules uncomfortably by force and who fears a revolution or a sudden,
calamitous fall from power. But unlike a dictator, he was not
essentially selfish or hard-hearted. To the poorer members of
his profession he was invariably kind and considerate and
encouraging. It was only when he was faced with a potential
usurper or a potential enemy to his own interests that he lost
all sense of charity.

In the theatre he was a vain and petty tyrant. But so
too have many other actors been with far less cause. So too
was David Garrick, who never in his lifetime knew a single
day of suffering. In the words of Charles Lamb, Garrick
"appears to have been as mere a player as ever existed;
to have had his mind tainted with the lowest players' vices,
envy and jealousy and miserable cravings after applause;
one who in the exercise of his profession was jealous even
of the women performers that stood in his way."

But while Garrick was diplomatic, restrained, and well-
bred, Edmund was blundering, blatant, and vulgar. He did
not make the smallest attempt to conceal his feelings—
worthy or unworthy.

He gave himself away, typically, when he added that
catty little postscript—"N.B. Perhaps the Great W.C.M.
may be got"—to the memorable letter which he sent to
Rae on March 22, 1816, explaining why he was unable
to appear in *The Duke of Milan*. "W.C.M." stood for
William Charles Macready who was, at the time, performing as a provincial actor in Dublin—and with such
uncommon success that the fame of his achievements
reached as far as London. A few months later—on September 16, 1816—he made his début at Covent Garden; and
then Edmund came along and sat conspicuously in a box
and was rather too obviously liberal with his applause.
Although he had reason to fear Macready, who would

eventually become his most dangerous rival, he might, had he understood the dignity which belongs to kingship, have affected to ignore him. But unfortunately he could not be reticent even about his jealousies.

It was his real fault to be always bombastically himself. He had no tact and no discretion. Every successful man fights hard, often unscrupulously hard, to keep his position: and even to-day there are few actors essentially free from a desire to dominate the scene. These are human weaknesses which in Edmund were particularly excusable. But he allowed them to appear glaringly unpleasant, because he made so much show of them. He would not gratify the British Public's demand for a sugar coating.

At Drury Lane things were going from bad to worse. The sub-committee had no policy, and apparently no authority. They were hopelessly divided among themselves. One wanted this, another that; George Lamb believed in lavish expenditure; Peter Moore in rigid economy. Consequently there were rows and ructions and resignations.

Meanwhile chaos ruled. Indifferent plays were badly put on, casting was all topsy-turvy, and the theatre was being plunged deeper and deeper into debt.

No one doubted that the sub-committee were largely to blame. In the outside world they were growing increasingly unpopular; and almost everything they did met with a storm of disapproval. At the beginning of the 1817–1818 season they lighted the stage of Dury Lane with gas, and this move, though in fact a major reform, was interpreted as an attempt to poison the public. "All admit," *The Times* reported, "that after having sat a whole evening in the theatre, they feel a burning and prickling sensation in their eyes, a soreness about the throat, and generally a violent headache which sometimes lasts for two or three days."

Several other structural alterations were greeted by an equally "bad Press." The theatre saloon was transformed into a Chinese Pavilion—"an assemblage of separate receptacles hung round with Chinese lanterns"—and "to this sinister improvement" at least one newspaper critic "decidedly objected." He feared that the Chinese Pavilion would become a kind of brothel and would keep many respectable families away from Drury Lane. A little while later his prophecy was proved correct, for a pitched battle was fought in the saloon between three ladies whose names —Miss Anastasia Bolt, Miss Caroline Rosa St. Albans and Miss Winifred Watlington Sparrow—were more picturesque than their manners were demure. They were eventually removed in custody!

But the encouragement of prostitution was among the minor charges brought against the sub-committee. They were chiefly attacked on account of their casual and unmannerly treatment of authors. It was alleged that they seldom bothered to read plays which were submitted for their approval and that they frequently mislaid them; that they put on cheap pieces written by their friends and that they wantonly ignored works of merit.

Whatever the truth of these accusations, there is no doubt that from 1816 onwards the new plays performed at Drury Lane were of a pretty poor order. Things came to a head when a tragedy in five acts called *Switzerland* was produced for the first time on February 15, 1819, with Edmund Kean in the leading part of Eugene.

The author—Miss Jane Porter—was a distinguished novelist, but she had had no previous experience of the stage and she had contrived to write an excessively cumbersome and boring play. According to the *Morning Post* " . . . The intricacies of the plot defied all attempts at unravelling them. There was a great apparent bustle, a succession of unconnected incidents, and yet upon the whole a decided want of action. Every character made long speeches, but did nothing, and this defect revealed itself so early that even in the Second Act, symptoms of disapprobation were manifested by the audience."

The audience—fed up with mediocre entertainment—let themselves go good and proper. During the last two Acts they shouted so loud and yelled "Off, off," with such vehemence that the actors could not make themselves heard. "Even Kean died in the midst of a storm of hisses and offs."

At the end of the play·there was pandemonium.

" . . . A loud shout and repeated call for the manager commenced. Though incessant for nearly half-an-hour it remained unanswered, and when the curtain at last rose no one had appeared to encounter the fury of an incensed audience but poor Mrs. Bland, who was about to open the After-piece. A general and continued roar of indignation, however, accompanied with a shower of orange-peel compelled her to leave the stage, which remained vacant for the space of ten minutes, during which calls for the manager resounded from all parts of the house. A second attempt to proceed with the After-piece only produced a second expression of indignation still louder than the former, and oranges began to shower upon the stage, instead of the peelings which had been previously thrown.

" . . . After a few minutes Mr. Stephen Kemble [now manager of Drury Lane] made his appearance. This was the signal for fresh vociferations, and even outrages, for an orange struck Mr. Kemble on the forehead as he advanced to the front of the stage. This outrage, however, excited a general cry of 'Shame' and in a short time silence was completely restored."

Mr. Kemble then addressed the house as follows:—

"Gentlemen, it is yours to make the law, and we must obey." (Applause and cries of "Why then did you not obey us before?"—"Why were you so long in coming?")

"Gentlemen, this tragedy is withdrawn."

So ended an unfortunate incident, quite typical of the early nineteenth century stage: and it would, in the ordinary course of events, have been quickly forgotten. But Miss Porter, who had a literary reputation to keep up, refused to lie down under so crushing a humiliation in the theatre, and she proceeded to blame her failure on Edmund. She maintained that he had given an atrocious performance. She accused him further of deliberately acting his part badly in order to ruin her play, in which (according to her) he had been forced to appear by the sub-committee against his will. In other words, she put herself forward as the innocent victim of a gross and revengeful act of sabotage—quite unsuspected, since, at rehearsals (so she said), Edmund had assured her, in the most flattering terms, that he was delighted with his part. She even suggested that, "on the night of public representation," the audience had directed their fury not against her but against her leading player. "Shame!—Shame Kean!" she wrote, "burst from every part of the house. . . . When the curtain dropped (though stunned by the cool, deliberate act of —— I will not give it a name—I had just witnessed) I yet sufficiently possessed myself, to insist on withdrawing the piece totally; though urged by a member of the committee, to permit a second representation, and with a new performer. I had been betrayed by the actor whose honour and talents I had trusted."

There was not much truth in all this. Clearly, Miss Porter's brave statement that *she* insisted on withdrawing her piece was a whopping lie. Though Edmund probably did put up a pretty poor show in what was a very bad part, it is remarkable that only one of the morning newspaper critics attacked him, whereas they were all agreed that Miss Porter's tragedy was beneath contempt and deserved its fate. Really, her assertions were nothing more than the hysterical whinings of a disappointed author; and they ought to have been dismissed as such. But unfortunately Edmund had, by his own indiscretions, made himself completely vulnerable to any form of abuse, and when the weekly newspapers appeared it was obvious that Miss Porter had won powerful support for her accusations against him.

The critic of the *Champion* in a long article, published on February 28th, under the heading "Conduct of Mr. Kean to Authors, Proprietors and the Public," was particularly violent. He claimed "undeniable authority" for stating that

Edmund had not bothered to learn his part, that he had invented his own lines, that he had embarrassed the other actors by his perpetual inaccuracies, and that "with arrogant carelessness, he had talked through his character, like a washerwoman over a tub."

Having got Miss Porter's complaints off his chest, the critic went off to affirm that the time had come for plain speaking. "The interests of the proprietors," he wrote, "and what is more of the Drama, must not be sacrificed with impunity to the whims and caprices of any actor. Mr. Kean, it is true, for want of a better, stands at the very head of his profession; and if he enjoyed his eminence with . . . moderation, we should be happy to swell the chorus of his reputation by dwelling on his excellences. But if he bashaws it—alike to actors, managers, and authors, and will suffer no other merit, among the first, to appear beside him on the boards—no production of the last to be accepted or to succeed, that does not make his character the *exclusive object of attraction* and no wish or promise of the second to be fulfilled that does not chime in with his ambition to shine, not only 'superior but alone, it is high time for criticism to look to the other side of the picture . . . William Hazlitt wrote him up: let him take care that he does not put himself down."

On paper, the critic of the *Champion*, and others who echoed his sentiments, had a cast-iron case. There was no doubt that Drury Lane was in very low water, and that Edmund's personal popularity was dwindling fast. During the past three years, Edmund had had only two genuine successes and he had appeared in flop after flop. *King John*, which he had produced on June 1, 1818, had been so disastrous a failure that the theatre had had to be closed down for three nights afterwards.

It was also indisputable that he boasted, both in public and in private, that he had little regard for the authority of his employers, that he was his own master and that "his reason was in his will." In effect, he was self-convicted of the charges brought against him: and his critics were able to argue, therefore, that he was ruining the theatre which he was supposed to serve.

But they did not pause to consider that he was in fact guilty of no worse offence than trying to look after his own interests. From his point of view it would have been professional suicide to have acted inferior parts in poor plays, to have encouraged the claims of his rivals, to have obeyed implicitly the dictates of a committee of amateurs who were incompetent to rule. In the fiercely competitive atmosphere of the theatre, no star performer could afford—even momentarily—to be dwarfed by another, and least of all Edmund, whose position depended on his being incomparable. It had been proved over and over again that the public were only interested to see him when he interpreted a character worthy of his powers, when he was complete master of the scene, when he was, in short, a show in himself. He had to electrify or he was as nothing.

His critics forgot, too, that he had once rescued Drury Lane from financial collapse and that even now the theatre would have been infinitely worse off without him. The house was often half empty on the nights that he appeared, but on other nights it was still emptier. His value to the box-office had lessened certainly; but that was not because of his refusal to co-operate with second-rate dramatists or to perform on the stage with actors who had the chance to eclipse him. On the contrary, it was due pre-eminently to the fact that neither he nor the Drury Lane sub-committee seemed capable of finding him new parts in which he could really shine alone.

But though Edmund had abundantly good reason for pursuing his policy—however arrogant and selfish and inimical to the true interests of the Drama it appeared—he was his own worst apologist. He *would* brag and bluster when he should have remained silent and serene. Consequently he laid himself wide open to criticisms of the most virulent kind, and ruined the strength of his own case.

Before he had had time to recover from Miss Porter's

fulminations, he was made a target for abuse by another outraged author. Charles Bucke had written a tragedy called *The Italians* which had been accepted by the Drury Lane sub-committee as long ago as the autumn of 1817, but which —much to Bucke's disgust—had never been produced. He now seized the opportunity to publish it together with a long preface in which he accused Edmund of perfidy. He alleged that Edmund, after having given him "a positive assurance that nothing should prevent" the play from being performed, had deliberately used his influence to have it shelved indefinitely, because he had been dissatisfied with the part intended for him and had feared that the other characters "would excite too much interest."

If Edmund had ignored these charges they would have attracted very little attention. Charles Bucke was an author of no distinction and *The Italians* was an excessively poor tragedy. But instead of maintaining a dignified aloofness from the controversy, he rushed headlong into print with an extraordinarily offensive letter which was published simultaneously in all the leading newspapers.

"On reading *The Tragedy of Deranged Intellect*," he wrote "(for that was the name the play was known by in the Green Room), to my professional brethren, the only feelings it excited were uncontrollable laughter, and pity for the author. From this criterion, I took the liberty of suggesting to the management the impossibility of producing a play, which must have been attended with considerable expense, when there was not in it one gleam of hope for its success. There is certainly some pretty poetry in the character which was to have been sustained by Miss Cubbitt; and after that I will say in good set terms Mr. Bucke's tragedy is the worst of the bad. In this opinion I am joined by the whole of the dramatic *corps* who were to have been concerned in it. . . . The publication of *Deranged Intellect* is all the answer necessary to the author's attack upon my judgment; and for his inventive fabrication I publicly tell him that he has not uttered one word of truth in the whole of his aspersions, and I thus leave him to his contemplation, with disgust for his falsehood and pity for his folly."

What a madly ill-considered statement! If Edmund had *intended* to injure himself, he could not have done so more effectively than by that coarse, common, mud-slinging letter! It turned a minor fracas into a sensational quarrel. It gave boundless scope for his enemies to attack him. It aroused widespread sympathy for Bucke, who was rather a pathetic person, poverty-stricken, with a wife and children to support. And it alienated those who were sincerely anxious to support Edmund. Even the critic of *The Examiner*, while defending him in principle, felt bound to remark, "The spirit evinced by Mr. Kean throughout the business has not been in good taste."

No wonder the public were enraged.

No wonder Sir Walter Scott wrote furiously: " . . . How do you think I could relish being the object of such a letter as Kean wrote t'other day to a poor author, who, though a pedantic blockhead, has at least the right to be treated as a gentleman by a copper laced, twopenny tearmouth, rendered mad by conceit and success?"

And no wonder, when Edmund made his next appearance on the stage of Drury Lane (in *The Dwarf of Naples* as it happened), he was greeted by hisses and by loud cries of "Off, off." He abandoned any attempt to speak the lines of his part but moved instead towards the footlights. Then he addressed the audience as follows:

Ladies and Gentlemen,

I apprehend that the interruption given to the performance is owing to an opinion entertained by some that I have failed in my duties to that public to whom I owe my reputation and existence. To the public it is my wish to explain—to their decision I shall submit and to them *only* I am willing to apologize. If in consequence of an unjust accusation I have been betrayed for a moment into passion or ill temper it is the fault of my nature—I cannot help it; but having done so, it remains for me to apologize to that Public whose support I now claim.

Although that speech was not nearly humble enough to silence the gentlemen of the Press, who thought that Edmund owed a grovelling apology to Bucke, it satisfied the audience. They ceased to protest and allowed him to resume his part. Once again he had seemingly been forgiven.

But nothing could alter the fact that he had behaved unpleasantly—without discretion and without magnanimity. "If Mr. Kean would play the great man properly," wrote the *Examiner*, "he should know that every true spirit owes modesty and sincerity to all the world." He had shown none.

When *The Italians* was eventually produced at Drury Lane on April 3rd—with Rae in the leading part that had been intended for Edmund—it was well and truly damned by an impartial audience: and the critics were agreed that it was a tragedy without merit and unworthy of serious attention. Its failure provided Edmund with a perfect answer to Bucke's charges against him. It was the only one that he had ever needed. But he had had neither the patience nor the wisdom to wait for it. Wantonly and unnecessarily he had convicted himself of "suspicious pride." He had damaged his reputation still further: and he had added incalculably to the number of those who would kick him without mercy when the moment of his downfall arrived.

Meanwhile, Drury Lane was £80,000 in debt and both creditors and shareholders had alike reached the limit of their endurance. On June 4, 1819, the sub-committee, yielding at length to irresistible pressure, resigned in a body. At a general meeting on June 12th, the shareholders were informed that the theatre would be let to an independent manager, and that £25,000 (including £1,000 from the Prince Regent) had been raised by subscription loan towards the discharge of outstanding liabilities.

Both these reports were received with enthusiasm. Mrs. Butler, proprietress of a celebrated brothel in Covent Garden, and one of the most voluble of the Drury Lane shareholders, remarked: "Better and better, but the devil a hair I care what is done, so as it's for the honour of ould Drury."

On August 7th, the following notice was published in the Press:—

"Mr. Elliston has the honour to inform the public that he has become the lessee of the Theatre Royàl, Drury Lane, for fourteen years. All letters respecting engagements should be directed (post paid) to Mr. James Winston at the theatre. Manuscripts of pieces proposed for representation to be addressed to Mr. Elliston at his house in Stratford Place."

That report may have afforded the public considerable pleasure, but to Edmund it came as a bitter disappointment. He had wanted Drury Lane for himself. He had promised to devote all his energies to restoring its fortunes, and he had offered to pay a rent of £10,000 per annum. He had looked forward eagerly to being at last a legitimate king in his own kingdom. Now the Drury Lane General Committee had turned him down in favour of Robert William Elliston— Elliston, a born impresario (as Edmund had once found out to his cost), but an actor who in recent years had frequently played second fiddle to him.

It was a cruel blow. It wounded his pride even more deeply than he cared to admit. It meant, in effect, that though he was the head of his profession, he was denied the right to rule.

4

Robert William Elliston had achieved the ambition of a lifetime.

He was at last the Great Lessee.

He had renounced all his other enterprises, with the exception of his provincial theatres, in order to become manager of Drury Lane. And now, with the instincts and energies of a super-showman, he lost no time in making a

tremendous splash. Money was no object. He redecorated
the theatre. He built tons of new scenery. He engaged an
exceptionally strong company of tragedians, comedians,
singers, and dancers—at exceptionally high salaries. He
lined up a number of well-known dramatists to whom he
paid handsome advances on account of future royalties.
And he took good care to announce that everything had
been carried out "under his personal direction."

On September 30th he gave a reception to two hundred
distinguished guests. They inspected the decorations, which
were very lavish; they watched, from the auditorium, the
new stage scenes which were exhibited *seriatim*; and they
stood up while the Drury Lane vocalists, led by the famous
singer Braham, sang the National Anthem in unison.
Afterwards they adjourned to the theatre saloon, where they
were all entertained by the Great Lesee to a Ball and Supper.

Elliston never ran short of projects, and even on this
night of triumph he had a few regrets. It was a pity, for
example, that he had been unable to tempt Mrs. Siddons
from her retirement. It was a pity that he had failed to
persuade Sir Walter Scott to write a tragedy for him. It was
also a pity that he had not had sufficient time to reconstruct
completely, at a cost of £7,000, the interior of Drury Lane.

But on the whole he had every reason to feel proud of
himself. Although he could not begin actual building
operations until next year, the architect, Mr. Beasley, had
completed his plans, and a model of his design would be on
show in the saloon throughout the coming season. The Great
Lessee hoped that, among those who would see it, there
might be a few professional men who would acquaint him
of their expert opinions.

Elliston could count it among his major achievements
that he had succeeded, after a tussle, in retaining the services
of Edmund Kean. Edmund had not wanted to return to
Drury Lane. He had been offered a small fortune to tour
America, and he had been very anxious to accept it. The
last few years had left him tired, depressed and embittered.

"The Great Lessee"

ROBERT WILLIAM ELLISTON IN THREE CHARACTERS

He wanted to find an escape from his comparative failure; from the attacks which had been made upon him in the Press; and from his ceaseless struggle to keep in the limelight.

He thought that he had reached a dead end. Once he had been discontented because he could not shine in Society. But now he was finding it difficult enough to squeeze applause from audiences who were no longer very enthusiastic about him. In London they took him for granted. Even in the provinces they had grown a trifle used to him. He was starving for want of admiration.

But in America, where he was still unknown, it would be quite different. In America he would find a vast new public eager to make his acquaintance. He would show them acting of a kind of which they had never dreamed before. He would bring them cheering to their feet every night that he performed. In America he would be able to amass dollars by the thousand. But more important—much more important —he would be able to startle and amaze so that he would become again a centre of universal adulation.

On July 21st he wrote, from York, to his friend Michael Kelly, the famous singer and composer:—

> Jack's married—can you do anything for his wife, he says, you can send her to Bath. I know you will if you can. He lives at No. 35, Southampton Street. I am taking in the natives of York in the very first style of swindling.
>
> Shall quit England for *America* by the end of September. When I go I shall delight myself in the recollection of many pleasant hours I have enjoyed in your society, and wishing you health, happiness, and all the blessings in the world, I sign myself,
>
> Your very Sincere Friend,
> EDMUND KEAN.

A few days after writing this, Edmund heard of Elliston's appointment to Drury Lane. Of course, if his own application had been accepted, he would have cheerfully abandoned the idea of going to America. But now that it had been turned down, he was more than ever anxious to escape from England, where he felt, in his bitter chagrin and disappointment, that he was no longer needed. Perhaps the British Public would miss him after he had gone. Perhaps the Drury Lane proprietors would realize then how badly they had treated him. Perhaps even the gentlemen of the Press would repent of their unfair attacks upon him. At any rate he determined that he would never serve under Elliston. He instructed his solicitor, Mr. Plumptre, to communicate his decision to the newspapers.

But in his anxiety for "revenge" he had overlooked one important consideration. Legally speaking, he was not at liberty to leave London. He was bound by his Drury Lane contract, which still had a year to run. If he broke it, he would be liable to pay crippling damages. The only alternative would be to persuade the Drury Lane management to release him voluntarily from his obligations. But unfortunately for him he was now faced, not with the feeble opposition of a vacillating committee, but with the purposeful resistance of Robert William Elliston.

Against this formidable opponent Edmund had been powerless once before, and he would soon discover that he was so again. But he was always incapable of making a previous calculation of the strength of an adversary: and so, heedless of the inevitable result of battle, he launched an impulsive attack.

At first, he tried, with a great show of ill-natured bravado, to present Elliston with a *fait accompli*. He wrote in a long letter that his plans were already made and that he could not possibly alter them. Perhaps, after his return from America, he would enter into fresh negotiations to act at Drury Lane, but for the moment he had decided irrevocably to "allow the field open to his compeers." (Had not Elliston engaged Vandenhoff, "an actor of the first consequence," who would be able to play all the leads in tragedy?) "Richards and Hamlets," he concluded in his most catty style, "grow on every hedge. Grant you may have a good crop of them."

Elliston, not in the least perturbed by these blundering
tactics, merely reminded Edmund of his contract. Edmund
offered to pay a £1,000 forfeiture. Elliston promptly refused
it. Edmund then toyed with the dangerous idea of breaking
his contract regardless of the consequences. But not for long.
When it was pointed out to him by his legal advisers that the
consequences would be, at the minimum, £10,000 worth of
damages, he realized himself that "it would be madness to
embark for America." On September 27th Mary informed
Elliston that although her husband was at present in
Scotland, he would return to his engagement at Drury Lane
immediately after the first week in November.

The squabble was over. Edmund had threatened,
quibbled, talked big and in the end had made rather a fool of
himself. But Elliston, who held every trump card, had
behaved throughout in the most courteous fashion. And so
he would continue to do. He would always get his own way,
of course. But he would treat his recalcitrant star with the
most grand and elaborate respect.

In truth, he regarded Edmund as a spoilt prodigy whose
will must only be crossed on matters of principle. Otherwise
he pandered to all his whims and vanities. He announced his
name in extra big lettering, in spite of several protests from
newspaper critics, who objected to this new-fangled *starring*
system. He allowed him to manage his own productions.
He gave him *carte blanche* to spend as much money as he
wanted on scenery, costumes, and effects. He consulted him
about casting. He even engineered a little indirect flattery,
for when Horace Twiss was about to publish his play, *The
Carib Chief*, Elliston demanded that the following paragraph
should be included in the preface: "The author cannot
allow this play to be hurried through the Press, without
recording his tribute of admiration to the splendid exertions
of Mr. Kean, by which its unprecedented success has been
achieved." Considering *The Carib Chief* had been performed
under the sub-committee's management and had been a
dismal failure, that was typical of Elliston's technique!

Yet, despite the careful blandishments of his employer, Edmund remained restless and resentful. He had been forced back to Drury Lane against his will and for the moment he was trapped. But he was still as anxious as ever to get away from England, and he was determined to leave for America as soon as his contract came to an end. He had only a year to wait.

Nothing happened during that time to make him alter his mind. The general business in the theatre improved, but his personal hold on the public weakened, if anything. Not even Elliston's enthusiasm and astuteness and flair for showmanship seemed capable of reviving Kean's pristine glory. From a crop of new roles he reaped only one success —*King Lear*, which he played for the first time on April 24th. (The play had been banned from the stage in recent years on account of the lunacy of King George III.) Even so, his performance, though supposedly very fine, was by no means universally acclaimed.

It was really a vintage performance—that is to say, it grew more impressive as the years went by. In time it would be regarded as one of his greatest achievements. At the moment it created only a mild sensation, and was considered far inferior to his Richard, his Overreach, and his Othello. Even Hazlitt, who, aware of the tremendous effect Garrick had once made in this part, had expected to be overwhelmed by Edmund's acting, was plainly disappointed. "To call it a decided failure," he wrote, "would be saying what we do not think; to call it a splendid success would be saying so no less. Mr. Kean did not appear to us to set his back fairly to his task, or to trust implicitly to the author, but to be trying experiments upon the audience, and waiting to see the result. We never saw this daring actor want confidence before, but he seemed to cower and hestitate before the public eye in the present instance, and to be looking out for the effect of what he did, while he was doing it."

Perhaps Hazlitt was right. Perhaps Edmund had strained after applause. Perhaps, in his present mood of discontent, he was incapable of "setting his back fairly" to any task. But whatever the case, his Lear was a veritable triumph compared with his other new offerings. *Coriolanus* lasted only four nights. And for the rest—he appeared in a succession of dreary, forgotten failures.

For him it was a miserable season. He had hoped to escape from it, and he had been prevented. Instead he had been forced to serve a manager whom at heart he resented; to suffer the continued humiliation of dwindling popularity and of abusive criticisms in the Press. He was still king of the British Stage. But he was a monarch without authority and without the power to raise cheers from his subjects or to silence opposition.

No wonder his affair with Charlotte Cox began about this time. It was the perfect psychological moment. What was there left for him but to fall in love? He, who could not survive without adulation, fled to a woman who was prepared to give it to him unstintingly. Charlotte had become "essential to his happiness." In her arms he found an exhilarating refuge from his wounded pride.

In the early April of 1820, he went off on one of his provincial jaunts to Lynn in Norfolk, and from there he wrote to her:

"Dearest of women . . . I am satisfied we were formed for each other; the assimilation of disposition in all its characters proclaims it. . . . The theatre was last night crowded to excess and the applause as enthusiastic as it could be for the country; but Charlotte did not hear it. The neighbourhood of Lynn is beautiful, the walks enchant- ing—Charlotte does not partake them. Thus everything that I might enjoy bears with it its counterpoise of mortifica- tion. Our separation is, however, but transient. I have not yet made any arrangement for the next week, and con- sequently expect to return on Sunday, and hold my dear little girl in my arms. . . . And now, my dear girl, banish from your mind every supposition of a change in my affections—they are unalterable. From the first moment I saw you, I loved every hour; and in possession of your heart, I acknowledge with gratitude, that I have obtained the very summit of my wishes. Dear, dear, dear girl more than fame, more than wealth, more than life, more than heaven—I love you."

He saw no fault in Charlotte. She had the same thoughts and feelings and tastes and impulses as he. And she worshipped him—not slavishly, of course, for she was a jealous mistress. But were not her suspicions and demands upon his leisure, though tedious at times, exquisitely flattering?

She gave him confidence even in his failings. She never suggested that anything he did was wrong or unworthy—unless, of course, he broke an appointment with her. His extravagance and dissipation were mere vagaries excusable in a genius. She did not make him feel in the least ashamed of his associations. She was all compassion and sympathy—except when his actions ran contrary to her own interests.

She liked those who were dear to him. She liked "Aunt" Tid and "Aunt" Tid liked her. "Aunt" Tid was made a party to their affair. She was their confidante and their go-between. Edmund had to be very careful to avoid detection, and so he addressed his letters to Charlotte in the fictitious names of Miss Alleyn, Mrs. Simpson, and so on, care of Miss Tidswell at Tavistock Row. It was an elaborate, despicable subterfuge and unnecessary as it happened. But it appealed enormously to "Aunt" Tid. At last she had got her revenge on Mary. And how sweet it was! Occasionally Edmund sent his passionate love-letters care of Mrs. Price at Craven Buildings. For Aunt Price—that shadowy figure of his childhood—was also in the plot.

Nor did Charlotte despise his friends who were humble. He introduced them all to her in turn, and she never afterwards shunned their company. In fact, she showed herself eminently suited to be the Queen of his little tavern kingdom. R. Phillips, his secretary, and Jack Hughes, his purse-bearer, became the organizers of her clandestine meetings with him; and she was empowered to give them his instructions. One night, when she was sitting alone in the stage-box at Drury Lane, a Mr. Crooke, who was a theatrical agent by profession, walked in and handed her this note: "Welcome, my life, my love, my soul, I cannot see you until after the farce. . . . How does my little darling? I introduce you to my friend, Mr. Crooke, an officer of the Wolves, whom I have commissioned to be in attendance and pay all honours to his captain's love. I shall hurry through the Tobacconist as fast as possible."

Edmund secured jobs for his poor actor friends through Edward Crooke's agency. Crooke, besides being his lieutenant in the Wolves Club, was also a director of his charitable enterprises! And, of course, Charlotte played up superbly to all Edmund's "human feelings," his generous impulses, his hatred of "false pride." She even showed herself eager to emulate them. "Your offer to assist poor ——" he wrote, "is like yourself—noble and unaffected; but, my love, keep your little purse for contingencies. I will send to ——. You charm me by your charity for I know it is not from ostentation: every day shoots up some unexpected tendril round the root of my affections . . ."

He was lavishly generous to her. It satisfied his mock kingly pride to be so. He gave her money, clothes, a horse—anything in the world she wanted. It was all part of this highly theatrical play. "I thank you, dear love," he wrote, "for asking for the plaid; it displays that undivided confidence which ever should subsist in hearts formed for each other. I hope my little darling will always tell me her wishes without disguise or reservations; and if love, money or industry can accomplish them, she is certain as she may be of the heart of her adorer."

What a sad, absurdly tinsel infatuation it was! At the age of thirty-one—with thirty-one years' experience of the world behind him—he had at last fallen in love, calf-like, with a beautiful image fashioned in his own vanity. He was deceived by a woman's wiles—so transparent that they did not delude him when he used them against himself. He thought that he loved her passionately—to the exclusion of all else. But did he love her more than fame? Oh, no! Not even Charlotte could extinguish his desire to go to America. Not even she could dull his wild craving for notoriety.

The season was drawing to a close. At his benefit on June 12th, Edmund announced that he would appear in a farce called *The Admirable Crichton*, and that he would, for the first time, show a London audience some of the tricks which he had learned as a strolling player. He would dance, he would sing, he would fence—and he would be Harlequin! The great tragedian would prove how versatile an actor he really was!

Hazlitt arrived at the theatre in a mood of amused expectancy. "We have longed ever since we saw Mr. Kean," he wrote, "to see him jump through a trap door . . . the leap from Othello to Harlequin! What an interval, what a gulf to pass! What an elasticity of soul and body too—what a diversity of capacity in the same diminutive person! . . . It is not being educated in the fourth form of St. Paul's School, or cast in the antique mould of the high Roman Fashion, that can do this . . . it is genius alone that can raise a man thus above his first origin, and make him thus various from himself."

But Hazlitt was doomed to disappointment. Edmund fenced, sang, danced, but while dancing with Miss Velancy broke his tendon Achilles and so was prevented from being Harlequin. "We do not think much of Mr. Kean's singing," Hazlitt wrote. "We could, with a little practice and tuition, sing nearly as well ourselves; as for his dancing, it is but *so so*, and anybody can dance; but for his jumping through a hole in the wall—clean through, head over heels, like a shot out of a culverin—'by heavens, it would have been great!' This we fully expected at his hands, and in this expectation we were baulked."

The remainder of his audience were not so gentle in their sarcasm as Hazlitt. They tittered and booed a little and suspected that Kean was drunk. At least they thought him

clumsy and ridiculous throughout and were not entirely
convinced by the story of his damaged ankle.

An eye-witness remarked: "This display will certainly
not raise his reputation." It certainly did not. It was an
absurd, undignified publicity stunt which a few years before
he would not have contemplated. Afterwards he regretted it.

But now the British public had at last woken up to the
fact that their "favourite" was about to leave them. And they
realized, on a sudden, how much they admired his incomparable talents and how grievously they were going to
miss him.

The season was over. But in August Elliston opened
Drury Lane, in spite of violent protests from the Haymarket
(for it was in the middle of the summer vacation), in order
to stage Edmund Kean's farewell performances in London.
Edmund played all his famous parts in turn, and for several
weeks the houses were large and enthusiastic. The last
night was on September 16th. He acted Richard III, and
at the end of the play he responded to the deafening cheers
with a long, grandiloquent speech. "It is with pain," he
began, "I announce to you that a long period must elapse
before I can again have the honour of coming before you,
and when I reflect on the uncertainty of life, the sentiment will
obtrude itself that this may possibly be my last appearance
on these boards." The audience cried, "No, no, we hope
not," and for a few moments Edmund broke down completely under the stress of his dramatized emotions. But he
pulled himself together, and concluded: " . . . I have now
to bid you farewell. My recollections will be gratifying, for
they will remind me of that honourable rank in my profession to which your kindness elevated me. If at any time I
have forgotten the dignity of that position, it would be
imputed to the delirium which your favour inspires, and it
is to you alone that I need apologize. With the deepest
sentiments of esteem and gratitude, I respectfully bid you
farewell."

Before leaving London, Edmund presented Drury Lane

with a plaster bust of himself, which he insisted should be placed in the principal Green Room. There was some doubt as to the propriety of this, but Elliston, in his most tactful, reverential mood, silenced all objections. He himself, followed by Edmund and the entire Drury Lane company in procession, carried the precious bust to the Green Room. There was a short ceremony. Elliston made a speech and then Edmund made a speech. In the course of the proceedings William Dowton, the celebrated comedian, who was jealous of Edmund and resented any honours being paid to him, spat in Elliston's face. But otherwise all went well. The party settled down to a bacchanalian feast which lasted until ten o'clock next morning, when it was time to begin the day's rehearsal.

Edmund went off for a short farewell tour of the provinces. He said good-bye to Mary and Charlotte. It would be a year before he saw either of them again. In London he left behind him both his wife and his mistress. He played in Leamington and Coventry, where the theatres were controlled by Elliston; and he concluded his final engagement—at the Liverpool Theatre—on the night of October 6th. At the conclusion of his performance he made the most extraordinary speech. He said that as an actor he deserved and expected applause, but that the Liverpool audiences were, in his experience, colder and less enthusiastic than playgoers anywhere else in the United Kingdom. What courage and impudence! These were his last words to the British public prior to leaving for America. On October 11th he set sail on board the *Matilda*.

A little while before, Alexander Rae had died suddenly. One newspaper reporter felt very sentimental He wrote:—

> Mourn, Drury, mourn, thy half-deserted scene,
> Thy triumph once, thy sorrow now is Kean:
> And in fresh gloom to wrap thy setting day,
> Lost is thy other son, extinct thy Rae;
> Hope's anchor raised, her swelling sails unfurled
> This seeks "another," that a "better world."

CHAPTER VIII

I

EDMUND could regard America as a kind of provincial Eldorado, which had been discovered only recently. There were some handsome, good-sized, fully equipped theatres in New York, Philadelphia, Boston, Charleston, and Baltimore. But they had none of them been built before the year 1790. There were famous actors of the American stage—Thomas Abthorpe Cooper, Elizabeth Powell, James Fennell, John Hodgkinson—but they had all of them emigrated from the Old World, and most of them had served, in their youth, some kind of apprenticeship in the English theatre. Native talent was still very scarce. Elizabeth Powell had been a colleague of Mrs. Siddons, James Fennell had come to New York in 1792, after having failed to reap success at Covent Garden. Thomas Abthorpe Cooper, the greatest of American tragedians, was the son of an Irish doctor and had first arrived in the United States in the year 1796.

In the gay Southern States the drama, though it had lacked organization, had never languished for support. But in the north it had been, through the greater part of the eighteenth century, ostracized by a Puritan community who still clung tenaciously to the superstition that play-acting was immoral and anti-Christian.

Intrepid adventurers from England battled painfully to keep the drama alive. During the 1730's an unidentified company of strolling players came to bustling, cosmopolitan New York and plied their trade in a loft over the Governor's house, using paper for scenery and crude hoops for chandeliers. In February of 1750 the loft was reopened, with a performance of *Richard III*, by the famous Murray-Thomas Kean troupe, who had previously confined their activities to the West Indies. A year later William Hallam, ex-manager of Goodman's Fields Theatre in London, landed in America with his wife, his brother Lewis, and his three children. He brought with him, besides, a company of twelve actors, a complete stage equipment, and a repertoire of twenty-five plays—including works by Shakespeare, Farquhar, Colley Cibber, Steele, Vanbrugh, and Fielding.

Hallam was the real pioneer of the American theatre. He had a pretty rough time of it himself, for it was not much fun travelling miles and miles of almost impassable roads in order to entertain a public who were hardly conscious of the drama. In the sparsely populated plantation villages of the south he had to be content with the crude wooden shacks which did duty for playhouses. And in the north he was continually opposed by popular prejudice and by the harsh bigoted laws enacted against stage shows. But he succeeded in paving the way for the Powell brothers, for Henry, and for Thomas Wignell—the great impresarios who came over from England shortly after the War of Independence was won, in order to put the drama in the New World securely on its feet.

In 1794 Thomas Wignell built a real theatre in Chestnut Street, Philadelphia. With its projecting wings, its colonnade of Corinthian columns, its Venetian windows and statues in niches, it was an imposing Georgian building. Its interior was "a perfect copy of the Theatre Royal at Bath." In the.same decade the playhouses of New York, Charleston, Boston, and Baltimore were opened. Contemporaneously the actors, who were to make their fortunes and reputations in the United States, arrived from England —Hodgkinson, Cooper, and the rest. A new and flourishing industry had been born.

By the beginning of the nineteenth century the drama in America was firmly established. The Puritan tradition still persisted—especially in Boston—but it was more distinguished by a crudity of taste and a susceptibility to sectarian assertiveness than by a moral objection to play acting.

Snelling Powell had started the Boston theatre. When he went bankrupt in 1795, his place was assumed by a native of the town—a certain Colonel Tyler. Colonel Tyler made himself a local hero by declaring:

> Let British lords their haughty birth declare,
> I boast of being born—in old North Square.

A little while later—during the war of 1812—a spectacular interlude, specially devised to celebrate the capture of a British frigate by an American vessel, was produced at the Boston theatre. It aroused immense enthusiasm. "In the course of the entertainment the following scenery, incidents, etc., occurred:

"Scene 1st. State Street. 'Huzza for the *Constitution*.'

"Scene 3rd. Cabin of the Ship. Song, 'A Cruising we will go.' Duet, 'Conquer or Die.' The *Guerrière* is seen through the cabin window under sail—orders are given to clear the ship for action, and scene changes to a view of the ocean. The *Guerrière* is seen under easy sail and the *Constitution* in chase. The action commences—the mizzenmast of the *Guerrière* goes by the board—the action continues and the *Guerrière* loses her foremast and mainmast—fires a gun to leeward and surrenders to the *Constitution*.

"Scene last. State Street. American officers, sailors, and marines enter with American colours, and the piece concluded with a song and chorus called the 'Good Ship Columbia.' "

But Boston was the most jingoistic town in the Union. Elsewhere the anti-British feeling, though latent, perhaps, was not nearly so patent. Certainly the famous actors of English origin who ruled the American stage occupied an exalted social position—of a kind which their confrères in the Old World might well have envied. John Hodgkinson, for example, was by no means a man of breeding or of unsullied character. He was a runaway weaver's apprentice from Manchester, with a considerable record of amorous intrigues to his discredit. But according to a contemporary account, "he lived in the most sumptuous style and a more tasty equipage than his did not roll through Broadway. One of his daughters married President Tyler's son."

George Frederick Cooke spent the last year of his life in America, from 1809–1810. He was virtually an outcast from his own country, for he had exhausted the patience of the English public, always exacting, by his consistent and flagrant errancy. But in the United States he became a kind of national hero. It did not matter that he was a dipsomaniac and supremely unreliable. Playgoers had not had the chance to see a star of the London theatre before, and they were swept off their feet by the incomparable power of his acting. They had never known anything like it. His arrival was the most sensational event in the short history of their drama.

Time after time he stumbled on to the stage so drunk that he could scarcely remember the lines of his part; and quite often he indulged in his habit of not appearing at all. But at his best he was still peerless and audiences continued to patronize him whenever he was announced to perform in the hope that for once they would discover him in full possession of his senses.

Socially, too, he was liked and respected; which seems strange because, even in his sober moments, he was perfectly equipped to upset Puritan and racial susceptibilities. Apart from his fatal weakness for alcohol, which was a mania, he was a punctilious, elaborately decorous man, and a stickler for etiquette. He was imbued with all the insular prejudices of the average Britisher. When he was asked to act before the United States President, he refused outright. He said that he had once had the honour of performing before the King of England and that he would not besmirch that record now by stooping to entertain the "King of the Yankee-Doodles."

But the hospitable American public forgave him even

that insult to their national pride. Nothing could really injure his popularity. His disreputable habits were accepted more in sorrow than in anger. And as for his insolence— admiring crowds used to gather in the streets to watch him walking gravely along, dressed in the fashion of an "English Gentleman." When he died, the doctors, the members of the Bar, and all the local celebrities of New York followed his funeral procession to St. Paul's Church.

The Americans paid Cooke greater honour than ever was or ever would have been accorded him in his own country. But it was natural that they did so. Though they were politically free, they still imported their culture from Europe: and though they were independently minded, they were still a trifle overawed by the famous personalities of the Old World. They called themselves, aptly enough, "a living Posterity." And Cooke was the first great star of the London stage upon whom they were able, from knowledge and not from hearsay, to pronounce a verdict.

Edmund Kean was the second. He arrived among them, in November of 1820, with a ready-made reputation both as an actor and as a man. For the past seven years they had read in their newspapers all about his successes and his failures, his histrionic merits and defects, his generosity and his arrogance, his courage and his weakness. Some of them were excitedly predisposed in his favour; others were violently prejudiced against him. But they were all of them as curious to see him as playgoers in our time would be. And they were called upon, not to discover his genius anew, but to decide for themselves whether or not the English had overestimated his faults and his virtues.

Or so they thought. But he showed them soon enough that he was not the kind of actor who could be judged dispassionately at first sight even by "a living Posterity." Like a whirlwind, he swept away their preconceived notions of him and startled them into surprised admiration. From his own point of view he had come to America for the purpose of reviving—in New York, Philadelphia, Boston,

and Baltimore—the historic drama of his London début.
And that is precisely what he succeeded in doing, not
because he was already known, but because he still had the
power to amaze. In America no less than in England he
triumphed because he was an original.

He wafted himself back to the glorious days of 1814,
and the details were the same. He became a centre of
controversy in the Press. There were his admirers who
hailed him as a perfect exponent of "nature." There were
his detractors who condemned him as a cheap trickster and
dwelt at length on his bad voice, his long pauses, his slow
delivery, his exaggerated contortions, and so on. And there
were the audiences who, without reference to the newspaper correspondents, disgruntled or enthusiastic, crowded
to see him whenever he appeared, applauded him to the
echo, and called him "the greatest creature they ever saw."
Once again he had the public at his mercy. He moved like
a conqueror from New York to Philadelphia, from Philadelphia to Boston, from Boston to Baltimore.

In sum, the Americans neither increased nor diminished
his fame as an actor. They merely confirmed it. And from
the historian's point of view, perhaps, their verdict was a
little disappointing.

But at least it gave Edmund the chance to prove how
well he thrived on success. At the outset of his London
career he had borne himself with becoming modesty. Now,
as then, all those who met him testified to the charm and
simplicity of his manner. They had read so much in recent
years of his jealousies, his tyrannical methods, his irresponsibility, and his love of ostentation that they had expected
him to be a veritable ogre of unpleasantness—vain and
vulgar and uncouth. They were relieved to find that he
was really quite endearing. "Kean . . . created no less
surprise in the green room than when before the audience,"
wrote W. B. Wood, director of the theatres at Philadelphia
and Baltimore. "All had heard . . . of his irregular habits,
his association with the Wolf Club and other persons most

likely to render his manner coarse and offensive. He appeared among us instead a mild, unassuming, and cheerful man, wholly free from every affectation of superiority or dictation. His suggestions as to business on the stage were always given with indulgence, and created even in the most careless of them a desire to excel. His presence in the green room was always a source of enjoyment. I speak of him and his deportment throughout a long series of performances. In private society, particularly in the company of ladies, he was distinguished for his modest and unassuming manner as well as conversation."

There were many such tributes to his kindliness and simplicity. They were all reminiscent of what Hobhouse and Kinnaird and others had said about him during his first Drury Lane season, when he had been supreme in his security and beyond reach of competition. But in one respect his reception in America was more satisfying to his vanity than his London triumphs had ever been. He was at last treated as a great man. The leaders of society who crowded his dressing-room and who invited him to their dinner parties and so on had none of the cynical brilliance and class-consciousness so typical of the English aristocracy. They were men of solid virtues—honest, straightforward, and slightly humourless. They were as much on the defensive as Edmund was himself: and when they found that he was unaffected, "accessible," and devoid of airs and graces, they were sincerely anxious "to pay homage to his renown." They encouraged him to express himself without the aid of foibles. And they decided that he had qualities of mind which his own countrymen had never suspected in him.

Doctor Francis, who became his particular friend, summarized the general feeling when he wrote: "He won my admiration from the moment of my first interview with him. Association and observation convinced me that he added to a mind of various culture the resources of original intellect . . . the drudgery of his early life had given a pliability to his muscular powers that rendered him the most dexterous harlequin, the most finished gentleman, the most insidious lover, the most terrific tragedian. Shakespeare was familiar to him: times, costumes, habits, and other manners of the age. He had dipped into phrenology, and was a physiognomist of rare discernment. His analysis of characters . . . often struck me with astonishment. His eye was the brightest and most penetrating any mortal could boast, an intellectual telegraph . . . I attribute his unrivalled success in so wide a range of characters somewhat to his extraordinary capacity for observation. He individualized every character he assumed. Wherever he was, he was all eye, all ear. Everything around him or wherever he moved fell within his cognizance. . . . He might have been called the peripatetic philosopher."

Of course Doctor Francis, as his literary style suggests, was a rather naïve character; and though a minor celebrity in New York, he would no doubt have cut an awkward, insignificant figure at Holland House. But he was not, on that account, unintelligent or lacking in perspicacity. He was well bred, knowledgeable, and fairly widely travelled. In his early youth he had spent a couple of years in Europe, and had been instructed by the great medical scientists of Paris, London, and Edinburgh. Now, at the age of thirty, he was a successful practitioner, a respected philanthropist, and a well-known patron of the arts.

Certainly he had nothing whatever in common with the tavern riff-raff and the extravagant hero-worshippers who had been members of the Wolves Club. And yet he understood how to win Edmund's confidence. His manner towards him was not condescending and superior, but simple, direct, and receptive. He put him at his ease and made him feel obliged neither to remain stupidly silent nor to become idiotically overbearing.

In the company of men like Doctor Francis, Edmund showed off his mind and his heart at their best. "I have given up all the frivolities of my nature . . ." he wrote to Charlotte Cox in March of 1821. And so he had. Now that he was appreciated by his fellow men he could afford to be himself and to do without his organized tavern orgies and his notoriety seeking stunts. In the words of Major Noah, editor of the New York *National Advocate*, he was a "modest, unassuming gentleman—securing the esteem of all who became acquainted with him—easy in manners —always accessible, refined and classic in conversation— and, when animated, the very life of the festive board."

The admiration of men of standing inevitably developed in Edmund his own inherent self-respect. He behaved with more balance and wisdom than he had ever done in his life before—or ever would again. He renounced displays. He saved his money. And he offended no one unnecessarily.

Of course, he got drunk occasionally. But his friends excused this weakness in him on the grounds that, while he could not resist conviviality, alcohol was poison to his enfeebled constitution. They realized that he was delicate. Both Doctor Francis and W. B. Wood testified to the fact that "whereas Cooke had been able to bear three bottles of port in an evening, Kean was upset by as many glasses."

Yet, in spite of his new-found prominence, Edmund was not completely at peace. He could only regard America as a temporary refuge from the tempest of his life in England. He knew that soon enough he would have to return to Mary and Charles who were his responsibility, to Charlotte whom he loved, and to Drury Lane which was still his real kingdom. Perhaps Drury Lane was the most important consideration of all. For he was continually haunted by the fear that some usurper would arise in his absence.

He wrote to Charlotte Cox: "I hear of all the adventures at Drury Lane Theatre. In your next tell me their successes, whether the humble spark of talent of the Kean still glows in the dramatic world; or if some unexpected meteor has dazzled the perception to the total extinction of the minor light. I am almost tempted to say, 'Come over and tell me all yourself,' but then you could never return and I must. Besides, you would by such an act lose your rank in society which you are so well qualified to adorn. . . . Your charming letters are a great source of delight, as of course my feelings are deeply interested in the success of Drury Lane and I receive all the events with double satisfaction when they come from you. . . ."

He could not remain indefinitely in America—not even if Charlotte consented to share his exile. And yet when the first days of summer came, and he looked back on six months of triumph almost unmarred, he decided to prolong his visit another year. He was still "making money and fame by bushels," and there seemed no indication that his popularity would ever dwindle. Of course, a few isolated newspapers continued to publish insulting criticisms of his acting, but he could afford to ignore these attacks now that he was again the public's idol.

After all, it would be silly to hurry away from a country where his reputation was secure in order to return to the weary struggle of maintaining his position at Drury Lane. Besides, from a material point of view, America was a gold mine. He was being paid, on an average, a thousand pounds a month—which was more than he had ever earned before. Since his personal expenses were negligible, he supposed that by the time he eventually left for England he would have saved a small fortune.

But Edmund's future, like his character, was always incalculable. His plans, though for once well laid, were destined to go sadly awry. On May 15th he concluded a three weeks' engagement at Baltimore and from there he returned for a second visit to Boston. (He had already played two successful seasons in New York and Philadelphia.)

His first Boston visit had been particularly glamorous. According to W. Clapp, chronicler of the Boston stage, the rush to see him had been so great that tickets had been sold by auction above their stated prices and the excess profits had been handed over to deserving charities. "We have before us," wrote Clapp, "a letter to the managers from Lewis Tapham, Esq., acknowledging a donation of

£90 for the Society for Employing the Poor, another from Annie G. Southack, in behalf of the Methodist Female Society."

Of course, in the usual way Edmund's acting had been "the all-engrossing topic of fashionable discussion," and he himself had become "the lion of the day." On his last night the audience had begged him to prolong his stay, and he had replied that "should any circumstances arise which he could avail himself of, to revisit . . . the literary emporium of the New World, he should certainly embrace it with heartfelt satisfaction."

Now he had come back in fulfilment of his promise and he anticipated a tremendous welcome. But unfortunately playgoing in Boston was unpopular during the summer months, and the public were inclined to stay away from the theatre, irrespective of the fame and attraction of the star performers. Edmund opened on May 23rd as Lear, and the house was poor and listless. On the 24th he played Jaffier in *Venice Preserved*, and the house was no better, in fact a little worse. Gone were the cheers and the giant box-office receipts of only three months ago.

Edmund was bitterly disappointed. He was incapable of regarding this unexpected failure impersonally. He did not pause to remember that he had been warned by the management against appearing so late in the season on the grounds that business was invariably bad immediately before the summer closure. What did statistics matter to him? It was his privilege to be an exception to every rule. Besides, he never allowed mere facts to interfere with his feelings. From his point of view, the apathy of the Boston playgoers meant only one thing—that his popularity had dwindled and dwindled more alarmingly than it had ever done in his own country. His American dream of security was shattered. He had hoped—he had believed—that the public in the New World were sincere and permanent admirers of his genius. But it was clear now that they had only come to see him from curiosity. And their curiosity was satisfied.

On Friday, May 25th, he was announced to act as Richard III. At 7 o'clock (the curtain was due to rise then) he walked on to the stage in his day clothes, peeped through the curtain, and saw that there were not more than twenty people in front. He had not expected a full house; but an audience of twenty for his Richard—that was too great an affront to be borne. "In the whole course of his professional career" he had never been so humiliated—not even on his worst nights at Drury Lane. He informed the manager, whose name was Dickson, that he would not play.

He refused to listen to Dickson's remonstrances. He gave him a parting drink and then, without further ado, left the theatre and returned to the house of some "literary friends," with whom he was spending the evening. Half an hour later Dickson sent Edmund a message in which he wrote that the boxes had filled up unexpectedly: that "Colonel Perkins and other distinguished citizens had come in"; and that the house, though not crammed, was of quite a respectable size. He begged him, therefore, "to keep faith with the public."

But Edmund thought he had been fully justified in walking out of the theatre, and in his present temper he was determined that he would never appear there again. Invariably he had the courage of his own impulses. And now, like a spoilt child in a huff, he was impervious to the most reasonable entreaties. Eventually Dickson was obliged to explain to the audience that "Mr. Kean had positively refused to play on account of lack of patronage."

What an admission! It was lucky for Edmund that he left Boston next morning, otherwise he might well have been lynched by an infuriated mob. One newspaper called him "an insolent pretender, an inflated, self-conceited, unprincipled vagabond," and urged that "he should be taken by the nose and dragged before the curtain to make his excuses for his conduct." There were many loyal Bostonians only too eager to follow this advice literally for the honour of good old Colonel Perkins and the other "distinguished citizens" who had been grossly insulted by the hoity-toity little *English* play-actor.

Although Edmund escaped physical injury, he was subjected to a fiercer and more savage verbal persecution than he had ever encountered before—even in his imagination. The newspapers—not only of Boston, but of New York, Philadelphia, and Baltimore—let fly at him with a violence of language which made the attacks that had from time to time been launched against him in his own country appear mild by comparison. No epithet was too abusive to describe his behaviour. His critics were convinced, illogically enough, that he had not a redeeming feature either as an actor or as a man. In the words of Major Noah who, among the gentlemen of the Press, was Edmund's one remaining supporter, "Had he robbed the banks; burnt all the books in the Literary Emporium; seduced all the women—and thrown all the printer's type into the river, he would not have been more roughly handled than for giving vent to vain feelings, and in a moment of peevish fretfulness, refusing to play on a certain night and disappointing a slender audience."

But although the Boston incident was trivial in itself, it *inevitably* brought about an explosion of popular resentment. For did it not prove to the American people that Edmund had made fools of them? They, who had refused to believe stories to his discredit, who had thought him modest, kindly, and intelligent, who had liked and respected him, now discovered that he was, after all, arrogant and tyrannical and jealous, that he was, in short, exactly as the English newspapers had painted him. He had come among them a "wolf" in gentleman's clothing; and the fact that they had failed to see through his disguise accentuated their natural anger beyond the bounds of reason. There is no one more detested than the fallen idol, for he has always deceived those who once idolized him. Edmund was in that unfortunate position. Consequently he was punished with far greater severity than his offence deserved.

He was himself overwhelmed by the onslaught, for he
still could not see that he had done wrong in leaving the
Boston audience to their fate. Perhaps he had been a little
hasty. But surely that was excusable in view of the acute
provocation he had suffered. He wrote to Dickson: "I much
regret the occasion of my abrupt departure, but you must
feel with me that my professional reputation must not be
trifled with. An indifferent house to such plays as *Venice
Preserved*, etc., *however well acted*, may be found in the
catalogues of histrionic events, but a total desertion of the
public to that character which has been the foundation of
my fame and fortune, requires a greater portion of philosophy
than I am master of. . . ."

That was the candid truth, which he later elaborated in
a long letter to the *National Advocate*. But, as always, the
truth did him far more harm than good. A grovelling lie,
a brazen lie, any sort of lie would have been well received.
In confessing the truth he convicted himself of those very
faults of which the public, in their own vanity, wished to
believe him innocent. And so he merely added fuel to the
fires which were already burning away the last vestiges of
his popularity.

The Democratic Press of Philadelphia summed up the
general feeling when it predicted that Edmund would
"never again be permitted to appear before an American
audience." And he himself soon realized that it would be
useless to accept further engagements. Instead of setting
matters aright by offering a suitable apology, he announced
that though unrepentant he had decided to leave the United
States immediately.

He spent his last day in New York (June 4th) with
Doctor Francis, who was one of his few friends who still
believed in him. Some months before he had become
obsessed with the idea of erecting in the churchyard of St.
Paul's a monument to George Frederick Cooke: and he
had asked Doctor Francis to help him carry out his project.
Together they had called on Bishop Hobart.

"Kean struck the attention of the Bishop," wrote Doctor Francis, "by his penetrating eyes and his refined address. 'You do not, gentlemen, wish the tablet inside St. Paul's?' asked the Bishop. 'No, Sir,' I replied. 'We desire to remove the remains of Mr. Cooke from the strangers' vault and erect a monument for them on some suitable spot in the burial ground of the Church. It will be a work of taste and durability.' 'You have my concurrence then,' added he, 'but I hardly knew how we could find a place inside the Church for Mr. Cooke!' "

Edmund's gesture, though generous and spontaneous, was essentially escapist. As an artist he was often compared with Cooke and as a man he had superficially much in common with him. No wonder he protested passionately that Cooke was the greatest actor who had ever lived. And no wonder he longed for his memory to be respected. Subconsciously he knew that in honouring Cooke he was paying honour to himself.

Now, on June 4th, when he was disgraced and virtually banished from the country where only a short while ago he had been so triumphant, the work of erecting his monument to Cooke was completed. In the afternoon he went with Doctor Francis "to pay his last devotion to it. . . . Tears fell from his eyes in abundance, and as the evening closed he walked Broadway, listened to the chimes of Trinity, returned again to the churchyard and sang sweeter than ever, 'Those Evening Bells' and 'Come o'er the Sea.' Doctor Francis, who played the part of a silent observer, "fancied that he saw a child of genius . . . deprived of the solace which the world cannot give, the sympathies of the heart."

Next morning Edmund began his journey homewards. He left behind him a monument to Cooke, but few fragrant memories of his own achievements. By one impulsive act of folly he had spoiled what might otherwise have been the happiest and most successful year of his life.

> Friends with new faces are common we're told,
> But a face without friendship is cheerless and cold;
> So Halpin let Face be the index of Heart,
> Let a smile be the welcome, a tear when we part.

Those were lines which Edmund himself had written some months before. But though the American people had welcomed him with a smile, they did not weep after he had gone. They laughed with malicious glee.

2

Robert William Elliston was cursed with the most mercurial temperament.

He had conceived the colossal idea of reproducing the Coronation of King George IV on the stage of Drury Lane. For weeks he had been working out his plans with that grand and feverish thoroughness of which he was so notable a master. He had determined that every detail of the ceremony should be perfectly re-enacted: and in pursuit of this object he had enlisted the co-operation of high Court officials. He had obtained facilities for his designers to inspect the royal robes in advance. He had secured for himself tickets of admission both to Westminster Abbey and the Hall.

But on the actual day of the Coronation—which was the 19th of July—Elliston's enthusiasm suddenly waned. He did not go to Westminster Abbey, he did not go to the Hall, he did not catch a glimpse even of the procession. Instead, he went off, for some unaccountable reason, to Walworth, where he got suitably drunk. Next morning he arrived at Drury Lane in a vague and apathetic mood. He vouchsafed very little information to his stage-manager, for he always loved to be mysterious. He contented himself with saying that the project of reproducing the Coronation would have to be abandoned for the simple reason that he had seen nothing of it. He had been to Walworth. And that was that. Since he had not another idea in his head, he lapsed into a tantalizing silence.

But a few hours later his spirits were completely revived and he was giving out orders right and left. At his bidding, "huge notices" were plastered all over the town announcing that Edmund Kean had landed in England, that he would arrive in the capital at noon on Monday, July 23rd, and that he would positively reappear that night in the character of Richard III.

On Monday Elliston, accompanied by a deputation from the theatre, went to meet Edmund a few miles outside London. Elliston organized a triumphal procession to Drury Lane which, in its essentials, was strikingly similar to those entries into New York which are now frequently arranged for film stars. "Six outriders, in a medley of costumes of all nations of the earth that do not go absolutely tattooed, constituted the vanguard; then came Elliston himself in solitary grandeur in his own carriage drawn by four greys. The hero of the triumph next—Kean himself, likewise in his carriage, supported by Russell and Hughes in cocked hats, drawn by four blacks. John Cooper, in the simple majesty of his undecorated form, followed drawn also by four . . . piebald. A troop of horsemen formed the flank, composed of bruisers, jockeys, tavern-keepers, and other friends of the drama: and the whole was brought up by the heterogeneous rabble which the progressive affair had from pillar to post enlisted."

This charade was followed by an official reception at Drury Lane and a formal dinner party presided over by the Great Lessee and attended by the entire *corps dramatique*. Elliston, of course, had his tongue in his cheek, but, as a master showman, he knew how well Edmund and the public would respond to these tinsel celebrations. And so he carried them through with elaborate mock solemnity.

That evening Edmund played Richard III before a packed audience who greeted his performance with such cheering as "had never been heard before." The house was again crowded for his Shylock on the 25th of July, and again on the 26th of July for his Othello. Elliston was announcing his name in huge red letters. London was giving him a wonderful welcome home. It seemed as if he had recaptured the power to carry Drury Lane on his own shoulders.

But not for long. On the 27th of July Elliston was obliged to close his theatre and to print, on his play-bills, a doctor's certificate instead of a programme. It read ominously as follows:

> Mr. Kean is very unwell this morning, and the medicine which I think needful for his recovery will not have completed my intent before late in the evening of tomorrow. I, therefore, think it most prudent to put off his acting until Monday; indeed, he might not be capable tomorrow and if called upon might be laid up for many days afterwards.
>
> (*Signed*) ANT. CARLISLE.

He did reappear on Monday, but the spell was broken. He had been unable to maintain it. His illness, though quickly cured, put an end to the idea that he had come back from America rejuvenated. It proved that he had not changed, that he was still the same Kean who had left England just under a year ago. Consequently the public began to take him for granted again. Their rush to see him on his return had been a mere flourish of excitement. After playing another week at Drury Lane, where the atmosphere was no longer particularly festive, Edmund deserted London to spend the rest of the summer in the provinces.

Elliston was not worried by Edmund's departure. His mind was now fully occupied with plans for presenting the Coronation. For he had, in his enthusiasm, revived that colossal idea. Indeed, he could not for the life of him imagine why he had been tempted to drop it. What did it matter that he had inadvertently missed seeing the actual ceremony? The newspaper descriptions were really very detailed. With a copy of the *Morning Herald* in his hand, he began rehearsals.

The splendid spectacle was eventually produced in August. It was a *succès fou*. Nothing like it had ever been seen before. Elliston himself, at the head of a cast of hundreds, impersonated George IV and with such feeling for his part that he soon believed that he really was the King. His manner on and off the stage became superbly regal. When Queen Caroline died, he engineered a rumour that he had killed her by putting poison in her coffee!

Edmund had none of Elliston's optimism and none of Elliston's magnificent ability to ignore setbacks. In spite of his passionate longing for the limelight, he had lost the will to fight. He could not, like his manager, go boldly after success. He was no bobber-up. He expected, as if by right, success to come to him and was immoderately peevish when it did not.

He returned to London in November of 1821 to begin another unfruitful year at Drury Lane. None of the new parts which he played caused the faintest stir; and even in his famous characters he was no longer much of a draw. The public's attitude towards him grew more apathetic than ever.

From his point of view the season was very humiliating. But from Elliston's it was financially disastrous. Spectacles like the Coronation, however splendid and however successful, were not sufficient by themselves to make Drury Lane a paying proposition. The theatre's prosperity depended to a large extent on the patronage given to tragedy. And in tragedy Edmund's was still the only name which counted for anything.

But while Elliston planned, in his vast, uncompromising way, to set matters aright, Edmund sank into a mood of bitter despondency. Far from making an effort to win back his popularity, he was suspicious of all suggestions which would entail a change in his position—especially when they came from his manager. He had no lust for battle. His one idea was to escape from the dreariness of failure. And so he fled to the brandy bottle, to his sycophantic friends, and to Charlotte.

In his home there was no peace at all now, for Mary had discovered that he was being unfaithful to her. She had come across one of Charlotte's letters and there had been a "terrible explosion." She had promptly cut off all relations with the Coxes and had made Edmund swear that he would never see his mistress again.

He did not keep his word, of course. But he had to make an elaborate pretence of doing so, if only to avoid Mary's hysterical recriminations which nearly sent him crazy. When he was with his family he felt like a prisoner, and he regarded his wife, unreasonably, as a gaoler who was trying to bar his way to happiness. She was continually suspicious, for she knew well enough that he was not to be trusted.

"The eyes of Argus may be eluded," he wrote to Charlotte from Hastings in August of 1821, "but those of a jealous wife impossible. Even now I am on tenter-hooks. I expect the door forced open 'and what are you writing?' the exclamation, or Susan to see if everything is comfortable, or Charles with a handful of endearments for his dear papa, all tending to the same thing, what is he about?"

And a little later he wrote from Carlisle: " . . . She left me yesterday for London; if that had not been the case I could not have written to you now. I am watched more closely than Bonaparte, independent of which I have never been more than three days in a place. . . ."

There were many such outbursts of resentment against his wife which, vulgarly, he confided to his mistress. Yet he knew in his heart that he would never desert his family. He was loyal to them in his own fashion. Though he had no bond of true sympathy with Charles, he was a proud and pitifully conscientious father. Charles was being educated as a gentleman, just as Edmund had always intended. He was a preparatory schoolboy now and would soon be going to Eton. Edmund was determined that his son should never become an actor. He flew into a passion once when Mary suggested, in her fond, motherly way, that dear Charles had leanings towards the stage and was already very gifted.

He was unfaithful to his wife. But he gave her all the worldly comforts that she demanded: and much as she bored and irritated him, he did not forget that she was his responsibility. He never hurt her maliciously. In one of his most abandoned letters to Charlotte, he wrote, "I will dare the worst . . . with the exception of not making them miserable whom I am bound to protect."

But while he found no pleasure in Mary's society, his mistress had the power to comfort him even in his blackest moments of despair. He wrote to her from Bath: " . . . In this infernal city my endeavours are totally failing. . . . My mind wants my own dear darling to condole with. My fevered head wants rest in the bosom of my Charlotte."

He was torn between his duty and his desire. He would not, for his family's sake, run away with his mistress. But at the same time it was impossible for him to give her up. And so he compromised perilously. He carried on his intrigue in a furtive, secretive way which stripped it of any romantic semblance and made it appear far more sordid and dishonourable than it actually was.

His precautions were elaborate. Just before his return to London from Sussex in November of 1821 he wrote to Charlotte: " . . . On no account come near the park. I shall cross over Waterloo Bridge on Tuesday between 1 and 2 oclock. I will see you on Wednesday at 12 in the saloon of the theatre. I have declared you are in the West Indies. If you are seen I am ruined."

Often when he was on tour and his wife was presumably in Clarges Street, he arranged his clandestine meetings with Charlotte outside London. But even so he was oppressed by the urgent need for discretion. There was always the possibility that Mary might follow him or turn up un-expectedly. He never felt safe—wherever he was. In town or in the provinces he was like a fugitive from justice: and his friends acted as his accomplices. For Hughes, Phillips,

"Aunt" Tid, Aunt Price, and the rest were all in league to protect the mistress and to make a fool of the wife.

Of course, there was the Alderman to be considered as well. But he was proving either very complaisant or extraordinarily blind. Far from sharing Mary's suspicions, which she had voiced so openly, he continued to allow Edmund every facility to consort with his wife. It did not seem to matter to the Alderman that, through Mary's intervention, he was no longer welcome at Clarges Street. He went on inviting Edmund to his own home—which was now in Wellington Street—as if there had been no change at all in their good relationship. Indeed, Edmund had the run of the Coxes' house where, unknown to Mary, he often used to spend the night. Sometimes he arrived unexpectedly and banged on the door with a vehemence which showed that he was considerably the worse for liquor. He enjoyed the kind of privileges which belong only to a great family friend!

The Alderman never tried to keep Charlotte away from her lover. On the contrary, when he was unable to take her to Drury Lane himself, he sent her there in the company of his niece, whose name was Anne Wickstead. On one occasion they all four of them drove off to Croydon together in the middle of the night. Next morning the Alderman returned to London "to settle some business," cheerfully leaving his wife in Edmund's tender charge. There were other excursions of a similar kind. And usually Edmund was permitted to pay for them.

In the circumstances Edmund might well have suspected the Alderman of willingness to be a cuckold. But he never did. He felt convinced that Cox was blissfully ignorant of what was going on under his very eyes. And he was as studious in his efforts to hoodwink him as he was to deceive his own wife. In fact, he was always fearful that the Alderman would discover his perfidy: and, in spite of his elaborate subterfuges, he had one or two uncomfortable moments.

In August of 1822, when he was touring the provinces

without much success, he had a sudden yearning for Charlotte's society. He begged her to meet him in Birmingham. "Meet me as soon as possible . . ." he wrote, "that is as soon as safety will permit."

She came to Birmingham at once. She assured Edmund that, though her husband was in London, she had fobbed him off with the plausible story that she was going to visit her mother in Brighton.

But apparently her husband was not so easily gulled as she had imagined. For once the Alderman had doubted her word! To confirm his suspicions he had sent his son Robert —a son by a former marriage—in hot pursuit. Robert discovered the happy lovers *in flagrante delictu*, and Charlotte returned with him to London.

Edmund was left behind in a blue funk. He thought that the worst must surely happen now. Charlotte would be turned out of her home and he would become responsible for looking after her. He dreaded the Alderman's vengeance even more than Mary's. Mary, he knew, would never wish to divorce him, however much she might rail and threaten. She was too fond of her own position to contemplate such a drastic move. But there was no telling what action the Alderman might take. He might create a public scandal by commencing legal proceedings against him. That would mean disgrace and probably the finish of his career and ruin for himself and his family.

In desperation he turned to "Aunt" Tid, who had made her last bow to a London audience on May 21st when Edmund had acted for her benefit. Now she lived in comfortable retirement on the money which she had saved during her forty years as a small-part actress, and on a generous allowance from her grateful nephew. She would come to his assistance as she had always done in the past. She would give his mistress a home while he thought out some way of putting matters right.

L.B. (that was his pet name for Charlotte. It stood for Little Breeches)—L.B. will explain the perplexities we are in (he

wrote to "Aunt" Tid) and I have so much confidence in you
that I am sure you will render us the utmost assistance. I place
her for a time under your protection. Her impudence is great
but her affection is unbounded. To your charge I trust her till
affairs are accommodated. She has plenty of money and I will
rather add to your comforts than diminish them.

Your affectionate friend and nephew,

EDMUND KEAN.

But in the end "Aunt" Tid's help was not needed. There
had been no cause for alarm. The Alderman neither showed
Charlotte the door nor even scolded her. "He treated her
with all his accustomed kindness and never upbraided her
in the slightest respect."

Had Robert Cox held his tongue? Or had the Alderman,
in his liberality, decided to ignore the incident? Edmund
did not care. He did not pause to consider how strange it
was that he had escaped disaster so easily. He merely
heaved a sigh of relief. The danger was passed.

In a sense he was glad of the Alderman's existence, for
it gave him the chance to impress upon Charlotte the
absolute necessity for secrecy. She did not really see things
his way. She was restless. She disliked the furtiveness of
their affair. She was no longer satisfied with passionate love
letters, with clandestine meetings, with money and presents
galore. She was weary of being a "hole and corner" mistress.
She wanted to be openly acknowledged. She wanted the
world to recognize her power. And, of course, in her tough
determination to get her own way, she cared little for
Edmund's career and nothing at all for his wife and family.

Edmund found it difficult to resist Charlotte's demands
and at the same time to protest that he was "all in all her's
forever." But her husband provided him with his best
defence against her accusations of timidity. He was the
"great cause" why Edmund could not do as his mistress
willed. It was love before honour, wealth and fame: but
not before the Alderman.

"Let but the great cause be removed," he wrote shortly

after the Birmingham scare, "and I shall laugh at all agencies though they may pursue in chaise and four; in other words let him but go abroad and I will dare the worst. . . ." And a little while later, " . . . Could the great cause be removed . . . I would hold my little darling to my heart and sleep in spite of thunder."

But Charlotte had far less respect for the "great cause" than Edmund had. She was becoming very indiscreet.

In January of 1823 a party was made up to spend a week at Salisbury. "Aunt" Tid and Anne Wickstead went by post-chaise. Mr. and Mrs. Cox travelled with Edmund in his coach. Benjamin Drury was also of the party. The week passed happily enough. But on the last night Charlotte behaved so obviously that the Alderman, out of self-respect, was no longer able to ignore the truth. He made a scene. He threatened a duel. And there was some talk of "pistols being produced."

Next morning Edmund paid all the expenses of the party and in addition lent Cox £10 for his fare back to London. But apparently the quarrel had not been patched up. At any rate Edmund felt certain that he had incurred the Alderman's everlasting displeasure: and, in his frightened anxiety to undo the damage, he sent him this foolish letter:

> My dear Cox,
>   I have been seriously considering the mass of nonsense uttered by us two last night at Salisbury. I must own likewise they have given me the greatest uneasiness. . . . I must be the worst of villains, if I could take the man by the hand, while meditating towards him an act of injustice. You do not know me, Cox: mine are follies, not vices. It has been my text to do all the good I could in the world, and when I am called to a superior bourne, my memory may be blamed, but not despised. . . .

At the same time he wrote to Charlotte:

> Dear Little Imprudent. . .
>   Your incaution has been very near bringing our acquaintance to the most lamentable crisis. Of course, he will

show you the letter I have written him; appear to countenance it, and let him think we are never to meet again and in doing so he has lost a friend.

Cox took no immediate action; and though Edmund steered clear of him from now on, he believed that once again he had avoided the Alderman's vengeance and was free to carry on his intrigue with Charlotte unsuspected.

Poor Edmund! In his flurried desire to escape from a temporary embarrassment he had forged the weapons which would later be used for his own destruction.

He might have learned much from the affair at Salisbury. He might have realized then that the Alderman was capable of turning nasty; and that Charlotte was either foolishly rash or dangerously determined to jockey him into a false position. He might have perceived that the time had come to call a halt.

But he could not look into the future. He only knew that Charlotte was still essential to his happiness. The world was using him badly at the moment: and he thought that without his mistress to comfort him he would not want to live.

3

At the beginning of the 1822–23 season Elliston announced his "new deal." He had at last found time to rebuild the interior of his theatre at a cost of £10,000. He had tempted from Covent Garden, with offers of largely increased salaries, several of the most popular comedians and singers of the day. And from Covent Garden, too, he had lured away the celebrated tragedian, Charles Mayne Young, who was Kemble's successor.

Everything was set for a particularly successful season. But it started without Edmund Kean. He was still fulfilling provincial engagements in Scotland. And when he learned that in future he would have to share the honours at Drury Lane with a rival, he flew at once into a tantrum.

From Dundee he wrote to Elliston on October 13th:
" . . . I find Mr. Young . . . is engaged for thirty
nights and my services are wanted to act with him—now
this I call exceedingly impudent . . . the throne is mine.
I will maintain it—even at the expense of expatriation—
go where I will I shall always bear it with me—and even
if I sailed to another quarter of the globe, no man in this
profession can rob me of the character of the first English
actor. . . ."

But there was fear in Edmund's heart as well as indignation. Though Charles Mayne Young was by no means a
brilliant performer, he was sound, reliable, and possessed
of many natural attributes which appealed to the public—
dignity, good looks, and a strong, melodious voice. He had,
besides, one rare advantage which inevitably made Edmund
feel inferior to him. He was, by birth and upbringing, a
gentleman. His father had been a London doctor with a
fashionable practice. He himself had spent his childhood
days hobnobbing with the Royal Family at the Court of
Denmark, and he had been educated at Eton.

Five years ago Edmund had not shrunk from joining
battle with Booth, and five years ago, perhaps, he would
have felt confident of vanquishing Young. But his health
had deteriorated badly since then. He had no longer much
reserve of strength. His energy did not always respond to
his will. Sometimes his voice let him down unexpectedly:
and sometimes he was unable, from sheer physical weakness,
to rise to the importance of an occasion. He dreaded comparison with Young, for the very reason that he could not
be certain of his power to exert himself to the full.

At the age of thirty-three Edmund was already so tired
in spirit that half of him yearned to withdraw from public
life. He planned to make the Isle of Bute, off the west
coast of Scotland, his fortress of retirement. It was many
miles from Drury Lane But it was within easy distance of
Glasgow and Greenock, and he had often stolen away there
for a few days' rest in between his theatrical engagements.

Rothesay, the capital of Bute, was a busy industrial town where they spun cotton, built ships, and launched schooners, and where a trumpet was blown every weekday morning at 5.30 a.m to arouse the working population from their slumbers. But Rothesay could quickly be left behind even on foot, and the rest of the island seemed almost deserted except for the farms scattered here and there about the rising landscape. There were lochs of clear water, and woods on the high ground, and green hills surmounting the trees. But the country, though richly beautiful and fertile in fact, had a wild, lonely, and uncharted appearance.

No wonder it appealed to Edmund, whose soul longed to soar far away from trouble and to find repose. He had been shown the secrets of the island by Duncan M'Corkindale, landlord of the Bute Arms at Rothesay. And a little while ago he had bought twenty-four acres of land overlooking "Sweet Loch Fad." Now a house was being built, to his order, on the site: and, idealistically, he looked forward to the day when he would settle down in it for good with his wife and family.

He was, of course, as always, alone in his enthusiasm. Mary hated the very idea of living in Bute: and she was convinced that Edmund did not really like it. With her suburban attachment to society, she could not understand what crazy impulse had prompted him to purchase a property which was completely cut off from the world— unless it had been a desire to get rid of her, while he pursued his intrigue with his mistress. She expressed her view— years later—in a letter to Barry Cornwall:

" . . . We took 22 acres of land from Lord Bute's factor—Lord Bute's property—as sterile—as damp—as forlorn—as desolate—as you can imagine—built and furnished a house in a spot where there was no . . . creature within three miles of the place. We paid pounds for what was not worth shillings . . . it was a madness done by the desire of Mrs. Cox to hide me in and ended in utter ruin to us all. . . ."

But Mary was always a dangerously prejudiced historian:
and in this case her word is refutable by direct evidence.
The property at Bute still remains much as Edmund left
it and during the past hundred years it has never lacked a
tenant. Anyone who cares to make the pilgrimage may judge
its beauty for himself and can understand why Edmund
called it, exuberantly, "his Island Paradise." His love for
it had nothing whatever to do with Charlotte Cox, as will
be made abundantly clear hereafter.

Of course, he never satisfied his inner craving for retirement. That was impossible. His faults of temperament
were weighed so heavily against him that a peaceful ending
to his life had already become unimaginable. But he would
have given a great deal to have avoided the battle with
Young which threatened him at the moment. And from
Rothesay, where he was staying on October 23rd (the
building of his house was not yet complete), he addressed
this incoherent, pathetically moving appeal to Elliston:

" . . . You must forgive my being jealous of my hard-
earned laurels. I know how Brittle is the ground I stand
upon—& how transient is public favour—Mr. Young has
many advantages that I have not—a commanding figure,
sonorous voice—& above all Lordly connection . . . I am
therefore coming to meet an opposition, made up of my
own enemies (which like locusts can almost darken the sun)
Mr. Young's *friends*—& his very great abilities—with
nothing but humble genius to support me, a mere ephemera
—always at the command of caprice—& the same breath
that nourishes the flame this day—to-morrow puts it out.
Aut Caesar, Aut Nullus, is my text. If I become secondary
in any point of view, I shrink into insignificance. . . .
I have taken a house in Scotland for the purpose of retirement with my family at the termination of my engagement
& all I ask of you—is to let me retire with my reputation
undiminished, that I may enjoy the retrospection, when I
am the world forgetting, & by the world forgot—as the
Covent Garden Hero—comes upon my ground the Chal-

lenger—I have doubtless my choice of weapons, he *must* play Iago!—before I act Jaffier I am told he is extraordinarily great in Pierre—if so—I am beaten—this must not be—I cannot bear it—I would rather go in chains to Botany Bay—I am not ashamed to say—I am afraid of the contest, will you take the *thousand pounds* & dismiss me? . . ."

But Ellison acted with his usual determination and would not allow his star tragedian to escape. He granted him only one concession—the choice of weapons. On November 27th Edmund Kean was billed as Othello to the Iago of Charles Mayne Young.

It was part of the paradox of Edmund's character that however greatly he was oppressed by fears of an event, he always faced up to it boldly in the end. Now a large, excited audience had come to see him fight the second biggest battle of his career, and inevitably he responded to their expectancy. He did not—to be sure—treat Young as murderously as he had treated Booth. But he more than held his own. He gave a very fine performance which was greeted with louder applause than he had heard for a long while. And when it was over the audience were satisfied that, while Young was certainly a good actor, Edmund was still supreme.

From Ellison's point of view the result could not have been better: for though Edmund had triumphed, his victory had not been so conclusive as to put an end to the pretensions of his opponent or to deaden the general clamour for further contests between himself and Young. This meant that Elliston had merely to announce the names of his rival tragedians on the same bill in order to be certain of record box-office returns. He made them play· together continually, not only in *Othello* but in other plays where there were two parts of equal importance—in *Venice Preserved* and in *Cymbeline*. The crowds returned to Drury Lane. Popular excitement over Edmund was again at fever pitch. And Young, too, became a star attraction. Nowadays it is hard to understand the lust which the public had a century ago for histrionic fisticuffs.

At the end of the season Elliston was delighted. He had made a handsome profit which he needed badly. For, during the last few years, he had, in his grand, irresponsible way, incurred heavy liabilities. But Young was far from satisfied. In spite of the financial reward, he had not enjoyed himself in the Drury Lane company. He complained, rather in the same fashion as Booth before him, that he had been fouled by Kean. He alleged that Kean had made use of all the vulgar tricks to which selfish actors resort, that he had, for example, invariably stood a few paces back stage of his fellow players. Young had only signed a year's contract with Drury Lane: and now that his engagement was over, he returned to Covent Garden, where his salary was less but where his position was secure and where the atmosphere behind the footlights was, he thought, more gentlemanly.

Elliston, however, was not content to return to the old, moribund policy of "Kean unaided." He had found the path to prosperity and he had no intention of abandoning it. So, to fill Young's place, he promptly secured the services of another celebrated tragedian, who, at Covent Garden, had steadily been adding to the stock of his reputation during the past few years and was now ranked by the leading critics as second only to Edmund Kean. The new Drury Lane season opened in due course with the announcement that William Charles Macready had been specially engaged to act leads in tragedy. On November 18th, Macready played the name part in *Caius Gracchus*, a new play by Sheridan Knowles.

But Edmund had flown away again. In spite of his successful encounter with Young, he was still as nervous as ever of meeting challengers on his own ground. This time he produced an excuse for avoiding Macready which even Elliston, with all his ingenuity, could not argue against. He was dangerously ill—according to medical report. After spending the summer vacation in the provinces, he had retreated to the Island of Bute under cover of a doctor's certificate.

On November 18th he wrote from Bute to his secretary, Phillips, who was looking after his affairs faithfully in London and keeping him minutely informed of all the latest developments at Drury Lane: "I thank you for your prompt attention. I must differ with you, about my coming to London. Fabius Maximus conquered not by fighting a powerful enemy, but by avoiding him. He weakened his resources, and saved the city of Rome.

"I shall not move from this heavenly spot, till Caius Gracchus meets his fate . . . the Christmas pantomime over—and a general stagnation of public excitement: and *then*—like a hawk I'll pounce upon my prey. Write and send bills, or those penny *critiques*, every day!!!"

He waited in vain for the downfall of his new rival. But at the beginning of December, Macready took a three months' leave of absence to tour the provinces and simultaneously Edmund reappeared at Drury Lane. The public gave him a wonderful reception, just as he had anticipated. They were delighted to see him again. They crowded to his Richard, his Overreach, his Othello, and applauded him with all their old fervour.

He had, for the time being, staved off the Macready peril. He had "saved the city of Rome." But he felt far from secure. He was, in fact, planning a second escape to America, for he knew that he would not be given more than three months in peaceful possession of Drury Lane and that sooner or later Elliston would insist on coupling him with Macready. He could no longer bear the strain of battle.

Besides, he had another reason for wishing to leave England. Charlotte was becoming very troublesome. For years past she had kept him on the run—teasing him, taunting him, accusing him of infidelities, and so on and so forth. Invariably her wiles had served her well, and she had had her way in most things. But now she was insisting on a sacrifice which, in spite of his protests to the contrary, he knew that he could never make. She wanted him to leave his family and to run away with her. A few days after his return to London she presented him with some kind of ultimatum.

On December 9th he wrote to her: "What can I say? I love you better than all the world—all beyond. I see no remedy for our disease but patience, and that must be exerted to the utmost. On my return from America all shall be as you wish, till then it is impossible. You must think for a man struggling to obtain competence for his family, which the circumstances of our connection must utterly destroy. I feel for you most sincerely, on my soul, my heart is breaking, but any rash steps would destroy our hopes forever. I long to see you but will not come to your house. If you enter the front door Theatre Royal Drury Lane, I will meet you thro' the other. . . ."

But Charlotte was inconsolable. She was weary of Edmund's hesitancy and secretiveness. In desperation she embarked on an affair with another man, who could be more dashing than Edmund if only because he spent most of his time in her own house. His name was Whatmore and he was by profession the Alderman's secretary.

Edmund did not know for certain that Charlotte had made division of her favours. But he suspected as much from her altered manner. She was cold, she was bored, she was casual. Obviously her feelings towards him had changed. He upbraided her and yet tried to blind himself to the truth. From Portsmouth, where he had gone to fulfil a brief engagement in January, he sent her this pathetic letter:

"My dear love, I wrote angrily to you yesterday, forgive me. *I was disappointed at not receiving a letter from you and wrote in irritation.* Indeed love I would not doubt you for worlds; for I live but thinking of you, and if I lose you I am sure my heart will break."

But events moved inexorably towards their climax. In March the Alderman suddenly awoke to the knowledge of his wife's infidelity. He walked out of his home determined that he would "never again live under the roof of that woman whose perfidy he had detected."

A few days later Charlotte left the house with Anne Wickstead to seek quarters of her own. The Alderman returned: and it was then that he discovered all Edmund's love letters "carefully, but most unaccountably left packed up." He at once consulted his solicitor and began proceedings to sue his false friend for criminal conversation with his wife.

The trial would not come on for many months yet, for English justice moved slowly. But rumours of its approach were printed in the Press, and all London was talking about "The Actor and the Citizen." It would certainly be a *cause célèbre*.

At the beginning of April, Cox created a scene outside an hotel where Edmund was presiding at a public dinner. Perhaps he wanted to collect evidence which might be necessary to show that he really had valued his wife's affections. At any rate he gave the passers-by a rare treat. He brandished a pistol and threatened to shoot the man who had wronged him. He was at length dragged away from the front entrance by the hotel staff.

Edmund remained comparatively calm. Now that the blow, of which for years he had lived in dread, had actually fallen, he did not think its effects would be very damaging. After all, Charlotte was obviously a bitch. In exasperation he had often called her so in the days when he had loved her. Now he hated her and called her a bitch in good earnest, and a whore as well. As for the Alderman—he was a liar and a cheat. No jury on earth, composed of decent men, would exalt the Coxes at his expense. On the contrary! Sometimes, of course, he was oppressed by lingering doubts and fears, but the brandy bottle soon disposed of *them*.

Meanwhile he was more concerned with theatre politics than he was with the Alderman's threats. For when Macready returned to Drury Lane in the middle of April he immediately scurried off into the provinces.

Elliston tried every means to lure him back again. On the 10th of May he actually billed his name as Richard III, but at the last moment Edmund furnished a doctor's certificate which stated that he had been taken seriously ill at Derby and was unable to move. The Press received the news sceptically; and so, too, did Elliston who was now determined to track down his runaway star. An incredible chase followed, with Elliston as the hunter and Kean as the quarry. Edmund began by attempting to stage a vanishing act. He left strict instructions at his home that all inquiries about him were to be answered with the laconic message that he was out of town and had gone to an unknown destination. But Elliston somehow managed to find out that Edmund was in fact staying at the Regent Hotel in Brighton. He at once despatched a trusted emissary in pursuit of him.

When the emissary, whose name was Dunn, arrived at the Regent Hotel, he heard "confused sounds of merriment issuing from an adjoining room" which convinced him of Kean's presence there. Although the landlord of the Regent had been warned to preserve his distinguished guest's incognito, Dunn persuaded him, by a ruse, to convey a note to Mr. Kean. The note contained Elliston's compliments and a gentle inquiry after the invalid's health!

Edmund was furious. "I hate a trickster," he wrote to Elliston. "You have employed unworthy means to disturb me in my solitude. That was neither manly nor open. It was necessary I should have repose—my health has suffered materially. Elliston, I must not be spoken to; you know what I am equal to when in vigour; but remember also, *ad nullum consurgit opus cum corpore languet!*

"You have pursued me by a trick, and I should deign you no reply; but I am here, Sir, under the direction of Sir Anthony Carlisle, and will not stir from this place until I have gone through all the routine of medicine and sea-bathing, prescribed for me by that great man. The medical gentlemen of Brighton declare also I need repose—on that

question there is no dissentient voice: 'Kean must have
repose.' If I am pursued either by trick or openly, I shall
retire to La Belle France for some weeks. . . .

"I leave you in no distress. You have Macready! Macready, Elliston!—why should you be anxious about poor
Kean? Yet, a breath—a breath, I say, of Kean shall confound
a generation of Youngs and Macreadys."

Before Elliston had had an opportunity to answer this
effusion, Edmund had fulfilled his threat of retiring to La
Belle France. Taking Mary with him, he crossed over from
Newhaven to Dieppe on the 21st of May. From there he
wrote to Jack Hughes:

" . . . The closer they pursue, the further I shall recede
—by the time you receive this Mrs. Kean and myself are
on our way to Paris—where I shall remain, till I see the
last night advertised of Drury Lane Theatre, the day after
you will see me in London. Settle all bills for me; I will
discharge them on the instant I return—I shall then quit
England for *ever*—but I carry with me the reputation of
the first English actor, which if I had allowed them to have
their way, I could not have done, if I had acted—I know
hundreds were prepared for hostility, and in the bad parts
they were forcing me to play with Macready he must have
skimmed the cream of my professional dish.—he may now
take the whole.—& the public may talk and be damned
I shall soon be out of hearing. . . . I was so ill, that if I
had attempted to act I am convinced I shou'd have fallen
on the stage.—Dunn was sent to Brighton & I immediately
got into the Packet & sailed—I shall not act now, till
August—my *Dublin engagement* & then—*Vale Patria*."

Edmund scarcely knew what he was writing. He was
obviously being driven almost insane by fear and worry
and wounded vanity. And yet it is strange that he sought
peace in company of the person who was least able to
understand him and most likely to irritate him.

Seventeen years of marriage had taught Mary no tact
as far as her husband was concerned; and at the moment,

of course, she was in one of her most antipathetic moods. She had not left Edmund on account of his proven infidelity with Charlotte, but she was none the less apprehensive of the pending action between him and the Alderman. She realized that if he were to come off badly at the trial, she also would be made to suffer. No doubt the world would sympathize with her. But his disgrace would inevitably mean the end of her own social aspirations.

In Paris the Keans were lavishly entertained by Talma, the great French tragedian. Mary treated him with that same wilting reverence with which she had once captured Edmund's heart. "The last time Talma came to the hotel to us," she told Barry Cornwall, "seeing me so delighted with his acting promised to act all his great characters for me but Mr. Kean hurried off and I lost a great treat."

Was she really surprised that Edmund "hurried off"? He, who had fled from England, because he had been unable to bear the public's applause for Macready, was hardly likely to relish his own wife's adulation of a rival actor!

In these times of stress, Edmund was cutting a pretty unadmirable figure. But when he reached Boulogne on his way home from Paris, he performed one of those kindly, impulsive actions which made his character lovable in spite of its many tragic blemishes.

There was a veteran actor in Boulogne called Penley, who earned a beggarly income at the head of a bedraggled company of English strolling players. Penley asked Edmund for his assistance. Would he be good enough to play one of his famous characters in the Boulogne Theatre?

Edmund consented. He had nothing to gain thereby— no money, no glory. On the contrary, he was putting himself to considerable inconvenience, for he had planned to leave France within a few hours and his luggage had already been placed on the boat. But he consented. He postponed his departure, played Richard that night, drew a packed house which enriched the resident company by a great many pounds, and refused to accept a penny for his own services. Next morning he returned to London.

On August 20th, while Edmund was fulfilling provincial engagements in Ireland, Mary and Susan and Charles travelled by carriage north to Bute. Mary wept most of the way up. Even after she had arrived, she remained obstinately inconsolable. Really, she had a great deal to occupy her mind, for though Edmund's house, which he had called Woodend, was habitable now, there was still a lot which needed doing to it. But Mary hated Bute, and she got no pleasure out of her duties as the wife of an estate owner. Susan agreed with her "that it was preposterous to think that a man as gay as Edmund would always be content to remain in Bute," but at the same time she understood the fascination of the place.

" . . . To say it is beautiful," she wrote to Margaret Roberts, "is not in my mind saying half enough—it is in fact perfectly enchanting, but so lonely one almost startles at the sound of their own voices—but its loneliness is no imperfection to me, indeed it gives me the idea that all nature was in repose—so very sweet and tranquil is all around.

" . . . The house stands in a pretty little lawn about sixty feet from a lake which is two miles and a half long and in winter very wide—the ground slopes up which ends in a high hill richly wooded and in summer enameled with flowers. This hill is at the back of the building which looks towards the lake and consists of a pretty stone vestibule and hall . . . on one side is a very good-sized dining parlour with folding doors of communication to Edmund's library —which is about four times the size of his London one— the windows of the whole are down to the ground—on the other side is a very pretty Bed Chamber in which I sleep —next to it is a large kitchen—a water closet in the hall— a large landing place which leads on one side to a drawing room thirty feet by twenty and high in proportion. One window looks to the woody hill, another to the lake and a third nearly takes in the whole compass which is about thirty-six acres—mostly indeed consisting of barren rocks with swamps interposed but all picturesque. On the other side of the landing place there are two excellent bed chambers—the one in front is my sister's, the Back Charles's— Mary's room has a beautiful little dressing room attached to it—with one door opening into the drawing room—the other into her own room. The whole of these appartments are beautifully furnished and when painted and papered . . . will be truly magnificent. To this building which certainly won't be too small Mary has added a couple of wings . . . the one has . . . a wash-house, coal cellar and larder in it, that on the other has two bed chambers . . . and wine cellar, so you see it is no cottage but a good chunk of thick set stone building."

Susan wrote this letter in December, when she was living alone at Woodend, for Charles had returned to spend his second term at Eton and Mary had gone to meet her husband in Glasgow. But she was quite content to be left behind. She liked running the house and looking after the gardener, who was paid twenty-five shillings per week, and the six labourers, who were paid one shilling and sixpence per day. Edmund had sent her a parrot to keep her company.

She was very interested in all the improvements which he intended to carry out in the near future. He said that soon they would all be able to live free, for he would get fish from the loch and would shoot rabbits and hares (he had already shot two hares). "When Edmund returns," she wrote, "he is to bring a low four-wheeled carriage such as I can drive in his absence. I am to buy a cow in the Spring when we shall have cream and butter of our own."

Poor Edmund! Even Susan realized on what very rickety foundations his plans and enthusiasms were based. For the trial between the Alderman and himself was now fixed for the 15th of January and "Heaven only knew what the end of it would be."

The Kean family spent Christmas together in Scotland.

But it was not a very happy celebration. Nerves were at breaking-point; and a few days later there was a first-class row between Edmund and Mary. The servants on the estate never forgot how the coachman came down from the house with an order from Mary "to yoke the horses" and how Edmund shouted after him, "There must be no carriage yoked here without my orders." The precise cause of the quarrel may only be guessed at; but its consequence was that Mary stayed behind in Bute, while Edmund went to London to face his trial alone.

He did not flinch from it. He was convinced that he would win. He had ordered his dresser at Drury Lane to get in a quantity of brandy, so that on the night of January 15th he would be able to drink with his friends to the damnation of "all whores and lying Aldermen."

CHAPTER IX

"*The Times*, January 15th, 1825"

Cox v. *Kean*

"SOME discussion occurred respecting the place this cause should occupy in the paper, in respect to the convenience of Mr. Scarlett, who was indisposed with a severe cold. At length it was agreed that it shall stand at the bottom for this (Saturday) so that probably it will not be tried before Monday."

It was, in fact, heard before the Lord Chief Justice and a special jury on January 17th. The Common Serjeant appeared for the plaintiff. Mr. Scarlett was leading counsel for the defendant.

The court, though newly built and exceptionally spacious, was packed to suffocation. A few of Edmund's friends were present to support him—Elliston and Jack Hughes took their places at an early hour. But the leaders of fashion, the shorthand writers of the Press, the noisy idlers who made up the rest of the throng were there to laugh, jeer, gloat, and get hysterical pleasure from the public exposure of a man whose conduct they had for years resented.

They knew beforehand what the outcome of the trial must be: for rumour had played its part to the full and they had already heard about the sensational letters which Edmund had penned and which the Alderman had found. Eight months before Mr. Creevey had written to his step-daughter, Elizabeth Ord: " . . . Another *slip* is Mrs. Alderman C—— with our tragedian Kean. . . . *He* has been at his letters too, one of which to the lady was intercepted by the alderman, and began, 'You dear imprudent little——' Can anything be more soft or romantic?"

The spectators at the trial were not expecting any unfore-

seen disclosures. They had come to wallow in the filth of
what they had been told would happen. They had really
come to revel in the discomfiture of a blindfolded man.
For only Edmund was still in the dark. Up to the last
moment he believed that he would "turn his accusers to
infamy and contempt."

Perhaps he did not understand the difference between
the histrionic and the forensic arts. Behind the blare of the
footlights a great actor can clothe a commonplace romance
with a lyrical quality. But in the chilly atmosphere of court
a clever counsel finds it easy to ridicule and debase the most
spiritual love affair. Inevitably the Common Serjeant made
mincemeat out of Edmund's crude, pathetic, half-educated
attempts at self-expression. He read the majority of the
letters aloud—the letters in which Edmund compared his
mistress "to sunbeams through the grating of the prison
house," the letters in which he called her a bitch, the letters
in which he swore that he would never desert his family.
At will, the Common Serjeant provoked loud laughter,
derisive titters, groans, coarse noises of every description.
Three times the Lord Chief Justice, in an effort to restore
order, threatened to clear the court.

The letters were Edmund's ruin. Of course, they established his adultery, but, more than this, they seemed to
show his perfidy, his hypocrisy, his deceit, his indecent
vulgarity. To have explained them away he would have had
to have laid bare the inner workings of his soul. And
unfortunately the soul is not evidence in law.

Mr. Scarlett did not attempt to excuse his client's conduct.
He admitted it; and remarked—*en passant*—that society
now looked back with disgust on the libertine age of King
Charles II. At the same time he suggested, first that Mrs.
Cox was a wanton, and secondly that the Alderman had
condoned her infidelity with Mr. Kean. For these reasons
he urged the jury to decide that the plaintiff was entitled
to no greater damages than those represented by the lowest
coin of the realm.

But the defence was not strong enough. Mr. Scarlett produced evidence which showed that Charlotte may have had affairs with a Sir Robert Wemyss and with a Colonel Pearson prior to her meeting with Edmund, and subsequently to it had certainly been guilty of adultery with Whatmore. He proved that the Alderman had often taken his wife to Edmund's dressing-room at Drury Lane and had once allowed her to stay there while Edmund changed his clothes in full view of both of them. He proved Edmund's repeated visitations to the Coxes' houses. He proved—to the plaintiff's discredit—the Birmingham, Salisbury, and Croydon incidents. And he called one witness who swore that to the best of his knowledge he had seen Mr. and Mrs. Cox walking arm in arm in June of last year—that is, three months after the present proceedings had been started.

But none of the evidence against the plaintiff was really substantiated. Most of it had to be got from Anne Wickstead, who was naturally hostile. And Mr. Scarlett was further embarrassed by the fact that all Edmund's letters went to establish the Alderman's innocence of complicity.

In his summing up, the Lord Chief Justice told the jury that Mrs. Cox's indiscretions with Sir Robert Wemyss and Colonel Pearson had not been proved, and that her affair with Whatmore was irrelevant to the issue. He also said that there was no reason for believing that the plaintiff had actually been aware of his wife's infidelity.

At the same time he pointed out that the Alderman's behaviour had been very far from that of a devoted husband, and he urged that this fact should be taken into consideration in assessing the damages.

The jury obediently followed the line suggested to them by the Lord Chief Justice. After ten minutes' absence they brought in a verdict for the plaintiff. They awarded him £800 damages, which was exactly £1,200 less than he had claimed. The case of Cox v. Kean was over.

But its sequel happened with such thoroughness and immediacy that it might almost have been rehearsed in advance. Verbatim reports of the trial appeared in all the newspapers. Indecent songs, ballads, playlets, and caricatures dealing with Edmund and his mistress sold like hot cakes. A pamphlet entitled *Secrets Worth Knowing*, which was a pornographic forgery of Charlotte's "suppressed" letters to her lover, was rushed through the press by an enterprising publisher. And in spite of this growing plethora of information—real and concocted—a Sunday newspaper advertised widely in advance: "Cox *v.* Kean—Verbatim report of this trial *with all* the letters, tragical and comical, will be given gratis in a supplement. . . ."

The Coxes did not win any sympathy. They were dismissed as being unworthy of it. But in spite of this, Edmund was mercilessly reviled, and held up to ridicule and contempt. A section of the Press, headed by *The Times*, conducted a ferocious campaign to arouse general indignation against him. On the 18th of January *The Times* wrote: " . . . It appears . . . that Kean . . . is advanced many steps in profligacy beyond the most profligate of his sisters and brethren of the stage. . . . It is of little consequence whether the character of King Richard or Othello be well or ill acted; but it is of importance that public feeling be not shocked, and public decency be not outraged."

A few of the more reasonably minded newspapers, it is true, revolted at this attitude of unrestrained recrimination. They urged that an actor's private conduct had nothing to do with his professional reputation, and was not the concern of playgoers. They also pointed out that Mr. Kean had behaved no worse than the majority of others who were guilty of his offence. " . . . In ninety-nine *Crim. Cons.* out of a hundred," wrote the *Morning Chronicle*, "there is evidence of treachery, and black, long-continued treachery. The confidence of the husband is always abused, and the adulterer seldom scruples to add falsehood to his other sins. . . ."

But fairness and a sense of proportion meant nothing at all to those who were determined to persecute Kean. For years they had waited for this chance to punish him for his arrogance and display: and now that he had, at last, delivered himself into their hands, they did not intend to let him off lightly. They wanted to drive him from the stage—for a while at least. They wanted to see him in the mud, grovelling and begging for mercy. Their mentality was beautifully betrayed in these extraordinary verses which appeared in a periodical called the *Literary Gazette* (they refer, of course, to Scarlett's mention of the libertine courtiers of Charles II's reign):

> No, Scarlett, no; the men were bad I own—
> Their manners loose, and profligate their tone;
> But they were GENTLEMEN! The heart and head
> Might be to morals and religion dead;
> But still the honour of their rank and race
> Kept them from grovelling taint of actions base
> And left to shabbier rakes the fame to win
> By joining inborn meanness to sin.
>
> Your client, bred to tumble for his meat—
> To act the monkey in plebeian street—
> To twist like serpents round the painted pole,
> To grin in barns, as Harlequin or droll,
> He—I'd have laid my fortune on the chance,
> That he'd have done just what I here advance,
> Taught us how differ'd gentlemen in heart
> From those whom we have hired to play the part.

That was why they hated him—because he was not a gentleman and yet had refused to be humble. He had flaunted himself in the face of society. It was his real fault not to have outraged morality, but to have outraged caste.

It had been announced that Edmund would play Richard III at Drury Lane on January 23rd. But a few days before, Sir Richard Birnie, the Bow Street magistrate, called on Elliston, "by direction of Mr. Secretary Peel," to express his fears that there would be serious disturbances if the performance took place so soon after the trial. He requested therefore that it should be postponed until popular excitement had had time to quieten down.

But there is a tradition in the theatre that a manager must stand by his players: and Elliston declined to make a decision without consulting Edmund. He found him at an hotel in Croydon, sitting up in bed with a cigar in his mouth and a glass of brandy and water by his side, being entertained, like some Eastern potentate, by a "broom girl" dressed in picturesque attire and an itinerant tumbler who was busily turning somersaults over the tables and chairs.

Elliston stated his business. But Edmund would not listen to any talk of postponement. He announced that he wished to face his enemies and said that "he was prepared for war." "In the meantime," he added, "see how quietly I am living here."

The Times was enraged when it learned that its victim intended to brave the storm of popular fury which it had been at such pains to create. "Mr. Kean is not merely an adulterer," it wrote in a leading article; "he is an adulterer anxious to show himself before the public with all the disgrace of the verdict of guilty about his neck, because that very disgrace is calculated to excite the sympathies of the profligate, and to fill the theatre with all that numerous class of morbidly curious idlers who flock to a play or an execution to see how a man looks when he is hanged, or deserves to be hanged. . . . When every person who can read knows that his offence is aggravated by the most shocking circumstances of indecency, brutality, obscenity, perfidy and hypocrisy—we do say that the public . . . ought not to be insulted by his immediate obtrusion before them, as a candidate for their applause. Let him hide himself for a reasonable time: his immediate appearance is as great an outrage to decency, as if he were to walk naked through the streets at mid-day."

The results of this kind of publicity were inevitable.

On the night of the 24th of January, Drury Lane was besieged by a seething, hysterical mass of humanity who,

"The Trip to Croydon"

A "COX v. KEAN" CARICATURE

in truth, had the lust to view an execution, not the desire
to see a play. Outside, the theatre was patrolled by a detachment of police from Bow Street, who had been given stern
instructions by their chief that they were not to enter the
building unless an actual riot broke out. Inside, the auditorium was jammed full half an hour before the curtain
rose, and a kind of suppressed pandemonium had already
been let loose. When Edmund made his entrance, a wild
shout went up, like the battle-cry of some barbarian army
on the march.

For three hours and more it continued unabated. But the
curtain was not lowered. The show went on. Edmund and
his fellow actors played their parts, though scarcely a line
that they uttered could be heard above the general din.

The audience entertained themselves. There were the
members of the Society for the Suppression of Vice—
"white-headed men"—who hooted fanatical abuse. There
were young bloods "who made good use of their hunting
halloos," and who bellowed "Little Breeches," "Heart
Strings," "Go back to Mother Cox," and so on. There
were Edmund's tavern friends who yelled at the top of their
lungs "Kean for ever," "Down with *The Times*," "Down
with Cant." There were bruisers, massed here and there,
who beat up everyone within sight. There were prostitutes
who screamed out obscenities. And there were indefinable
sensation-seekers who swelled the inane, prurient row
indiscriminately.

The fun never died down. When Edmund was on the
stage neither his supporters nor his opponents let him alone
for an instant. And when he was off, a series of side-shows
took place. Private brawls broke out in the pit and in the
boxes, hats were thrown in the air, dirty handkerchiefs were
waved, missiles were hurled across the auditorium, and
placards with lewd inscriptions were raised on high. Then
Edmund re-entered, and the persecution began again.

He himself was apparently unmoved. He tried once or
twice to address the house, but in vain. And so heedless of

the showers of orange peel which fell around him and the maniacal shouts which drowned his utterance, he played his part to the bitter end.

No one who saw him that night could have doubted his courage. Throughout a terrible ordeal he had not flinched. Perhaps the hostile newspapers which reported the proceedings next morning in detail, with gleeful indignation, felt satisfied that the experience must have unnerved him and that he would not come back for more. But they were wrong. On the 28th of January *The Times* was forced to announce: "That obscene little personage (Mr. Kean) is, we see, to make another appearance this evening. . . . His real friends and supporters, who have hitherto upheld him, because they thought his frailties over-balanced by his talents, must now desert him, when they see him dead even to the lowest degree of shame which distinguishes human from animal nature. We suspect he will scarcely find adequate consolation among his 'Wolves' and—we need not add the alliterative adjunct."

He appeared as Othello: and he had to contend with another prolonged exhibition of mass hysteria which was no less humiliating than the one which he had already suffered. In fact, Othello gave his audience an even better chance for coarse enjoyment at his expense than Richard III had done. Many of the lines which he was obliged to speak were greedily interpreted as references to his own morals. And, of course, during the scenes with Desdemona there were shrieks of disgusted delight.

Midway through the performance a placard was raised with the inscription "Let Elliston be summoned." The cry was vehemently taken up, and after the play was over Elliston did appear. He was greeted with a couple of full-sized oranges which narrowly skirted his person, but, placing his hand on his heart, in his best managerial manner, he at length gained a hearing.

Elliston discharged his own responsibility by explaining that it would not become him to take part in a quarrel and that he had signed a contract with Mr. Kean, who had himself chosen to face the public according to its terms. He then left the stage and Edmund reappeared in person.

Edmund was received with mingled cheers and hisses, but this time he was allowed to speak. He addressed the house briefly and under stress of obvious emotion. He disclaimed any intention of justifying· his private conduct, though he suggested that he had been victimized. "I stand before you," he said, "as the representative of Shakespeare's heroes. . . . If this is the work of a hostile press, I shall endeavour with firmness to withstand it; but if it proceeds from your verdict and decision, I will at once bow to it, and shall retire with deep regret, and with a grateful sense of all the favours which your patronage has hitherto conferred on me."

After that speech the issue was really settled. In spite of the frantic efforts of his enemies, Edmund had neither retreated nor begged for mercy. The odds had appeared to be overwhelmingly against him, but heroically he had refused to yield, and it was obvious now that he would never do so. Next morning *The Times* published a leading article in which it stated, with shameless hypocrisy, that though it disliked discussing theatricals "in the more distinguished part of the journal," yet it felt bound to protect even actresses on the stage from Kean's love-making. "Is it not shocking," it wrote, "that women should be forced to undergo this process with such a creature, for the sake of bread, before an assembled people?" And then it added irrelevantly: "Woe be to us as a people if the *circenses* occupy our thoughts as objects of national interest."

The Times made several further efforts, "in the more distinguished part of the journal," to whip up mass hysteria. But it had played itself out. Though there were minor disturbances when Edmund acted Overreach on January 31st, these were so tame in comparison with what had gone before that it was evident that he would soon be allowed

to perform in peace. By a supreme effort of will and courage
he had restored order to his kingdom.

But he had not brought back peace to his own mind.

In spite of his superb bravado he emerged by no means
unscathed from the battle which he had chosen to fight.
His enemies had dealt him cruel and shattering blows
from which he would never recover.

He was an artist with an artist's sensitivity. And he had
been paraded as a kind of monstrous freak for the delight
of the masses. Those who had rushed to gloat over his
disgrace had scarcely been representatives of the élite among
playgoers. Prostitutes and tipplers had cheered him; boun-
ders and fanatics had execrated him. But the true connoisseurs of the drama—"the decent part of society"—had
expressed their feelings in a less noisy and more telling
way. They had ignored him.

And so, in a sense, they continued to do. Of course they
returned to Drury Lane, after he had beaten off the *vociferous*
onslaught of moral indignation which had been launched
against him; for they were sane enough to realize that,
however base his personal habits might be, his histrionic
powers were still matchless. But at the same time they
could not forget or forgive his reputation. Between him and
themselves they now regarded the footlights as an insur-
mountable barrier. They applauded the actor; but they
would not shake hands with the man, let alone receive him
as a guest in their houses.

Socially he was ruined. Had he really been the vulgarian
that he liked to paint himself, he would have accepted this
fact with indifference. But he was a man who cried out
pathetically for the admiration and respect of his fellows.
Unconsciously *The Times* had prophesied correctly that he
would not find adequate consolation "among his wolves and
his whores." It was his misfortune that he never had done
so. He worshipped "culture." He had always longed, in
spite of his fierce protestations to the contrary, to be a
gentleman among gentlemen. Now he had placed himself

for ever beyond reach of gentility. And the realization of this was unbearable.

Perhaps if he had believed that his punishment was deserved, he would have accepted it with more fortitude. But he still could not understand why the world had turned against him so suddenly and so brutally. He thought that he had been foolish, not vicious. He was convinced that he had been the innocent victim of a conspiracy and that it was the Coxes not himself who merited the public's fury. He was bitterly unrepentant.

Night after night at Drury Lane, although he was no longer being actively attacked, he lashed out at his unseen enemies in absurd, unrestrained, futile speeches. He made himself appear completely ridiculous. He was like a hurt bull charging madly about the arena where his tormentors lurked in safety. And like a bull, too, his suffering would seem endless. Suddenly and unexpectedly his skin would be pierced by fresh wounds.

At the beginning of April he went off on a tour of the provinces and then organized persecutions began all over again. In one town he was ostracized; in another he was hooted and pelted. In Manchester, men walked through the streets with banners urging all decent playgoers to boycott the theatre where Edmund Kean was due to appear. Eventually a vast audience, consisting almost exclusively of males, succeeded in ruining his performance. The same thing happened in Glasgow. In Edinburgh, where the Presbyterian conscience was particularly alive, the manager of the playhouse was generally assailed for daring to engage the immoral actor upon whom no respectable woman could be expected even to cast an eye. One public-spirited citizen stated, *coram populo*, that he would withdraw his patronage from the theatre if Kean ever acted there again.

This outburst drew forth a plea for sanity from the London periodical, *John Bull*. "If Mr. Kean," it wrote, "(like Mr. Coutts) had made an overwhelming fortune and were to be received at the gates of Edinburgh, to have the keys tendered to him, to be escorted . . . by galloping cavalcades and made the associate of noble and virtuous women—we might say, 'For God's sake, Scotsmen, consider what you are doing—this man has no merit but his wealth—he tipples and swears—he drinks gross porter, aye and spirits—he is an adulterer, he is moreover a stage player—do not degrade your national character by trashy processions for this wretched creature, merely because he is rich.'

"But this is not asked of the Scotch people. Mr. Kean is engaged to act, to do his professional business for their amusement."

John Bull expressed the view which was already held in London, and which would eventually be held throughout the rest of Great Britain. But it did not satisfy Edmund. He had never been content merely to be an actor. And now it was miserable consolation to him that he had—after the most galling experiences—saved his professional name from the total wreck of all his aspirations. No amount of applause from playgoers could make him forget the world's injustice or could alter the fact that his pride had been savagely mutilated.

He had stood up to the public's first outbursts of fury and had apparently come triumphantly through his repeated ordeals of being hooted by the mob. But his life was none the less in ruins; and he looked on it angrily, hopelessly, as a child gazes on a favourite toy that has been broken beyond repair. He knew of no way to dull the pain which he suffered except by drinking himself into a stupor.

Grattan, who called on him some months after the trial, was moved to pity by his mere appearance. "I never saw a man so changed," he wrote. "He had all the air of desperation about him. He looked bloated with rage and brandy; his nose was red, his cheeks blotched, his eyes bloodshot. . . ."

He told Grattan that from all the vast sums of money which he had earned, he had not more than a hundred

pounds left in the world. But otherwise he did not moan.
He sat down at the piano and sang "Lord Ullin's Daughter." Grattan noticed with astonishment how much his
voice and piano-playing had improved since last he had
heard them. Even now, when his tragic plight was the
inevitable consequence of his own folly, Edmund proved
that his hours of leisure in the past had not been entirely
wasted.

Meanwhile, though he could not afford idleness, he had
decided that it was impossible for him to remain much
longer in his own country where he had been so mercilessly
persecuted and where he was still socially taboo. He would
revisit America. He would go into voluntary exile and
would bid an everlasting good-bye to his enemies. He
believed that playgoers in the United States had not heard
of Mrs. Cox, and that they would therefore be willing to
heal his injuries. He hoped that in America he would be
able to rebuild his fortune and recapture his self-respect.

No ties bound him to England. He had already made up
his mind that he would never live with his family again.
On July 21st he wrote from York to Jack Hughes: "Damn
Drury and Buonaparte then *for America* . . . I have
promised a *Snuff Box—Brutus* to Major Downes, can send
it down by my wife, who comes to Buxton on Sunday. I
think you had better meet me in Edinburgh as I shall
never be able to stand separations. I shall go to Greenock.
I cannot return to London again. . . ."

Mary was still in Bute. Her happiness was jettisoned no
less than Edmund's, for everything that she valued had
been torn away from her. The house in Clarges Street had
been disposed of. And her days of playing the society
hostess were obviously at an end.

She was completely wretched. Even Edmund must have
pitied her, if she had shown any sympathy towards him in
his distress. But, nursing her own grievances, she only
knew that he was the whole cause of her misery: and
although she had condoned his infidelity with Charlotte

Cox, she could feel for him nothing but loathing now that he was publicly disgraced.

In her heart there was no affection left. Had she been moved by the merest tingle, she would have rushed to his side the moment the result of the trial became known. But, instead, she kept well away from him. She left him to endure his agonizing adversity alone. Worse than this, she added to his troubles by conducting a personal vendetta against him and by assisting to drag his name through the mud.

She recriminated cruelly. She intended to desert him for good. She threatened to sell his property at Bute—lock, stock, and barrel—and to collar the proceeds for herself. She even went so far as to publish the fact that she was suffering from a malignant venereal disease which she alleged she had caught from him.

No doubt she was blinded by self-pity, and in her mad concern for her own immediate future did not realize what she was about. Certainly after she had discovered that her husband was still capable of earning an income, she protested that she did not desire a permanent separation from him. But her repentance came too late. She had at last offended Edmund beyond hope of reconciliation. He could not find it in his heart to forgive her.

Edmund left for the United States in September. " . . . He parted very kindly from me when going . . ." Mary told Barry Cornwall. Perhaps he did. But he knew —and she knew—that they would never live under the same roof again. Their matrimonial affairs were now in the hands of the lawyers.

Several letters passed between Henry Sigell, Edmund's solicitor, and Mary during the months of October and November. Mary's style verged from supplication to anger. On the 6th of October she wrote from Bute: ". . . Tell me at once does he want me to remain here—will it give ease to his mind my doing so? Does he wish to see me again? Oh, pray answer these questions. I am too ill to leave here. I write from bed, and if I was well I cannot go without money. . . . I do not want a separation from my husband—not for worlds would I bring such a thing before the public—I thought it best to live away from him as he has behaved so strange—speak to me friendly and tell me Mr. Kean's wishes—*all I can do I will.* . . . Tell me truly what will make him happy? I am heartbroken."

In reply Sigell explained that Edmund would make her an allowance of £504 per annum, out of which he would expect her to keep Charles at Eton and provide him with clothes. He would also let her have the use of his house and furniture at Bute, provided she made no attempt to sell the property. She would thus be able to live rent free.

Sigell urged her to accept this offer. "It is in your power," he wrote, "to restore to Mr. Kean much of his lost happiness by acting up to his wishes. . . . If it is not too much to ask of you I should feel greatly indebted if you would spare me one of the many portraits you have of Mr. Kean. I should like some token of remembrance of him in recollection of the many excellent qualities he possesses. . . . He left for U.S.A. in excellent health but almost broken-hearted, his mind much depressed with conflicting thoughts."

But this letter did not please Mary. The last paragraph alarmed her particularly—and no wonder, since she had accused *Edmund* of having given her venereal disease. "Sir Anthony Carlisle having attended me yesterday," she wrote, "I told him I was made very uneasy by your saying Mr. Kean was quite free from ailment . . . in that case my character must suffer, for if this can be proved what must be thought of me—Sir Anthony said, '. . . . Should the least hint be given that Mr. Kean was not ill I shall come forward for your sake—leave it entirely to me—no one ever yet doubted the truth of my assertions' . . . Mr. Kean must pay Sir Anthony everything."

She was also furiously indignant, in spite of her previous protestations, that Edmund expected her to live in Bute. "He has deprived me of health," she moaned, "the finest and greatest of blessings—happiness he has forever destroyed—my name he has taken from me and left me without any inquiry as to what I might need in the situation, the *dreadful* situation he left me."

She herself had determined to leave Bute. She was not going to be kept there against her will. But she was peevishly angry at being baulked in her design to sell the property. "No one will take charge of it," she concluded exultantly. "Take my word, Mr. Kean will never live here, say what he likes. It is a sin to let it go to desolation, decay, and so see to it *directly*."

By April Mary had taken rooms in London at No. 6 Spring Street, Portman Square. She lived there with her son on an allowance from Edmund which was paid with faultless regularity, and which, though small, was sufficient to defray Charles's school fees at Eton and to satisfy her own immediate needs. As the cast-off wife of a vicious husband, her contemporaries pitied her greatly. Posterity, too, has deluged her memory with sentiment. But in view of the facts which have now been published for the first time, it may be wondered whether she was not, in a measure at least, responsible for her own misfortune: and whether, in the end, she did not receive at Edmund's hands better treatment than she really deserved.

2

Poor Edmund! It is strange that he regarded the United States as a potential haven, for back in 1821 he had been virtually thrown out of the country, and the screams of outraged newspaper editors had still rung in his ears as he had sailed homewards across the Atlantic.

But with him the wish was always father to the thought. In one of his most bombastic speeches at Drury Lane he had expressed the hope that "for the honour of his countrymen, the machinations of his enemies would never be reported in Foreign Journals." No doubt he had really believed that playgoers in the United States would be blissfully unaware of his moral turpitude, and would rush to give him a wonderful reception.

Of course, he had harboured a sad illusion. The American public had been well fed by their Press with all the details of the Cox *v.* Kean trial: and since they had not yet got over the insult to their national pride which Edmund had perpetrated at Boston they were now thirsting for vengeance. When he reached their shores they were ready for him.

He opened as Richard III in New York on November 14th. But though a huge audience filled the theatre, he might just as well have stayed at home. Not a word that he spoke could be heard above the noise of hisses and counter-cheers which was kept up unremittingly throughout the action of the play. Evidently the Americans were determined to prove that they were every bit as adept at staging "Kean" riots as the English had been.

In their detailed accounts next morning the newspapers reported that there had been more applause than anger, and that Kean's enemies, though successful in spoiling his performance, had been outnumbered by Kean's admirers. But what did these considerations matter to Edmund? They were merely academic. He only knew that he had come to America for peace and had got war. The persecution had begun again: and he could no longer bear it.

In desperation he fell back on his last line of defence. All his life he had refused to beg for mercy; but now that he had not the spirit to fight, what else was there left for him to do? The *New York Commercial Advertiser* had written:

"We think that no manager should allow such a lump of moral pollution to contaminate the boards. Every female must stay away and males hiss with indignation."

The *New York Daily Advertiser* had written: "Americans, do your duty just like London and Edinburgh."

To these attacks and others of the same kind Edmund

sent the following reply, which was published in the *National Advocate*:

> I visit this country now under different auspices and feelings than on a former occasion. Then I was an ambitious man, and the proud representative of Shakespeare's heroes: the spark of ambition is extinct, and I merely ask a shelter in which to close my professional and mortal career. I will give the weapon into the hands of my enemies; if they are brave they will not turn it against the defenceless.
>
> EDMUND KEAN

This letter soon stemmed the tide of public resentment against him. Its effect proved that Edmund would certainly have minimized—might even have avoided—his previous disasters had he chosen to face them less aggressively. He conducted the remainder of his New York season not only peacefully but almost triumphantly. Before it came to an end he was able to send a £500 bill to his London bankers. He was encouraged to regard his audiences as his friends again; and he could justly suppose that he was in truth beginning to rebuild his fortune.

But that first outburst of popular frenzy had shocked him none the less. He was now miserably apprehensive of the future, for he dared not foretell what would be the nature of his reception in other towns which he had contracted to visit. After all, he had learned from bitter experience to expect new troubles wherever he performed. Birmingham and Glasgow had booed him months after he had restored order to Drury Lane. On this hypothesis, peace in New York did not necessarily mean peace throughout America. On the contrary.

In his tortured state of mind he might well have been tempted to run away. But even now he was no coward. Though he had at length been driven to self-abasement, he had lost none of his amazing courage. Otherwise he would never have ventured to Boston—to a town where, even in happier times, he had narrowly escaped being lynched.

He went there towards the end of December. He must have realizèd the fearful risk he was running, for on arrival he once again took up the shield of humility. From the Exchange Coffee House, where he was staying, he addressed a moving plea to the *Columbian Sentinel,* in which he besought the citizens of Boston to show him "liberality and forbearance" instead of "prejudice and cruelty."

"That I have erred," he wrote, "I acknowledge; that I have suffered for my errors and indiscretions, my loss of fame and fortune is but too melancholy an illustration. Acting from an impulse of irritation, I certainly was disrespectful to the Boston public; calm deliberation convinces me that I was wrong. The first step towards the Throne of Mercy is confession—the hope we are taught, forgiveness. Man must not expect more than those attributes which we offer to God."

But this time his appeal for mercy was useless. He had made it exactly four years too late. Though he had returned to the scene of his crime voluntarily, he had come none the less in the role of an escaped felon who had already been convicted and condemned. His judges had waited long enough for the chance to execute their sentence upon him: and now that they had him in their power they did not intend to let him off lightly. They were out for his blood.

Physical fear was an emotion which Edmund had never before experienced. But he was made to understand it on the night of December 21, 1825, when he played Richard III in Boston.

All day long rumours of approaching vengeance had spread round the town. In the afternoon small boys had collected to jeer at the very placards on which Edmund's name was announced. In the early evening the street outside the theatre was already blocked by an angry, jostling crowd who had been unable to secure tickets of admission. They were obviously in a bellicose mood and were not easily going to be dispersed.

Edmund must have guessed what was in store for him

as he walked through the stage-door. He must have been certain of it as he sat in his dressing-room putting on his make-up. For by then he knew that, although there was a packed house in front, not a woman was present. The audience resembled a sea of leering male faces. And that sight, so familiar to him, was not only ominous. It was horribly final.

He stood in the wings listening to the uproar which had already begun, and which was the gentle prelude to his own reception. When the appalling moment came for him to make his entrance he must have felt like a doomed prisoner mounting the guillotine. No wonder he looked pale and dejected.

But his enemies did not pity him on that account. They were as men maddened by bloodlust, and they revelled in his discomfiture. "Off, off," they yelled, and to enforce his obedience pelted him with "nuts, pieces of cake, a bottle of offensive drugs," anything they could find.

Of course, Edmund withdrew. There was no alternative. But even now he was not faint-hearted. He was still prepared to risk another onslaught in an effort to quell the disturbance. The audience would not allow him to speak; so he sent a message to them through Mr. Kilner, who was dressed up for the part of King Henry.

"Mr. Kean wishes to make an apology," Kilner announced, "a humble apology from his heart and soul; but he will not do it at the risk of his life."

This inspired the stockholders of the theatre, who sat in the boxes, and who for obvious reasons wanted peace, to shout lustily, "Silence! Hear Kean! Let him apologize!" and so on. They did not, it is true, succeed in drowning the wild shrieks of disapprobation from the rest of the house, but they made themselves sufficiently heard to encourage poor Edmund to venture on a second entry.

He reappeared. But he came like a lamb to the slaughter. Once again he was greeted by howls of "Off! off!"; once again he was pelted without mercy; once again he was driven ignominiously from the stage. This time he rushed to the Green Room, where he flopped down and "wept like a child."

He wept tears of anguish and defeat. After having fought so many bitter duels with the public, he was at last beaten and had to give in. A few minutes later a placard was brought on to the stage with the inscription "Mr. Kean declines playing." It was received with a bellow of unkind, exultant laughter.

Meanwhile the situation looked ugly. Outside the crowd had grown bigger, angrier, more restless. Inside the rowdies were already beyond control. The management, afraid for Edmund's personal safety, smuggled him from the theatre by way of a back alley "through Mrs. Powell's house."

But the audience, like all bullies, were paradoxical in their desires—and capricious. They had not let their victim speak, they had not even allowed him to stand silently before them; and yet they could not leave him alone. After the first act of *Richard* had been played in a dumb show (with another actor in the leading part) they began to shout for him again. They wanted a further chance to torment and humiliate him before the kill.

When they were told that he had gone their fury knew no bounds. In the pit they rose up as one man and swept on to the stage like a tidal wave, breaking up seats and smashing lamps and wrecking any other obstacles which blocked their way. Their purpose was presumably to drag forth Kean from his hiding-place and tear him limb from limb. But simultaneously the crowd outside stormed the playhouse doors, the more respectable men in the boxes swung themselves up on to the windows twenty-five feet from the ground in an effort to get away, and the confusion became so great that a semi-organized lynching expedition got caught up in a general riot. In result only the theatre was damaged—and the public peace.

Edmund escaped. It was said that "Tom Divol," a local hack driver, drove him to Brighton, where he took the stage-coach to Worcester. He had seen the last of Boston. He had heard the last Bostonian shout. He had suffered the worst experience of his life, and one which, he thought, no other could equal. He must have sunk back into his seat wearily, dejectedly, but a little thankfully.

Before the end of the year he was safely back in New York, planning to begin another successful season. On December 31st he wrote to his London banker, Mr. W. Clarke of Messrs. Coutts:

". . . I enclose you a bill for 500£ [*sic*]—to be placed to my account which with another bill of the same sum, sent on the 29th November, you will be kind enough to acknowledge by means of the next Liverpool packet. I am convinced, Sir, from your great attention & politeness to me in England that you will be pleased to hear that the scales of fortune have once more turned in favour of an unjustly persecuted man . . . whatever information you can give me, regarding my own affairs, or those of Drury Lane Theatre, I shall feel obliged for. . . . I commenced acting only the end of November . . ."

Whether that letter was sincere or mere bravado or a cry of satisfaction that he had now passed over the peak of injustice, it proved at least that his will was indomitable. Within the framework of a mind and body that were already shattered the flame of his art still burned, and nothing save death could put it out. No experiences, however bitter, could drive him into retreat or could make him lay down his grease paints even for a while. Without a pause he went on to further encounters. During the next few months he played in Philadelphia, New York, South Carolina, Charleston, and Baltimore.

His courage was rewarded. It is true that in Philadelphia he was hissed on his first appearance; and that in Baltimore another riot broke out, and he had to conclude his engagement with unbecoming haste. But these were isolated examples of opposition. More often he was cheered; and nearly always his performances were well patronized.

"Kean in America"

A CARICATURE OF KEAN PUBLISHED DURING HIS SECOND VISIT TO THE UNITED STATES

Inevitably public opinion had begun to take his side. It realized that he had been punished to excess. As one newspaper put it: "Has any man been so persecuted in any profession as Mr. Kean?" His sin was not particularly uncommon; why, therefore, had he been singled out for such extraordinarily brutal treatment? In fairness there was no reasonable answer to this question; and people thought the time had come to make amends.

But popular sentiment was not the only cause of his revived favour. He was still a supreme actor. Though he himself was broken, his genius blazed forth challengingly and could not for ever be downtrodden or ignored. Though his health had deteriorated so badly that to go through one of his famous parts completely exhausted him, yet he was still capable at his best of hiding his own weakness and of mesmerizing his audience. Sometimes he was forced to rest for weeks on end. Sometimes playgoers could not help noticing that he was ill and feeble when he appeared on the stage. But more often they agreed with Doctor Francis, who wrote:

"His devotion as an actor was not less earnest than when I first knew him. His Sir Giles in New York abated not of the vehemence and terror that characterized it as I had witnessed it at Old Drury in London in 1816. . . . There were sometimes with him moments of renewed study, and he threw himself into several new characters which he had not previously represented here; his Jew of Malta, his Zanga, his De Montfort, and Paul, were of the number. His Othello was received with louder plaudits than ever, and his Lear, as an inspiration beyond mortals, was crowned with universal praises. . . ."

By the beginning of April Edmund had saved £2,250. He wrote to Cooper, stage-manager of Drury Lane, telling him this joyful news, and also introducing a certain Mr. Mills, who was apparently anxious for a London engagement: ". . . he is good enough to undertake the whole management of the *boat* which I shall call the United States,

a trifling but sincere tribute of grateful feeling to a country
that has given new life to my talent, my health & fortune
. . . I am not really the people's actor—but their Idol. I
had entrusted this commission to Reynolds, but I hear of
his being in France, in Devon & and devil knows where
besides, & perhaps when I wanted him on the Thames I
should trace him in Seringapatam . . . do you know anything of the unworthy being that bears my name? I hear
she has left my paradise to spend that money in London
which if she had an atom of maternal feeling should be
hoarded for her son . . ."

That, of course, was not the letter of a happy man, in
spite of its nervous exultancy. Edmund was blinded by
confused feelings of anger, weakness, pain, desire; lurching
about like a drunken man in the dark, not knowing what
he wanted or where he would go, but unable to remain still.

He was only thirty-seven years old. Yet the drama of his
life was already played—struggle, triumph, downfall. What
was there left to him?

He talked a great deal about death both in his speeches
and in his conversation. Once when he was with Doctor
Francis he threatened to throw himself from the roof of
Bethlehem Asylum, which he had come to visit in order,
in his own words, "to learn if there were any difference in
the insanity of John Bull and of the Americans." Doctor
Francis seized him and dragged him to safety. Otherwise
he would have shared the fate of his father before him. Had
he at last come into a share of his family inheritance? Had
he gone off his head?

Back in England a year ago a provincial audience had
thought him mad when he had interrupted his performance
of *Sylvester Daggerwood* to point to his whip and exclaim,
"I keep this little instrument to punish cheating aldermen
and lying editors." Now his behaviour was often so strange
that even his friends had begun to despair of his reason.
On one occasion he suddenly started to turn somersaults in
a public park. On another he rushed out of his hotel in the

middle of the night wearing only his shirt, and awoke the whole street crying "Fire! Fire!" The alarm, of course, was false.

But although he was obviously a little unbalanced, he no doubt exaggerated his symptoms of brain fever in an effort to attract attention to himself and to the wrongs that he had suffered—just as in moments of desperation he made wild statements which he did not really mean.

He said that he never wanted to see his own country again, that he would be quite content to spend the rest of his days in America, that America was now his home. And yet he sent his savings to London. He scrutinized the English newspapers and begged his correspondents to tell him "all about the affairs at Drury Lane." His interest in England was far from academic.

Protest as he might, "the spark of ambition" was not really extinguished. It could never be so long as he held the stage; for his genius—no less than his anguish—depended upon it, and without it he would have been as nothing.

In his heart he fretted against his exile and clung tenaciously to life. He yearned to prove that he was still "the first English actor," and that he was capable of further triumphs. He could never forget that he belonged to Drury Lane, and that Drury Lane by right belonged to him.

He would gladly have returned to England at any time, had he been certain of his welcome there by the public. But he shrank from facing his own countrymen again, for fear that they would continue to treat him as a social outcast. Before he would even contemplate a journey homewards he needed some proof that he had vindicated himself, some indication that the English people really wanted him back and would accept him, not as their fallen player, but as "their idol."

During the summer of 1826 he visited Canada. And then —perhaps because he had never been there before or perhaps because he was so obviously owed reparation—

Fortune suddenly began to shine upon him again in all its radiance.

He acted in Montreal and Quebec. In both towns he was given a wonderful, exhilarating reception of a kind which he really appreciated and which he had not known for long enough.

Audiences flocked to see his performances and applauded him with royal acclamations. He was entertained by the leaders of society, he was flattered and lionized. He was treated like an ambassador of the theatre. As one newspaper put it, the Canadians were doing their best to wipe out the injustices of his past and to rebuild the glories of his future. They were teaching the English "a salutary lesson."

In Montreal, Edmund was entertained at a public dinner. During the course of his speech he said: " . . . How shall I thank those beings who have rekindled the social spark, almost extinct, and have lighted up my heart again to friendship and esteem? It is . . . the key unlocking the barriers to society . . . the symbol that I have not *wholly* lost the affections of my countrymen. . . . More than on my own account, I hail this day hallowed—fast as the winds can bear these tidings to the British shores, it will enliven those who in spite of my inconsistencies and errors, watch with anxious eyes my progress, and whose grateful hearts will beat like mine at the receipt of that friendship which restores me again to the rank of a gentleman!"

How he hoped that those words were true! And in Quebec he was paid an honour which convinced him that they were. He was received into the Huron tribe of Red Indians. The ceremony was elaborately conducted in the presence of four native tribesmen—Abarathaha Tsawanhootei, Tsione, Teacheandahe, Tsodhahissen—and several local celebrities including Captain Sir William Wiseman of H.M.S. *Jupiter*. He was given the exalted rank of chieftain and the name Alanienouidet.

Who could doubt now that he was a gentleman? He had

a title. The disgraced actor, the pernicious adulterer, the social outcast, had become Alanienouidet, the Red Indian Chief. That would surely silence his most obstinate enemies and would make even *The Times* bow down to him. For was he not, in truth, a kind of king? He adored his status in the Huron tribe. At the moment it meant more to him than all his Drury Lane triumphs put together. Over and over again he played, in his own imagination, the part of Alanienouidet and his wonderful exploits—his feats of horsemanship, his stirring speeches, his wise and powerful rule. To add the zest of reality to his daydreams, he painted his face and decked himself out in his tribal raiment whenever he could find the faintest excuse to do so—either in public or in private. He had special visiting cards printed with Edmund Kean on one side and Alanienouidet on the other.

After his return to New York in the autumn, Doctor Francis received a mysterious command to call on a certain Red Indian Chief at his hotel. Doctor Francis obeyed. He was shown into a long, darkened room and "at the remote end perceived something like a forest of evergreens, lighted up by many rays from floor lamps, and surrounding a stage or throne; and seated in great state was the chief."

Doctor Francis, still unaware of his host's identity, was a trifle nervous and overawed. "I advanced," he wrote, "and a more terrific warrior I never surveyed. Red Jacket or Black Hawk was an unadorned, simple personage in comparison. Full dressed, with skins tagged loosely about his person, a broad collar of bear-skin over his shoulders, his leggings, with many stripes, garnished with porcupine quills; his mocassins decorated with beads; his head decked with the war eagle's plumes, behind which flowed massive black locks of dishevelled horse hair; golden-coloured rings pendant from his nose and ears; streaks of yellow paint over his face, massive red daubings about his eyes, with various hues in streaks across the forehead, not very artistically drawn. A broad belt surrounded his waist, with tomahawk; his arms with shining bracelets, stretched out with bow and arrow, as if ready for a mark. He descended his throne and rapidly approached me. His eye was meteoric and fearful, like the furnace of a cyclops. He vociferously exclaimed, "Alantenaida!" And it was only then that Doctor Francis recognized his friend Kean.

Edmund had decided to return to England. His experiences in Canada had heartened him enormously and he was longing to show off Alanienouidet to his own countrymen. Besides, he had another—more potent—reason for wishing to reach London as soon as possible. He had always said —even in his blackest moments of despair—that before he died he would like to control the destiny of Drury Lane. Even after the world had robbed him of the joy of living, that had been his one remaining ambition.

Now it seemed that his chance had come at last. Elliston, having failed to pay the rent of the theatre, had been forced by the proprietors to resign. Someone had written to Edmund assuring him that the vacant lesseeship was his for the asking. He required no better proof that the London public wanted him back again.

He was very ill when he sailed from America on December 8th. His last few performances in New York had been marred by physical weakness. But he was excited, and his spirits were buoyed up by more genuine stimulants than brandy. He felt confident of a wonderful reception on the other side of the Atlantic. He had triumphed over his enemies. He was going home as Alanienouidet, the Red Indian Chief, to become at last the rightful king of Drury Lane.

3

In spite of his brave hopes, nothing would ever happen again as Edmund wished it.

Six days before he left New York so gleefully—on December 8th—King George IV paid a state visit to Drury

Lane. The occasion was remarkable since it was the first time that the new management of the Royal Patent House had had the chance to welcome His Majesty. But Edmund Kean was not mentioned as the real or even the titular head of the régime which the King was pleased to honour. Stephen Price, once director of the New York Theatre, where Edmund had often played, now filled the place of the banished "Great Lessee."

It is strange that Edmund was unaware of Stephen Price's appointment; for London had learned the news months before—in July, in fact, shortly after Elliston's dismissal. It is true that on November 3rd *The Times*, quoting a paragraph from the *Quebec Gazette*, had stated that Price had only taken up the Drury Lane lease "on Mr. Kean's behalf." But this rumour must have been vigorously denied, for on December 19th, when Edmund was already halfway across the Atlantic, *The Times* wrote: "By last accounts received from America, relating to Mr. Kean, the actor, his health is represented to be in a most shattered condition, and it is even doubtful if he will ever be able to return to England."

Had he, then, been double-crossed by Stephen Price? Or had he been the victim of some cruel hoax? Whatever the case, it is certain that he left New York on the understanding that he had been called to the vacant throne of Drury Lane and that he was bitterly hurt when he discovered his mistake.

It is also certain that the Drury Lane proprietors would not have given Edmund control of their theatre in any circumstances. They had really got rid of Elliston, not because he had failed to meet his outstanding liabilities (that had merely been their excuse) but because he had had a stroke. They had considered him no longer strong enough to guard their interests satisfactorily. They would, therefore, have been resolutely opposed to replacing him with a man like Kean whose health, according to report, was broken and who had proved himself woefully irresponsible.

On his return Edmund sensed this, and it added gall to his other disappointments. He was back in his own country and yet he had no status and no home. He had never liked his house in Clarges Street, but he must have regretted it a little when he awoke to the fact that even in his native town of London he had to drag himself to an hotel. He took rooms at the Hummums Hotel in Covent Garden, where he went straight to bed and sent for a doctor. He was very ill; but no one would tend his ailments now, except those whom he paid for the purpose.

Debts had accumulated during his absence from England. One bill shocked him in particular—and enraged him as well. It came from Sigell, his solicitor. It was so large that it would drain nearly all his resources—a staggering thought. Sigell, Edmund decided, was obviously a villain and a swindler. What work had he done that he dared to send in such a preposterous demand? Edmund would meet it—that was his way. But—by God—he would never speak to Sigell again or to any member of Sigell's family.

In all this there was only one consolation. He had signed a contract with Stephen Price whereby he was engaged to play on a specified number of nights during the season and was to be paid the colossal salary of a hundred guineas per performance. His first appearance had been fixed for January 8th, and already the rush for tickets and the newspaper comments foretold a house which, in its size and enthusiasm, would be reminiscent of his happiest days.

But, in the nature of things, London playgoers were passionately anxious to see Edmund *act* again. He had kept away from them for longer than a year; and although they had not forgotten, during his absence, that he was an immoral man, they had had time to remember that he was a great tragedian—infinitely the greatest of his age. At the moment, indeed, they could not help remembering it. For Elliston was carving out a new fortune for himself as manager of the Surrey Theatre; Macready had gone to America; and the stage was sadly bereft of personalities.

No wonder London hailed delightedly the return of its National Player.

Was it from sentiment that Edmund chose to make his reappearance as Shylock? It pleased the public to think that he was coming to receive their forgiveness in the same part in which he had first won their applause. But Edmund was only anxious to prove to his audience that he had lost none of his power; and he realized that as Shylock he would have a better chance of doing so than as Richard or Othello or Overreach. For the character is not consistently on the stage, and he knew that during the lengthy intervals which separate its big scenes, he would have time to rest and to husband his strength for another supreme effort.

There were many graphic accounts of Edmund's performance and of his reception on the night of January 8th, when he reappeared before the English public. But perhaps the most interesting one was printed in *The Times*, because it might so easily have been prejudiced against him and was certainly not exaggerated in his favour. "When the curtain rose," *The Times* wrote, "a general cry of 'Kean! Kean!' resounded from every part of the densely crowded house; the call was persevered in, so as to prevent any of the earlier scenes from being heard. At length Kean made his appearance: he was received with a shout of acclamation. He made no speech, but expressed his feelings by many obedient bows. Mr. Kean appeared to be in excellent health, and took more than ordinary pains in the delineation of the ruthless Jew. He gave with a force which no man on the stage but himself could display that energetic speech in which the follower of the Mosaic creed argues that he has a right, from Christian example, to satisfy the feelings of revenge. His scene with Tubal, where he is alternatively delighted with the information of Antonio's misfortunes, and depressed by the announcement of Jessica's extravagance, was acted in a masterly style. The transitions from joy to grief, and vice versa, in this very difficult portion of the play were forcibly imagined and finely executed. The last, the trial scene, was not inferior to any that preceded it. The exultation of Shylock in the earlier part and his utter dejection at its close . . . were justly and powerfully contrasted. During the whole of the fifth act, in which Shylock does not appear, the cries for 'Kean' were incessant. At the close of the play the uproar continuing, Mr Kean came forward, bowed to the audience, and, amidst their greetings, retired."

Strange that Edmund, who loved making speeches, remained silent on this occasion when there was such an overwhelming demand to hear him. Perhaps he was so exhausted that he had not the strength to utter another word; or perhaps his heart was so full that he did not trust himself to speak.

He had certainly re-established his histrionic fame. He had given a wonderful performance. Doctor Doran, the stage historian, who still treasured memories of it in his old age, wrote that he had never heard a shout so loud as that which greeted Kean on his entrance. To him it signified a complete reconciliation between the actor and his public.

And so, in a sense, it did. But the men of fashion who sat in the front and cheered and clapped their hands were not seen in the Green Room afterwards. To them Kean would always be a social outcast. They looked upon his vices now more in sorrow than in anger. But they avoided his society like the plague.

Next day the newspapers wrote glowingly of Kean's triumph without a trace of their former rancour. But the hero himself, feeling the pangs of physical exhaustion, understood how false and hollow it had really been. He lay uncomfortably in bed at the Hummums Hotel, dosing himself with brandy, playing with the trappings of Alanienouidet and looking dejectedly into the future. Had he any cause for joy? True, he had climbed painfully back on to his histrionic pedestal. But something which he valued far more than a myriad successes on the stage still eluded him

—his honour and prestige as a man. He was angry, resentful, and acutely aware of his loneliness.

Still, he had to go on working. He played Richard III on January 15th, Richard III again on January 22nd, Overreach on the 25th, Macbeth on the 29th, and so through the whole round of his famous characters. He found that he could muster just enough energy to act every Monday and Thursday, provided he stayed indoors throughout the rest of the week. Of course, if he obeyed his doctor's orders—drank no spirits and led an invalid's life—he might recover his strength completely. But would it be made worth his while? Would he ever be returned his self-respect? He hardly thought so.

He tried desperately to impress the world with his recently acquired title. Dressed up as Alanienouidet, he paraded himself in his own room, in the streets, in his wherry on the Thames, and even on the stage at the close of his performances. But he did not inspire the respect due to a chieftain. His few friends, who were not sycophants, regarded his sudden preoccupation with Red Indians as an instance of lunacy, and humoured him rather in the same fashion as they would have a spoilt child who has built a toy castle out of bricks. Public opinion, in general, accepted Alanienouidet as another example of Kean's love of vulgar ostentation—now more pitiable than annoying.

He was buoyed up by only one genuine enthusiasm. He wanted to appear in a new part. He remembered vividly his sensational success as Overreach and the wonderful aftermath of his triumph—the social whirl, the dinners in his honour, the flattery, the lionizing, the presents that had been showered upon him, the sword that Byron had given him. He still treasured Byron's sword. It was his favourite relic of former glories, the only one which he had required Mary to send from Bute when he had supposed that she would go on living there.

Perhaps if he could take London by storm in the same sudden, dramatic way as he had done as Overreach, he might indeed become the people's idol as well as their actor. Besides, from a purely professional point of view it was very necessary for him to prove that he was still capable of fresh achievements, great and startling. As a man of the theatre he could not rest indefinitely on laurels already won.

He was convinced that he had found the right play. His friend, Thomas Colley Grattan, had written a tragedy, and on hearing of his return from America had immediately sent it to him. Of course, it was typical of Edmund, liking Grattan, to like Grattan's work. But he really did think that the name part—Ben Nazir, the Saracen—would provide him with superb opportunities to show off his virtuosity. He was very excited about it.

Grattan, on his side, was equally delighted, and he was surprised also. He had written *Ben Nazir*, which was his first attempt at a play, especially for Kean. But he had completed it some years ago; and after the Cox *v.* Kean trial he had given up hope that it would ever be produced. At the time he had convinced himself, in common with the majority of his fellow countrymen, that Kean's career was irretrievably ruined. Now the fallen man had—amazingly— staged a histrionic come-back, and Grattan felt convinced that he would do *Ben Nazir* full justice. Certainly there was no other English actor whom he would allow to play the part.

Of course, Grattan was not so carried away as to minimize Edmund's moral and physical abasement. He had only to look at him to realize how grossly he had deteriorated even in the last year. "He presented," Grattan wrote, "a mixture of subdued fierceness, unsatisfied triumph and suppressed dissipation."

Grattan called on Edmund one day at the Hummums Hotel; he was ushered into his room by a black boy in livery; and the sight which met his eyes would have been laughable had it not been so nauseating.

Edmund, propped up in bed, was holding court as the Huron Chieftain. He was appropriately dressed in his tribal robes. With one hand he grasped a tomahawk; with the other he was aimlessly engaged in making up his face "for a savage look." A supply of hot white wine (he had temporarily forsworn brandy) stood close beside him within his reach.

By the window, at the far end of the untidy room, an unknown artist, his form partially hidden behind an easel, was painting Alanienouidet's portrait. Two grubby courtiers lounged near Edmund's bed; they were apparently assisting their master to while away the hours by drinking copiously of his liquor.

When Grattan walked in Edmund rolled his eyes, flourished his tomahawk, and then, as if satisfied that these theatrical tactics had produced their effect, shook him warmly and sensibly by the hand. He must have warned his hired artist and his attendant satellites of Grattan's approach, for they soon excused themselves; having drained their tumblers and spouted some extravagant farewell compliments, they took their leave. Edmund and Grattan were left in peace to discuss the pressing business of *Ben Nazir*.

But a little while later their interview was interrupted by the unheralded entrance of two veiled young ladies, who flitted mysteriously through the room. Edmund explained, *sotto voce*, that they were the daughters of a respectable clergyman, and were both madly in love with him. Grattan, however, from the brief glimpse he had of them formed a less flattering opinion of their station in society.

Inevitably Grattan decided that Edmund had "lost all the respectability of private life." He realized, too, that he was suffering from a painful malady. And yet he felt satisfied that his histrionic powers were as great as they had ever been. The critics, in their most recent accounts of his acting, had all said so.

Besides, as an artist Edmund himself still inspired trust. He assured Grattan, with the most disarming confidence, that *Ben Nazir* would be a *succès fou*. He predicted that it would run for a hundred nights. He had decided to spend fifty guineas on a costume of special magnificence—over and above any dress allowance that the Drury Lane management might make him. He had made arrangements for his portrait to be engraved in character. He had ordered his next annual prize wherry to be called *Ben Nazir*. And, apart from these flourishes of enthusiasm, he seemed genuinely determined to work hard at his part. He kept a prompt copy of the play underneath his pillow. And he had already begun to study his lines.

At the end of February Edmund left London to fulfil a series of provincial engagements. He played in Manchester, Dublin, and Edinburgh, and in each of these towns he received ovations no less cordial than those which had greeted him at Drury Lane. In Dublin, however, he appeared one night as Alanienouidet and harangued his audience with a long, lunatic speech. Grattan was slightly alarmed when he read news of this in the Press. It augured ill for *Ben Nazir*.

But at the beginning of May Edmund returned to London apparently invigorated and in a calm, conscientious state of mind. He set Grattan's fears at rest. He took lodgings at Duke Street, Adelphi, and embarked eagerly on a new routine of life which was quiet and sheltered. He renounced alcohol, went to bed every night before eleven o'clock, and shunned low company.

Ben Nazir was put into rehearsal at Drury Lane. It would be produced on May 21st. Edmund was present at the first two rehearsals, when he delighted Grattan with the vigour and intelligence of his reading. He excused himself from attending the remaining rehearsals on the grounds that his fellow actors disturbed his concentration and that he preferred to work in the peace and solitude of his own surroundings. No one objected.

Every morning after breakfast Edmund ordered his carriage and drove in it to Kensington Gardens, where he spent two hours in the shade of the trees studying his part. In the afternoons he sometimes had himself rowed in his wherry on the Thames. He lay comfortably back, the book of *Ben Nazir* in his hands, and spouted away for the benefit of the watermen and the *naiades*.

In the evenings Grattan generally kept him company at Duke Street. Grattan came as a kind of guardian angel. He wanted to make sure that Edmund was not tempted into the night by any of his unwanted guests. He never left him until he was safely in bed. When May 21st arrived at last there was no doubt in Grattan's mind that Edmund had worked hard and undistractedly, although he had refused to attend even the final rehearsal.

But there was, none the less, cause for apprehension. In the morning Grattan went alone to Edmund's lodgings to wish him luck. He found him striding about in his drawing-room, already arrayed in his gorgeous stage costume and declaiming his part with the utmost conviction. He was conducting his own private dress rehearsal. He seemed excited, proud, and brimful of confidence. And he boasted that *Ben Nazir* could not possibly fail.

This was all very assuring. But Grattan noticed with dismay that Edmund still carried a prompt copy of the play in his hands. He spoke his lines magnificently, but not without the aid of the written text.

Grattan did not give up hope. He was nervous when he took his place at the theatre—well hidden from the public view in a small private box near the side of the stage. He had resigned himself to the fact that Kean would be "fluffy" and uncertain; but he felt confident that the actor's experience would pull him through and that his imperfections, however numerous, would not be glaringly obvious to the audience. Although he feared a rough, unpolished performance, he did not think it would be disastrous. There would be time for improvement later. Allowances always had to be made for a first night.

But if Grattan had had the power to see through the curtain at that moment, he would probably have refused to have allowed his play to go on. All Edmund's self-confidence had fallen from him like a loosely girt mantle. He was in his dressing-room weeping his heart out—so nervous and so miserable that he had not the spirit to change his clothes. The curse which strikes most actors down in their old age had hit him cruelly in the prime of life. He was a player who could no longer learn a part. In spite of all his efforts, all his good resolutions, he had failed to make the lines of *Ben Nazir* lodge in his memory.

Day after day, up to the last moment, he had avoided the truth and had tried to beguile himself into thinking "that everything would be all right on the night." But now, when his memory was still barren of any of the words which he should speak, he realized that such miracles do not happen. If he had been unable to say his lines in the quiet and solitude of his own surroundings, how much less able would he be to repeat them in full view of a critical audience! Inevitably he would disgrace himself and ruin the first play of a man to whom he owed much obligation.

Wallack, the stage-manager, finding him thus, suggested that he should ask for a postponement. But Edmund rejected Wallack's advice. A few hours, more or less, what would they avail him? At the moment he felt that even if he worked for a century he would still not know *Ben Nazir*. He would have to face the ordeal sometime—so better now than later. He dried his eyes, put on his make-up, and walked down to the stage in a kind of stupor.

The first two scenes of the play, in which Edmund took no part, had gone off well enough. But in front Grattan was still anxious and uncertain. Success or failure depended entirely on Kean, and Kean had not yet made his entrance.

He did at length appear. He looked extraordinarily impressive in his rich costume of which he had been so proud. The audience cheered him wildly and settled down to enjoy what they supposed would be a fine performance. But Grattan was dumbfounded. He curled up in his seat. He knew now that his worst fears must be fulfilled. Obviously Kean had no notion of what he was about.

"The intention of the author and the keeping of the character," Grattan wrote, "required him to rush rapidly upon the stage, giving utterance to a burst of joyous soliloquy. What was my astonishment to see him, as the scene opened, standing in the centre of the stage, his arms crossed, and his whole attitude one of thoughtful solemnity! . . . He spoke; but what a speech! The one I wrote consisted of eight or nine lines; *his* was of two or three sentences, but not six consecutive words of the text. His look, his manner, his tone, were to *me* quite appalling; to any other observer they must have been incomprehensible. He stood fixed, drawled out his incoherent words, and gave the notion of a man who had been half-hanged and then dragged through a horse-pond. . . ."

As it had begun, so it went on. There was no reprieve. A cold sweat broke out on Grattan's brow, and he experienced a feeling of revulsion of which he was ashamed. But he remained, in his secluded seat, to endure the cumulative agony of fiasco. He watched his play being mutilated, and his reputation as a dramatist being sacrificed on the altar of Kean's "exhaustion and decay."

When the curtain fell on the first act, there was complete silence—"the voiceless verdict of damnation." At the end of the play there was loud booing. Wallack appeared to offer Kean's apologies. But the audience, exasperated by what to them had been an incredibly bad entertainment, wished neither to listen to excuses nor to censure anyone in particular—except the unfortunate author. They shouted abusively at Wallack until he had announced that *Ben Nazir* was withdrawn and that in its place, next Thursday, Kean would play Sir Giles Overreach. Then, illogically enough, they cheered him lustily.

Grattan braced himself to go behind the scenes. He thanked his actors who, in their turn, commiserated with him. He saw Edmund being led off the stage by two dressers, and spoke to him as consolingly as possible. But Edmund was too upset to say much in reply. He merely bowed his head, waved his hand despairingly, and muttered some half-choked, incoherent words of regret.

Next morning the newspaper critics—with few exceptions—were more derogatory of the play than of the acting. *The Times*, for example, while admitting—*en passant*—that Kean was imperfect, reserved its main invective for Grattan. No player—it concluded—could have saved the tragedy of *Ben Nazir* from the fate which it had encountered and had deserved.

But Edmund did not attempt to shelter behind the Press notices. He had already admitted, through Wallack, that he had been responsible for the failure of *Ben Nazir*, and he never tried afterwards to shift the blame on to Grattan, who was his friend. In his own mind there was no escape from the truth. "He had ruined a fine play," and in so doing had disgraced himself. His last hope of retrieving his happiness was gone beyond recall.

A few days later Grattan returned to France, disillusioned and determined that he would have no more concern with the theatre. But before he left he went to bid Edmund farewell. He would never meet him again. He had every reason, of course, to be angry with him, and yet when he saw him, broken and miserable and tragically repentant, he could feel for him nothing but sorrow. He forgot his own grievance in his compassion for the man who had caused it.

It was, after all, impossible for Grattan to recriminate against someone who was obviously helpless and infinitely more injured than he was himself. Grattan had met with a temporary setback. He was disappointed. But before him stretched a life rich and varied.

Edmund, on the other hand, had suffered a crowning blow. Already he had lost home, health, honour, position —the things which, in retrospect, he valued as a man. Now he had been forced to realize that even as an artist he was crippled. For six years he would go on working, fighting, earning, spending, lusting, hating, drinking, regretting, indulging in false pleasures which gave him no joy and seeking peace which persistently eluded him. But all the while he would know in his heart that there was nothing before him save death. He would slither towards it painfully, slowly, and unwillingly. But he would go towards it directly.

CHAPTER X

I

EDMUND was like the captain of a damaged vessel who, in spite of the inevitable end, continually puts out to sea. His estate on the Island of Bute, which he still owned and still cherished, was his harbour. But though he visited it frequently, he never stayed there long. For him there was no hope of permanent retirement. He had to go on working.

He acted feverishly both in London and in the provinces. In pursuit of his calling he still travelled north, south, east and west of the United Kingdom. He wrote to the manager of the Scarborough Theatre, "I shou'd be happy to pay my respects to the residents, it is the only town in his Majesty's dominions that I have never seen . . ."

He had courage and the enterprise which is born of courage. At the beginning of the 1827–8 season, as a result of a quarrel with Stephen Price, he passed over from Drury Lane to Covent Garden. In his dotage, as it were, he broke with the theatre where he had won his fame and whose stage he had dominated for thirteen years. It was a cleavage which must have hurt and frightened him. But he still placed his pride before all other considerations.

Charles Kemble—John Philip's younger brother—who was now in charge of Covent Garden, welcomed Edmund with open arms, not because he liked him, but because he realized that his services would be of incalculable value to the box-office. In spite of his failing powers and his apparent inability to learn a new part, Edmund had no difficulty in getting work and in being paid handsomely for it. He was earning as large an income as always.

At Covent Garden they crowded excitedly to see him, partly because he was in new and strange surroundings, partly because he was pitted against such brilliant rivals as Charles Mayne Young and Charles Kemble himself, but chiefly because it was thought that he was nearing the end of his tempestuous career. At the age of forty he was already history. And he had the glamour and pathos about him that invariably attaches to history which yet lives.

He was still the first English actor. On most nights he could summon enough energy to electrify his audiences and to make his famous characters seem vigorously alive. Only those behind the scenes knew for certain how much of his strength was artificial. Before his entrances he sat in a chair in the wings, his face blotched and puffy and distorted under its make-up, his body bent double with exhaustion. He sipped continually at a glass of brandy and hot water. He called impatiently to his dresser, who hovered near him, for another glass "stronger and hotter." Someone gave him his cue warning. "He looked about, as from a dream, and sighed, and painfully got to his feet, swayed like a column in an earthquake," then gathered himself together, stood erect and walked firmly on to the stage.

But though he seldom disappointed those in front, his attacks of illness were now so frequent and so serious that no one believed that he could last much longer. From the alarming reports of his health, which crept from time to time into the newspapers, it seemed obvious that he was fighting a losing battle with death. Young men who would prattle about his splendour to their grandchildren, and old men who had thrilling memories of his first achievements, wanted to see him again and yet again before it was too late.

He himself encouraged the popular suspicion that his career was approaching its close. He often threatened retirement. And in his speeches he let it be known that he would not bother the world much longer with his presence. And yet, while he posed as a figure of the past, he tried bravely to believe in his own future. Time after time he collapsed, but always recovered amazingly and plunged once more into the fray.

He did not jib at taking on any fresh engagement, however arduous. In May of 1828 he went over to Paris to act for Emile Laurent, who had established a company of English players at the Odéon Theatre. He opened a two months' season on May 12th, and one may judge how busy he had been before then by this letter which he had written to Laurent in January: "I am sorry you did not apprise me of your wishes previous to your departure from London, as I shou'd then have made any sacrifices on my part to have complied with them, it is now not in my power as I have made theatrical engagements in Yorkshire which will fill up my time till the seventh of May. . . . A word once given cannot be in honour revoked . . ."

The French playgoers did not give Edmund a very heartening reception. In April they had been swept off their feet by Macready, and now they found Kean unexciting by comparison.

Of course, they expected too much of him. They knew him only by his tremendous reputation and made no allowances for his weakness and fatigue. Though he had been well heralded in their Press, they had never seen him before and were not hypnotized by any lingering memories of his former glories. They were inevitably disappointed in him, because they judged him unsentimentally and strictly on his own merits. They were dazzled by his occasional flashes, but on the whole they decided that his light flickered feebly beside the brilliant star of Macready.

Edmund returned to England at the end of June, moody and disgruntled. He had hoped to win fresh laurels in Paris, and instead he had been engulfed in the aftermath of another's triumph. It was unwholesome medicine for a dying man.

Throughout the summer he went on fulfilling provincial engagements. But he had decided that he was in need of a long rest. On August 27th he wrote from Liverpool to the Covent Garden manager:

"I wrote you from Southampton, requesting you to

favour me with a line at Liverpool, this is more than a month since, I stated, that the longer leave of absence you allowed me, the more I shou'd feel obliged. I play here till Monday next, & intended then to put my helm towards the Isle of Bute, if you & the Winds permit. I beg you therefore to let me have my orders instanta, & I shall implicitly obey command."

He spent September in Bute, and did not reappear at Covent Garden until October 13th. But by then his health was so far improved that he was able to carry on for nearly three months without a breakdown, which was now a considerable achievement for him.

He was, of course, by no means well. The quality of his performances varied from night to night, according to his physical condition, as one may gather from reading the criticisms in any contemporary periodical. For example, one finds in the *Theatre* that his Richard on October 13th was "very tame and unimpressive." His pauses were often misplaced through breathlessness. However, on October 16th his Shylock was so bold and vivid that criticism was disarmed and plunged into verse:

> What ere thine errors, Kean, what ere thy shame,
> We cannot part with thee, we cannot cease,
> To own thy worth: enjoy thy well-earned fame,
> And may that fame still with the years increase!
> Thou art the Sun's bright child—then pause, and let
> Prudence direct thee, for thy sun must set!

But even this mood of ecstasy was impermanent. On October 30th his Othello was pronounced to be "sinking gradually into a premature debility both of body and mind."

And yet he was doing his best to merit the public's applause and the gratitude of his new employers. From November 17th to December 3rd Covent Garden had to be closed down on account of a gas explosion, and the company played during the interim at the English Opera House. In the circumstances of financial loss, which was the

inevitable consequence of such a move, Edmund refused
to accept more than half his salary.

He gave an even better proof of his devotion to duty
when he agreed to attempt a new character. He chose the
name part in Sheridan Knowles' *Virginius*—a play which
had originally been intended for him but which, through
lack of foresight, he had allowed Macready to produce. In
spite of his experience of only a year ago, in spite of his
inner knowledge that his memory was irreparably impaired,
he embarked on the perilous task of learning lines which he
had never spoken before and which had already been made
famous by his foremost rival.

And by some freakish, superhuman exertion of his will
as an artist, he succeeded. It cost him days of anguish,
anxiety and despair, but in the end he knew his part. On
December 15th—after repeated announcements and with-
drawings on the bills—he appeared as Virginius.

He created little sensation in the character. Criticism, on
the whole, thought him inferior to Macready. "His parting
with the child was exquisitely played, and in the more
subdued parts he was eminently successful. But when
Virginius is made a slave, rage appeared more the frothy
ebullitions of a choleric man than the terrible indignation
of a noble Roman. His physical powers are unable to
execute his design. In all scenes requiring great exertions
he became exhausted . . ."

No doubt his performance had the sad blemishes of his
own weakness. And yet it was an heroic effort, and deserved
more generous recognition and wider testimony than the
handsome tortoiseshell snuff-box, lined with gold, which
was presented to him after the final rehearsal "as a trifling
but cordial acknowledgment of his most valuable assistance
and most liberal conduct . . . by his brother performers."

The strain of learning *Virginius* heralded another collapse.
On January 12th Edmund was taken ill in his dressing-
room immediately before a performance of *Richard II* and
had to return to bed. A few weeks later he left London for

the avowed purpose of enjoying a protracted convalescence at Bute. Kemble had agreed that he should not reappear at Covent Garden until the season after next; and that in the meantime he should employ his months of leisure in rebuilding his strength and in studying several new parts. Kemble was not sorry to be rid of him. He wrote him a kind, fatherly letter speeding his departure. After all, a failing, doddering Kean, virtually incapable of producing anything new, would soon cease to be much of an asset. From Kemble's point of view the arrangement that he should stay away for a year or more was altogether admirable. For it meant that, while Kemble was spared a large salary, he was also secure from Kean's rivalry at Drury Lane. And if and when the first English actor came back Covent Garden would profit from the wave of public interest in him which would inevitably arise.

Edmund always welcomed the chance of going to Bute, and pined for his "paradise" while he was away from it. A year ago he had written to Dan M'Corkindale:

". . . You will oblige me therefore by acting as my agent during the interval of absence, & direct Reid to let me find the grounds on my return precisely as I have been accustomed to see them. I do not understand gardening technicalities, but they always looked very beautiful, and beautiful I wish them to remain. My health is very fast improving & the public favour greatly increasing, and yet I do not know how it is, amidst the blaze of popularity that is the natural attendant upon the favourites of caprice, I cannot help envying the poorest peasant that doffs his cap to the visitor of Rothsay—however, if the world & my profession prevents my living there, it remains with myself the power of dying there, & even that I look forward to with gratification. . . ."

At Bute Edmund sought happiness in a world of make-believe which he had fashioned from the paradoxes of his own nature. He glorified the past and planned for the future and pretended that the present was not fleeting. He revealed all his conflicting faults and virtues—his generosity and extravagance, his simplicity and his love of display, his craving for solitude and his plungings into dissipation.

Since his return from America he had lavished a small fortune on improving his property. He had had a road built through the woods, so that he could now drive from Rothesay to his front gates in his own coach. The local workmen had warned him beforehand that the road would cost him a great deal of money. But he had replied confidently that he would earn enough to pay for it from a three nights' engagement at Glasgow. Above the gates he had placed four busts—one of Shakespeare, one of Massinger, one of Garrick, and one of himself. When the moon showed up their whiteness after dark they looked like spectres and frightened the peasants. On the night that they had been unveiled Edmund had given a firework display, and had invited half the inhabitants of Rothesay to attend it.

He had papered the walls of his drawing-room with an expensive wall-paper which had been specially designed for him in Paris and which depicted scenes from his famous plays. In his wardrobe he kept a supply of stage costumes. Sometimes he would wander about his grounds dressed up as Richard or Overreach. More often he would appear in the kilt or in a loud tartan suit.

He pictured himself, through a fog of tinsel, as a great Lord living in retirement. He had had a moss house built for him on a mound which was sheltered by the trees. He used to sit in it for hours on end and gaze down on Sweet Loch Fad and on the country behind. Above the entrance to his moss house these words were inscribed:

'Tis Glorious
Through the loopholes
of
Retreat
To Peep at such a world.

And beneath the inscription was placed his "coat of arms"!

When he spent his birthday at Woodend (as he did in
1829) he would order a blunderbuss to be fired in the
morning as a kind of royal salute. In the evening he would
give a dinner-party to his notable acquaintances from
Rothesay.

He entertained on a lavish scale. But he was a surprising
host. Before the meal ended he would invariably find some
pretext to rush from the room, and would return a few
minutes later through another door, having changed into
fancy dress. Then he would embark on a song or a recitation, and would expect his guests to applaud him effusively.

But in spite of these curious displays, so alien to his
surroundings, he was by no means unpopular with the
natives of the island. He was in the first place free and easy
with his money; and a wonderful patron to local labour
and local trade. John Duncan the draper, Nanny Lochley
the butcher, and the Old Mill Shop where he bought his
groceries, were all very thankful for his custom. And with
his extensive building operations he put a deal of work in
the way of Robert Orkney the mason, and Archibald
Mackirdy the joiner, and John Crawfurd the handyman.
He paid handsomely for it, too. There was nothing mean
about him.

His servants on the estate—born and bred in Bute—were
devoted to him. And though they were convinced that he
was fabulously rich, he did not have to buy their respect.
They had an instinctive understanding of his true qualities.
They were mystified, of course, by his eccentricities. But
they were drawn to him because of his generosity and
modesty and simplicity and his gay love of their own
country.

John Reid the gardener lived with his family in the lodge
by the front gates. He had a daughter, who was a small
child at the time, but who later became Mrs. M'Fie and
who was still alive at the beginning of the present century.
She had the most charming recollections of Edmund.
"I min' Kean liked a wee drap," she said, "and he always

came into the lodge for it every time he passed out or in the gate. He had a press there to keep it in, but he would never take it unless my mother was there to give it to him. Any time we saw him coming along we would run and tell my mother 'There's Mr. Kean coming,' and she always had it ready for him."

Edmund gave her a pony, so that she could ride in and out of Rothesay by herself. And once he gave her and her mother tickets for a performance of his Richard III at Glasgow. Some time afterwards he asked her whether she had enjoyed it. As she had not recognized him in his make-up she remarked naïvely that "Richard was a very ugly man." Edmund laughed delightedly at this. "Ah," said Mrs. M'Fie, "Kean was a very kind man and very charitable to all around him."

He liked to be with children, perhaps because he had himself a child's inquisitiveness about animals and flowers and all the other things in Nature which he did not understand. He used to be seen carrying Bailie Muir's son on his back, or walking about his grounds with Sandy Nisbet the herdboy by his side. (He called him the "cow boy.") Sandy Nisbet, like Mrs. M'Fie, lived to be an octogenarian, and he too had his tender memories of Edmund.

"He was very fond of hearing me speaking Gaelic," said Sandy. "He always carried a bottle containing wine or red stuff, and plenty of bread and cheese. One day, when taking lunch outside, there were some sheep feeding about, a black sheep being among the flock. 'Do you know, Sandy,' he asked me, 'why black sheep do not eat as much grass as white ones?' 'Well, I don't know, sir,' I replied, 'unless it is because there are not so many black sheep as white ones.'" For this information Edmund gave Sandy half a sovereign. And he gave him a whole sovereign when he learned that his mother could speak nothing but Gaelic!

Sandy also said of Edmund: "He was always very fond of sitting at a big oak near a burn that comes down from the Glen at Woodend. He would be looking at some little trout in the burn, and one day he said to John Reid that if he died in Scotland he would like to be buried beside that tree."

Edmund dropped all his pretence when he was with children—he had a touching respect for their innocence, and expected others to respect it too. Once he caught his coachman, whose name was William Bedlam, amusing himself by shooting a bonnet off Sandy's head. He flew into a temper and snatched the pistol from Bedlam's hand. "If it wasn't for your wife and small family," he shouted dramatically, "you would never handle a rein for me again." "He was a drunken devil that coachman," said Sandy, "but Kean would never say a word to him for that."

Neither Sandy Nisbet nor Mrs. M'Fie had much to tell of the life which Edmund led inside his house. That was largely hidden from them. Sandy said that Edmund had little regard for the Sabbath—that he stayed in bed till the late afternoon, and then went fishing on the loch. Mrs. M'Fie remembered that after his return from America he used to come to Bute with a woman who was not his wife— "an awfu' bonny woman." Mrs. M'Fie knew her as Ophelia Lemans.

Her real name was Ophelia Benjamin. By nationality she was an Irish Jewess. According to one account she was the daughter of a tailor and a prostitute, the sister of a professional bruiser. She was certainly a hardened strumpet herself.

Edmund called her officially Mrs. Kean. It is likely that he had first taken her to live with him shortly after the failure of *Ben Nazir*—in the summer of 1827. About that time he had written to his tailor: "I forgot this morning to tell you, my wife wants a plaid silk coat. Send it with mine on Monday. *Oh, these women are damned plagues.*"

Ophelia was a "plague" in every sense of the word. She was young, vigorous, strong, unscrupulous, and frequently tipsy. She had no affection and no respect for her invalid lover. She regarded him as a weak-willed, doddering, profligate old fool, who was crazy for her well-used body; and she treated him accordingly. She was abusively rude to him. She humiliated him in public. When she could not get her own way by any other means, she was not above resorting to physical violence. One celebrated instance of this was immortalized in these lines. (They describe how a party of Edmund's was broken up through Ophelia's intervention.)

> The lesser tribe of low buffoons,
> And high-flown tragic ranters,
> Had plenteous showers of knives and spoons,
> And volleys of decanters.
>
> I'll pull the house about the ears
> Of each belligerent Tyke,
> And, like the sun, let fall (she cry'd)
> My beams on all alike.
>
> Full late the pair retired to sup;
> For after several rounds,
> Inglorious Richard gave it up,
> And gave her fifty pounds.

Ophelia had added a hundredfold to Edmund's loneliness and degradation. She had virtually isolated him from the love and companionship for which in his heart he yearned. Most men, of course, avoided his society in any case; and inevitably Charles Kemble politely refused an invitation to Bute, in spite of the warmth with which it had been extended. But even his oldest friends were deserting him because they could not tolerate his offensively unamiable mistress. Ophelia had cost him the devotion of his little clique of followers. She had even cost him the respect of his son.

Charles was now a young man of eighteen, and was on the stage. He was still under Mary's influence. As an Eton schoolboy—two years ago—he had angered his father by declining a cadetship in the East India Company which Edmund had found for him. He had said that he would not go to India unless his father would agree to increase his mother's allowance by £100 per annum. At this Edmund had lost his temper and had told Charles that henceforth he could expect no more help from him and would have to find his own way in the world.

Of course, Edmund was severely blamed for behaving so callously towards his son. But from his point of view, why should he have allowed Mary to use Charles as a weapon with which to blackmail him? She was being paid her allowance regularly: it was small, but it was enough and as much as she deserved. Certainly she had the most extravagant ideas about her just claims on Edmund's purse. In August of 1829 Tom Moore called on her to ask her some questions about Byron and Kean. "In talking of the circumstances of Kean's first appearance in London," Moore remembered, "I said that some memorial of it ought to be preserved; on which she exclaimed eagerly: 'Oh, will you write his life? You shall have all the profits if you'll only give me a little.' "

In due course Charles became an actor. He began at the top. Simultaneously with Edmund's breakaway to Covent Garden, Charles made his début at Drury Lane as Young Norval in *Douglas*.

It was a stunt, of course, engineered by Stephen Price; and deservedly it failed. The boy Kean had had no training, and he was possessed of very little natural talent. The critics handled him roughly, and the public soon lost their interest in him, for it had been artificially aroused.

After a few weeks' experience of failure Charles realized that, in spite of his mother's blandishments, he was not yet fit to face a London audience. He went into the provinces, courageously so it has been said by his biographers. But he went to learn his job, as every actor and every craftsman must. And even so he never had to endure the hardships which his father had suffered before him. Edmund allowed his son to fend for himself, but he gave him a fine education, and—more important—he gave him the name of Kean. From the beginning Charles played leading parts in big theatres, and he was paid considerably more than a starvation wage.

Father and son were not permanently estranged. By the summer of 1828 they had composed their differences, and in September they actually played together at the Glasgow Theatre. Edmund was incapable of bearing malice towards his own kith, and though he had never wished his son to become an actor, he was now possessively proud of him. Charles Kean! The name looked well on the bills.

Charles, for his part, was not above profiting from his father's histrionic experience and advice. But he remained none the less his mother's child. He was a born prig. He had been spoiled and pampered. He would grow into a vain and pompous man. He was righteous and devout. He would lead a model life. He would earn and save money. He was persevering. He would become a leader in his profession and would have a good influence on the theatre. He would be honoured by a host of distinguished acquaintances. He would avoid all his father's failings and would suffer none of his father's misery. But he would never be lighted up by a spark of his father's genius.

His attitude to Edmund even now was more parental than filial. He treated him as the brilliant black sheep of the family. According to newspaper report, he visited him at Bute during the summer of 1828. He did, it is true, go to Bute. But he did not enter Woodend House. He stayed at the lodge with the Reids. Out of loyalty to his mother, he refused to sleep under the same roof as Ophelia Benjamin.

Loyalty to his father might have prompted him to take a more drastic course. For Ophelia was hurting Edmund far more than she could ever hope to injure Mary. She was robbing him of life itself. She was driving him to such feats of extravagance that he could not possibly enjoy the rest that was essential for his health's sake. She was digging her spurs into an old war horse, making him gallop after gold who had not really the strength to walk.

The year's peaceful convalescence in his "Paradise"—to

recuperate and to study new parts—which Edmund had promised himself at the beginning of 1829 was woefully upset. During April and May he was in Ireland fulfilling provincial engagements, or at least attempting to do so. Most of his time was spent in recovering from a series of dangerous collapses. At the beginning of June he returned to Bute—"still miserably ill"; and then another crushing disaster overtook him. He lost the services of his secretary Phillips, who for fifteen years had looked after his business interests.

Ophelia was naturally the cause of the trouble. Apparently Phillips protested to her about her wanton disregard for economy. She answered his complaint by insulting him so monstrously that he decided he could not stay another minute in Edmund's employ. From Rothesay he wrote to Edmund explaining the circumstances of his hurried departure and regretfully announcing his resignation. Edmund sent him this reply:

> DEAR PHILLIPS,
> I am shocked but not Surprised. in error I was born in error I have lived in error I shall die, that a *gentleman* should be insulted under my roof, creates a blush that I shall carry to my grave, and that you are so in every sense of the word is unquestionable. from Education, Habit, and manners. it is too true that I have fostered a worm till it has become a viper but my guilt is on my head, farewell . . .

Edmund despised Ophelia, yet he was her slave. He wanted to be rid of her, yet in his decay could not do without her. He was bound by the shackles of his own physical desires. And he had resigned himself to his fate.

Phillips had left, and Edmund was powerless to do the one thing which would bring him back. Not long afterwards he wrote these lines to the "viper":

> I break your slumber, sweet but pray forgive
> For you alone my love I wish to live.

2

In August of 1829 Charles Kemble faced bankruptcy. During the six years that he had had control of Covent Garden (he had taken possession from Thomas Harris in 1822) he had accumulated a debt of £22,000. Now the rate collectors threatened to distrain upon his property and to sell his theatre without his permission.

The sympathy of the whole profession went out to him in his distress. Several distinguished players offered to appear for him without pay during the coming season. Edmund was among them. He wrote from Bute to say that in spite of his precarious health he would come to London and would give three gratuitous performances.

But when he arrived to fulfil his promise at the beginning of November, he was not accorded a very enthusiastic welcome by the Covent Garden management. It was made plain to him that his services were no longer urgently required. Charles Kemble was out of danger, and was heading towards a new prosperity. He had been saved from bankruptcy in a full-blooded, dramatic fashion by his eighteen-year-old daughter, Fanny. She had made a sensational stage début as Juliet on October 5th, and was now the idol of the town. Three times a week she was impersonating the heroines of tragedy and was drawing huge, excited, adoring crowds to Covent Garden.

She was not, for several reasons, within measurable distance of being a great actress. She had had no proper training and had never suffered for her art. She was unambitious and even out of love with her calling. On her own admission, the theatre—"from the preparations behind the scenes to the representations before the curtain"—was repugnant to her. "My task seems so useless," she wrote, "that, but for the very useful pecuniary results, I think I would rather make shoes."

And yet her triumph is easily understandable. The mere announcement that Fanny Kemble—the niece of Mrs.

Siddons and of the great John Philip—was coming from
the nursery, as it were, to rescue her harassed father from
the threats of angry creditors, struck deep into the hearts
of the British public. On the night of October 5th she sat
in her strange dressing-room, surrounded by anxious relatives, clutching her hands convulsively together and weeping
large, heavy tears which washed away her make-up. But
she need have had no fear. The battle was already won. In
front, a vast audience were waiting impatiently for her
entrance. They were longing to applaud her. They cheered
her wildly when she appeared at last, looking so fresh and
innocent and timid. They went mad about her when they
found that her voice was clear and that some of her
mannerisms were reminiscent of her Aunt Sarah.

It was not the time for dispassionate judgment. In
many scenes Fanny Kemble was stilted and artificial and
obviously "taught." But none cared. She was irresistible.
Next morning the critics, overcome by their softer
emotions, mistook Fanny Kemble's brave sweetness for
genius.

Leigh Hunt, who saw her a few weeks later, was proof
against her immature charms. "We doubt not from that
ingenuous face of hers," he wrote in the *Tatler*, "that she
is a very nice girl and we think that she has very cleverly
seized what has been taught her. But we see nothing in
her at present, that we should not expect to find in twenty
others."

Leigh Hunt was the first of the great critics. A quarter
of a century ago he had stood out alone against the Master
Betty hysteria. But now as then he was a solitary exponent
of reason. The Fanny Kemble boom was on.

And Edmund Kean was expected to support it. He wrote,
on November 19th, to Bartley, stage-manager at Covent
Garden, "I am very unwell . . . the fatigue of travelling
such an immense distance, has nearly overcome me, &
nothing but the *cause*, the *cause* my soul cou'd reconcile me
to the exertion. Numerous engagements are pouring in

upon me, & I shou'd like to get rid of the three nights as fast as I conveniently can—what say you to next Monday, Wednesday Friday & give the management to understand that I play on no other nights but those I have been accustomed to in both the London theatres."

He sent that letter as a challenge and he knew what answer to expect, for the stage has little sense of the courtesy which is owed to age and experience. He was duly informed by Bartley that Mondays, Wednesdays, and Fridays were engaged for Miss Kemble's appearances. He would, therefore, have to make his arrangements accordingly, though in regard to any other matter the management were anxious to accommodate him.

Bartley's reply was politely phrased, but its implication was none the less obvious, and Edmund could not tolerate it. He had already made up his mind that nothing would induce him to take second place to Fanny Kemble by playing on the "off" nights; and now he decided that he must leave Covent Garden altogether. He would go back to Drury Lane, where he was really wanted. Drury Lane had been faring very badly since his defection two years ago, and by making his reappearance there he would help to restore the fortunes of the theatre "which had first fostered his talents." He would also be unchallengeably the star attraction. Without deigning another word to Bartley, he entered into a new contract with Stephen Price.

The inevitable row followed. Charles Kemble, in his anger, invoked the agreement signed last January, and tried to injunct Edmund from performing anywhere in London. His action failed, as it happened, but he publicized it well and he succeeded in enlisting the vigorous sympathies of a section of the Press. The old cry was taken up once again. Kean was petty and vain and jealous. In his unpardonable arrogance he had stooped to insulting the defenceless Fanny Kemble.

The charges, as usual, seemed well founded. They were proved, in fact, by Edmund's own letter to Bartley. And yet, for once, the furore in the newspapers failed to arouse the public's indignation.

Perhaps it was realized that Edmund, in spite of his lack of magnanimity, had at least some right on his side. Magnanimity is a precious virtue, but it requires the strength and confidence of which Edmund was so sadly in need. He was tired and sick; he was still struggling to keep his position in the theatre against overwhelming odds; and before he had attained it he had already shown an infinite capacity for suffering. Was it not a little hard to expect him suddenly to play second fiddle to a prim and proper girl who had neither fought nor yet been hurt? When he reappeared at Drury Lane as Richard on December 2nd, he was given a grand reception. And did he not deserve it?

Audiences were, in any case, beginning to treat him more tolerantly than of old. Even when he exasperated them, they tried to curb their anger. No doubt they understood that a man so lacerated as he could not bear the infliction of many more wounds. And he was, after all, a treasured thing. They did not want him to die.

Throughout December and January he played at Drury Lane to packed houses. Sometimes he was apparently ill, and his performances were very disappointing. But, in front, they sat patiently, hoping against hope, that his feebleness in the early scenes merely meant that he was "husbanding his strength" for a terrific effort later on. They who had once consigned him to damnation were now satisfied by a few, brief glimpses of his true genius.

His failures to rise above his physical weakness were becoming more frequent; and he was himself mortified by them. At the beginning of February he wrote to Dunn, the Drury Lane treasurer: "I am almost ashamed to ask for payment for so feeble a performance as my last Richard, nor would I but for Doctor's bills—for Lancets & Boluses—however I hope all will soon be better than ever, these little casualties of nature teach us to be cautious."

And yet it was not only for money that he acted. "The

spark of ambition" still burned. While the doctors bled
him and dosed him in order to keep life in his body, he
was again attempting to learn a new part. He was going
to impersonate Shakespeare's King Henry V. Rehearsals
at Drury Lane had already started, and the management
were planning an elaborate, expensive production.

The announcement caused great excitement, and they
were all there to see him on the night of March 8, 1830
—the critics, the connoisseurs, and the eager throng in the
pit. They were restive; for already the play had been once
postponed at the last moment and now it was very late in
starting. Three times the orchestra had repeated the over-
ture, but the curtain still remained obstinately down. Was
Kean ill again? Or was he drunk? Or was he being coaxed
on to the stage against his will?

He looked well enough when they saw him at last,
dressed in a magnificently regal costume of purple and
crimson and gold, seated on a throne, with his courtiers
around him. But as soon as they had finished applauding
him and were silent, he revealed himself as a mere dummy
decked out as an actor. His very fineries added to his tragic
absurdity. He did not know his words.

He spoke a few lines haltingly and waited for a prompt;
then echoed the prompter's voice and stopped again. He
floundered, gagged, cut, transposed, and made his part
quite meaningless and ineffective.

It was like *Ben Nazir*; only, unlike *Ben Nazir*, the play
was by Shakespeare, not by Grattan. This time the audience
had no doubt as to who was the real culprit. For two acts
they endured the travesty, hoping in vain that Kean would
recover his faculties; and then their patience snapped. The
tumult and the shouting began.

Midway through the fifth act Edmund tried to quell the
row by a humble appeal for mercy. He removed his royal
hat and walked towards the footlights. "I have worked
hard, ladies and gentlemen, for your amusement," he said,
"but time and other circumstances must plead my apology.

I stand here in the most degraded situation, and call upon you as my countrymen to show your usual liberality."

A few members of the audience cheered him. But the majority, who had wasted their shillings, were for the moment too annoyed and too disgusted to be moved by pity or sentiment. They interrupted his speech brutally. "Why do you get drunk?" they yelled. They continued to hiss him until the curtain had come down upon his first and last performance of King Henry V.

When Edmund left the theatre that night he feared that his career was smashed. The humiliation of failure was bad enough in itself, but worse—far worse—was the memory of those angry howls from the audience. Of course, he would never again attempt to learn a new part. But would the matter end there? Would he even be allowed to play his famous characters in peace? He had been made to pay so heavy a price for his sins in the past that he lived in terror now of the public's vengeance. Perhaps he would be booed on his next appearance; and if so he would have to retire from the stage, for he knew that he could not bear to face another persecution. He would rather end his life as he had begun it—by picking up pennies in barns and fairgrounds.

He sent an appeal to *The Times*: ". . . want of memory is not want of heart, and while a pulsation is left it beats with gratitude and affection to that public who brought me from obscurity into a light I never dreamt of, and it over-powered me. I find too late that I must rest on my former favours. My heart is willing, but my memory is flown. All that I have done I can and will; what is to do I leave to a rising generation. Kindness and urbanity will remember how long and zealously I have made my grateful bow to the British public, living on their smiles, destroyed by their censure, both of which I have comparatively deserved. Let me once more have to say that the old spoiled favourite is forgiven; let me once more pursue that path which led me to your favour, and die in grateful recollection of the debt

I owe to a sympathizing though sometimes an unjustly angry public."

At the same time he wrote to W. H. Halpin, editor of the *Star*: "Fight for me, I have no resources in myself; mind is gone, and body is hopeless. God knows my heart. I would do, but cannot. Memory, the first of goddesses, has forsaken me, and I am left without a hope but from those old resources that the public and myself are tired of. Damn, God damn ambition. The soul leaps, the body falls."

But Edmund was always a bad judge of popular feeling. The days when he required apologists were over. Humility would have saved him much agony in the past; but now his own lamentable state was all the protection which he needed against excessive punishment. When he made his entrance as Richard on March 15th "his frame was almost convulsed, and perspiration rolled down his cheeks": but he never heard the hisses which he dreaded. Instead "he experienced a kind reception." The pit rose up and cheered him. And in the boxes they clapped condescendingly. What else could they do? They shrank from breaking the nerve of an actor who was still capable of giving them intense pleasure. And in common humanity they could not harbour a grudge against a man who was so obviously helpless.

He pulled himself together and gave one of his best performances. With the line "Richard's himself again" he brought the house down. The audience did not really think that it was true, but they hoped that it might be. And so they shouted out their applause. They were as much moved as he. He was their wayward lover, and though they had often treated him heartlessly in the past they clung to him desperately now, because they were in danger of losing him for ever.

A few days later Edmund wrote almost buoyantly to Halpin, "I am reinstated in all my dignities and privileges." He meant, of course, that his worst fears had not been realized; that he had been spared the horror of another persecution; and that, in his world of precarious values, he was at least secure in the knowledge that he would never have to go a-begging for his bread.

But his relief, though great at first, was not a permanent cause for joy. From the beginning it had been his tragedy that he could not accept a limit to his own achievements; and now, both as an artist and as a man, he rebelled hopelessly against his incapacities. His body ached, and his mind was failing. But his "soul still leaped." Ambition would not be God damned.

He knew that it was impossible for him to learn a new part. And yet he could not resign himself to the prospect of "resting on his former favours." In spite of his protests to the contrary, that was not his way; it never had been. His feelings were as intense, as impulsive, as emotional as always. They fought against his ailments for expression. He submerged them with brandy, but they came to the surface again and drove him on. There must be something he could do which would be fresh and startling.

In March, Stephen Price resigned the lesseeship of Drury Lane. He had found out that it was impossible to make the theatre pay. He had tried his hardest. He had cut salaries, had reduced the cost of tickets, and had been dubbed Stephen *Half Price* (which proves that even the most esoteric stage jokes are never new). But the days of the Patent Houses were numbered. Soon they would lose their legal protection and their national status. Already the minor theatres were beginning to encroach upon their monopoly with impunity. The way was being paved for the polite, intimate school of acting.

Edmund at once applied for the place left vacant by Stephen Price. But, of course, he was refused. The Drury Lane committee preferred the claims of Alexander Lee, a man of no particular distinction in the world of the theatre.

Edmund was again baulked from attaining the important post which he still coveted. So in June he stimulated popular excitement by announcing that he would close his professional career after a last grand, remunerative tour of the United States. From June 16th to July 12th he gave a series of farewell performances at the Haymarket, which were naturally well attended. On July 19th he moved a few doors down the road to the more spacious King's Theatre for the purpose of making what was supposed to be his final appearance before a London audience.

That night no one could have doubted his magnetism. An hour before the curtain went up every inch of space in the vast auditorium was filled by a huge crowd who had already experienced a surfeit of waiting in the sultry heat outside the closed doors of the playhouse. Those who had seats breathed foul air and listened to the angry shouts of men and the piercing shrieks of women. But they were fortunate even if they were uncomfortable. At least they were envied by others who stood, closely packed together, in the lobbies, on the stairs, in the orchestra pit, and even in the wings of the stage itself: £1,370 had been taken at the box-office—a figure which must still be something like a record in spite of the increased prices of theatre tickets.

Edmund fully exploited the drama of the occasion. He had specially engaged a glittering cast of actors to support him and to do him honour. He did not impersonate just one character, but appeared in scenes from five of his famous plays. He was first discovered dressed as Richard III and mounted high up on a throne. He arose and bowed in acknowledgment of the applause which greeted him. Then he began to act his part.

For three hours and more he held his suffocated audience under his spell. He gave them something to remember of his Richard, his Shylock, his Othello, his Overreach and his Macbeth. They noticed that as time went on he became increasingly exhausted; that in Overreach he was feeble, and forgetful even in Macbeth. But they did not care. They grasped frantically at the points which were as fine as always, and merely regretted the lapses.

At the end there were scenes of wild, emotional enthusiasm. The stage was drowned in flowers, and the cheering thundered so long and so loudly that it was minutes before Edmund could speak. That was the moment for which he had been waiting, the climax of his evening.

"Ladies and Gentlemen," he said, "I hope that none of you can understand the . . . acute suffering I endure now that I am about to quit the country that has given me birth, and the people whom I have adored, to visit a land where perhaps nothing but ill-health and sorrow await me. I feel it quite impossible to express my gratitude for the constant ebullitions of your approbation which you have this night and always bestowed upon me. For the favour and popularity I have always enjoyed, the fact of performing in one night all my favourite characters was the best, the only return my gratitude could make. I will not particularly allude to past or to future events, but now that I am about to leave you for ever, most earnestly from my heart I entreat that you will suffer no empirics to usurp the dramatic throne, to the ruin and disgrace of the drama. I must and will venture to assert that the well-being of the stage is of the utmost consequence to a nation's morality. . . . Ladies and gentlemen, the time has now arrived for me to return you all my most fervent thanks, and to bid you a long, a last farewell." He bowed repeatedly and slowly disappeared from sight. The audience remained a little while, cheering an empty stage; and then in their turn solemnly left the theatre.

But it was all so much pathetic make-believe—the advertised intent, the carefully prepared speech, the sorrowful departure. How could Edmund, who had saved nothing from his huge earnings, ever hope to retire? And how could he, who scarcely had the strength to walk across the stage, brave the risks of a further adventure on the other side of the Atlantic Ocean?

Perhaps in his desire to test the heart of the British public he had deceived himself. Perhaps he really did believe that he would go to America, that he would accumulate a vast fortune there, and would eventually return to his

own country rich and independent. But the events of the
next few months served to awaken him from his dream.
They proved to him that in the United States he might
meet, not merely "sorrow and ill-fortune," but death. He
was afraid to die, especially in a strange land where he
would be far away from those few who were still dear to
him.

He spent the summer, according to plan, bidding "good-
bye" to his provincial audiences. He played in Brighton,
Liverpool, Norwich, Yarmouth, Cheltenham, Peterborough,
and Manchester. But his tour was hardly triumphant. It
was painfully arrested by frequent bouts of illness. In
Manchester, according to the *Theatrical Observer*, "he had
a most dreadful attack of 'purulent ophthalmia.' " He dared
not entrust his case to a local physician, so he sent for
Mr. Douchez, one of his London doctors. Douchez found
him "acting Richard so blind as not to be able to distinguish
Lady Anne from his 'Cousin of Buckingham' except by
'their sweet voices.' " And this was the gallant warrior who
had wanted to reconquer the American public!

In October he went to Bute for a short rest. He did not
guess then that he was spending his last holiday in his
island paradise, but he must have known that he would
never live there in retirement. His idea of a farewell visit
to the United States had already receded beyond the bounds
of possibility; and now he was uncertain whether he even
wished to retire. He was so lonely that there was no joy in
his heart and very little will to be alive except that which
was induced by his fear of the unknown. Ophelia had
deprived him of friends and of the money with which he
should have purchased peace. Now she, in her turn, had
deserted him. He hated her with the hatred of an ill-used
lover, yet still desired her passionately. To her he attributed
his misery, yet was miserable without her. He felt that if
he did not go on working he would fall down dead. But he
could not work without the aid of those artificial stimulants
which were eating away the last vestiges of his stregnth.

He left Bute after Christmas to fulfil engagements in
Bath, and later in Hull. In January he returned to London,
and on the last day of the month reappeared at Drury Lane
as Richard.

The newspapers, of course, could not resist printing
some jibes at his expense, and hastened to make fun, in
retrospect, of all the meaningless fuss which had attended
his "farewell" performance. But the public were delighted
to have him back again. Leigh Hunt, who reviewed his
Richard in the *Tatler*, stated that he was infinitely the
greatest actor "he ever saw," that he still reigned Lord
Paramount, and that he was as far ahead of Macready as
Macready was superior to the rest of contemporary tragedians. Of course, there were moments when he grasped
his sceptre with less firmness than of old. In the tent scene,
for instance, where he started up from his horrid dream,
he made such a feeble business of the rush forward (or
coming rather) that the house seemed inclined to be angry
with it. "But how fine he is, when he *is* fine!" wrote Leigh
Hunt. "How true! how full of gusto! how intense! What
a perfect amalgamation there is of the most thorough
feeling, and the most graceful idealism! The first four lines
which Richard utters on coming on—

> Now is the winter of our discontent, etc.

were as beautifully delivered as they ever could have been,
especially the last—

> And all the clouds that lower'd upon our house
> In the deep bosom of the Ocean buried.

"Kean, in speaking this last line, held forth his arm, and
in a beautiful style of deliberate triumph, uttering his words
with inward majesty, pointed his finger downwards; as if
he saw the very ocean beneath him from some promontory,
and beheld it closed over the past."

"We could not help persuading ourselves," Leigh Hunt

added, "that Mr. Kean might recover all that he wanted.
There is nothing in his time of life to hinder it."

Edmund was, in fact, forty-two years old. But there
were many sad reasons why he could not retrieve the past.
Leigh Hunt hit on one of them a few months later. He
noticed that while the playgoers in the pit applauded Kean
unstintingly, the people of quality in the boxes seemed
loath to display even the mildest enthusiasm. They behaved
as if they had been dragged to the theatre against their will
—by some magnetic power which, in spite of themselves,
they could not resist. Leigh Hunt sensed that Edmund was
hurt by their attitude and so he took the opportunity to
address them as follows:

"Do at least justice to your own discernment, be at the
trouble of applauding what you think worth going to see,
and let not the town-talk with which a man of genius has
been mixed up, and with which his genius has nothing to
do, induce you to sit as if you were afraid to applaud him,
and had no business where you are. Pray let the generous
reader think of this . . . and do his best to hinder some
of the finest points of acting in the world from being blunted
against the dull doubts of the boxes. If people are ashamed
to express their pleasure, they ought to be ashamed to be
pleased."

Leigh Hunt made his plea. But, of course, it was
disregarded. In truth, society *was* ashamed to be pleased
by Edmund's acting. The man had proved himself despicable; and though nothing could alter the fact that he
was a great tragedian, no words, however ably and reasonably
and forcibly expressed, could ever wipe out the memory of
Cox v. *Kean.*

3

Edmund realized that he could never retire from the
stage. But he longed none the less to settle down in some
kind of permanency. During the past six years he had had

many different addresses but no home. He was sick of dragging himself to the hotels and lodging-houses where he had spent most of his time.

So when he learned that the King's Theatre, Richmond Green, was in the market, he at once offered to rent it. He had always fancied himself as an actor-manager, and now it would suit him perfectly to be in control of a small country playhouse. Although he knew that he could not afford to stay in Bute, he felt that it was essential for him to breathe good, clean air. And where better than in Richmond, which was within easy distance of London?

He wrote to Mr. Budd, the agent, on February 10, 1831:

> . . the fact is I am weary of scampering about His Majesty's domains, and till I make my final bow to the British Public, I think a good company, well appointed and governed by a man of forty years' theatrical experience, would fix upon my retreat both pleasure and profit. If you would do me the favour to let me know if my name would not be objectionable to the proprietors, or my industry to the public, the rent, taxes, etc., etc., you will confer an obligation on
>
> Yours truly,
>
> EDMUND KEAN.

His offer was accepted, and gladly no doubt, for Richmond scarcely ranked among the most prosperous of playgoing towns. Before the spring of 1831 was over he had become lessee of the King's Theatre, and had taken up his abode in the picturesque cottage which adjoined it.

It was not altogether a wise move. For Edmund soon discovered that management added to his responsibilities rather than diminished them. Far from enabling him to live in comfortable seclusion, as he had hoped, it forced him into a veritable orgy of exertion. His theatre was a costly, not a profitable business. In order to pay for its losses, he had to chase madly after money elsewhere.

He appeared frequently on his own stage during the next eighteen months, but he appeared on many other stages besides. Indeed, his professional commitments were so arduous and so varied that they would have exhausted an actor whose strength was unimpaired, and would shock even the imagination of a modern player. In May and June of 1831 he caused a sensation by giving a series of performances at two minor theatres—the City and the Coburg. On June 7th he paid a fleeting visit to Drury Lane as Sir Edward Mortimer in the *Iron Chest*. From August 2nd–5th he acted in Birmingham, and on August 10th was bound for Cheltenham. On August 29th he opened a six weeks' season at the Haymarket, and immediately after left again for the provinces—for Bristol, Dublin, Edinburgh, and so on up and down the United Kingdom. No wonder his progress was often arrested by illness. No wonder his health worsened under the strain. He was killing himself as much by overwork as by drink. It seemed as if he knew the end could not be long delayed, and for the sake of a final fling, was prepared to throw away heedlessly his last reserves of strength. And yet when he *was* at Richmond, his life was more sheltered than it had ever been before. He had a home. He assumed an invalid's role. And he was well protected from the blasts of the world by a devoted entourage.

There was John Lee who looked after his business interests. He was a young ex-actor, and had only recently taken up Phillips' duties. But he had worshipped Edmund long before he had even known him. Five years ago, when Edmund had arrived in America—an outcast from his own country—John Lee had stood on the quay, a solitary Englishman, to welcome him.

There was James Smith—a local physician—who was Edmund's medical attendant. He visited him daily, and liked him so well that he consistently refrained from sending in an account. He considered himself sufficiently rewarded by Edmund's friendship.

And lastly there was "Aunt" Tid. She was an old lady now, in her seventy-first year, but she had come from her retreat in Chelsea (she had at last left Tavistock Row) to nurse her nephew, who needed nursing, and to keep house for him. According to Dr. Smith she was "tall, erect, grey haired, and exceedingly well conducted." She often used to be seen with Edmund walking on the green, and he looked small and bent beside her. Her fondness for Edmund puzzled Dr. Smith. One day he asked her outright whether she was "Mr. Kean's mother." She answered that she was not, but that she had known him since he was a little boy. "And it is hard, very hard," she added, "to see him fading away like this in the best part of life." Then she burst into tears.

He was, in truth, fading away. From his very appearance—so old and pallid—it was obvious that death was closing in upon him, and would not be kept at bay. He had about him an air of mystery and other-earthliness which usually belongs only to men who have reached a great age. There was something almost miraculous in the fact that Edmund Kean was alive at all. Those of the new generation, who were at the outset of their stage careers, regarded him as a kind of oracle and made pilgrimages to Richmond to seek his advice while it could yet be given. "Can you starve?" he said to one of them.

It was impossible to suppose now that he would ever recover his health and fortune. He was still prodigiously extravagant, still spent money as fast as he earned it, and was still wildly generous. It became known in Richmond that he was incapable of turning a deaf ear to any hard luck story, however fanciful or far-fetched. And there were several who abused his charity.

He survived on brandy. Neither "Aunt" Tid nor Doctor Smith could persuade him to eat solid food. He had no appetite. While he was under their care he did behave otherwise in a sensible, dignified way. He never left his house unless the weather was fine when he went, well wrapped up, for a walk on the green or for a row on the river. But the moment he was out of their sight, fulfilling provincial engagements, he became again the carousing, gallivanting vulgarian, a prey to all his weaknesses.

From some town in the Midlands he wrote to John Lee on April 10, 1831:

> DEAR LEE,
>
> What day do I open in Cheltenham. The stupid son of a bitch has not dated his letter, write me Birmingham. Get as much money as you can and save it for me, I shall send you——money as soon as I get it—I won't say—I wish her dead but I'll be damned if I don't.
>
> Yours truly,
>
> EDMUND KEAN.

To this letter he added a playful little postcript for "Aunt" Tid's benefit: "Tiddy no sausages out of season capitol [sic] cigars & grog."

The sharp contrasts in his character persisted to the end. And nothing reveals them more clearly than the distinct impression of two celebrated figures of the Victorian stage —Samuel Phelps and Helen Faucit—who in their youth both had the privilege of a single meeting with him.

Samuel Phelps remembered him professionally. "He was," he said, "like thunder and lightning, wild and extravagant and frequently incorrect. But . . . terribly in earnest. He lifted you off your feet."

Phelps was a young member of the resident company at a theatre in York, and when Edmund came there to star as Shylock he was cast as Tubal. Edmund did not bother to attend rehearsal; and though Phelps had been put through his paces by John Lee he was a trifle puzzled at the actual performance, for Edmund "prowled about the stage like a caged tiger." However, he did his best. "He dodged him up and down, and crossed when he crossed." Everything seemed to be going smoothly, when Edmund hissed into his ear: "Get out of my focus—blast you—get out of my focus." Phelps looked into the wings where John Lee was standing. Lee motioned him to stand higher up. He had committed the unpardonable sin of blocking the floats' light from shining into Edmund's face.

After the play was over Phelps was summoned to Edmund's dressing-room. He found him drinking copiously of brandy with Bill Anderton, a well-known provincial actor and a notorious dipsomaniac. (Apparently Edmund spent most of his time during this engagement drinking with Bill Anderton, whom he had known in his strolling player days. They got up drunk. And when they appeared together on the stage they were both "more than half seas over.") Edmund welcomed Phelps: "Have a glass of grog, young stick-in-the-mud. You'll be an actor one of these days, sir; but mind, the next time you play with me, for God's sake steer clear of my focus." Phelps never had occasion to heed this advice. And no doubt he was glad to see the last of Mr. Kean.

But Helen Faucit's impression of Edmund was touchingly different. She was still a schoolgirl at the time when she formed it, and she used to spend her holidays with her sister, who lived at Richmond. "One of my earliest and vivid recollections," she wrote, "was a meeting with 'the great Edmund Kean,' as my sister called him. He was her pet hero. She had seen him act, and through friends had a slight acquaintance with him. Wishing her little 'birdie,' as she often called me, to share all her pleasures, she often took me with her to the green for the chance of seeing him as he strolled there with his aunt, old Miss Tidswell. The great man had been very ill, so that all our expectations had been frequently disappointed. At last about noon one very warm sunny day my sister's eager eye saw the two figures in the far distance. It would have been bad manners to appear to be watching, so in a roundabout way our approach was made. As we drew near I would gladly have run away. I was startled, frightened at what I saw—a small pale man with a fur cap, and wrapped in a fur cloak. He looked to me as if come from the grave. A stray lock of very dark hair crossed his forehead, under which shone eyes which looked dark, and yet bright as lamps. So large were they, so piercing, so absorbing, I could see no other features. I shrank from them behind my sister, but she whispered to me that it would be unkind to show any fear, so we approached and were kindly greeted by the pair.

"Oh, what a voice was that which spoke! It seemed to come from far away—a long, long way behind him. After the first salutation it said, 'Who is this little one?' When my sister had explained, the face smiled (I was reassured by the smile, and the face looked less terrible), and he asked me where I went to school, and which of my books I liked best. Alas! I could not then remember that I liked any, but my ever good angel sister said she knew I was fond of poetry, for I had just won a prize for recitation. Upon this the face looked still more kindly on me, and we all moved together to a seat under the trees. Then the far-away hollow voice—but it was not harsh—spoke again, as he put his hand in mine, and bade me tell him whether I liked my school walks better than the walks at Richmond. This was too much, and it broke the ice of my silence. No indeed, Greenwich Park was very pretty—so was Blackheath with its donkeys, when we were, on occasions much too rare, allowed to ride them. But Richmond! Nothing could be so beautiful! I was asked to name my favourite sports, and whether I had ever been in a punt—which I had; and caught fish—which I had not. My tongue, once untied, ran on and on, and had after a time to be stopped, for my sister and the old lady thought I should fatigue the invalid. But he would not part just yet. He asked my name, and when it was told exclaimed, 'Oh, the old ballad—do you know it?—which begins:

> O, my Helen,
> There is no tellin'
> Why love I fell in;
> The grave, my dwellin',
> Would I were well in!

I know now why with my Helen "love I fell in"; it is
because she loves poetry, and she loves Richmond. Will my
Helen come and repeat her poetry to me some day?' This
alarming suggestion at once silenced my prattle, and my
sister had to express for me the honour and pleasure I was
supposed to feel. Here the interview ended; the kind hand
was withdrawn which had lain in mine so heavily, and yet
looked so thin and small. I did not know then how great
is the weight of weakness. It was put upon my head, and I
was bid Godspeed! I was to be sent for some day soon.
But the day never came; the schooldays were at hand. Those
wondrous eyes I never saw, and that distant voice I never
heard again."

Edmund was still the man who wooed beauty and courted
vulgarity, who displayed arrogance and simplicity, swagger
and charm, coarse anger and sweet gentleness, who had
two personalities which were seemingly irreconcilable. He
was more than ever the slave of his own impulsive feelings.
But whereas he had once been able to give vent to them in
actions—great and petty—he was now so largely hemmed
in by physical infirmity that he had become morbid, introspective, and repentant. His strength was gradually ebbing
away. His appearances on the stage grew less frequent as
the months went by, for there was a limit to the revivifying
powers of brandy. During long periods of enforced idleness
at Richmond his energy, lust, ambition were all frustrated,
and he was thrown back upon himself.

His body rebelled painfully against exertion. But while
he rested it he suffered agonies of mind for which there
was no relief. He was then the prisoner of his remorse and
was face to face with the awful realization that his tragedy
was of his own making.

> This is the hour, when sluggards are in sleep,
> That genius soars the air, or scours the deep,
> Brings to the vision, all the days gone by,
> This heart, the good and ill which in it lie,

Looks on proud man, but as a worldly thing,
Scarcely a shade twixt Beggar and a King,
Whipt in his childhood, in manhood trained,
In all the voices which the fallen strained.

That was a poem which he wrote during his hours of solitude when he had nothing else to do but contemplate his melancholy. He hated his thoughts, yet could not escape from them. Sometimes he tried to lull himself into forgetfulness by playing the piano and singing and listening to the sound of his own voice. Doctor Smith remembered one such occasion. It was on a summer's evening in 1832. "I crossed the green," he wrote, "and went into his house, the door being open. In the twilight I saw the figure of Mr. Lee, not very clearly defined, standing at the door of Mr. Kean's sitting-room. The secretary, who was attentively listening to something, raised his finger to enjoin silence. The tragedian was sitting at his piano, accompanying himself to an inexpressibly beautiful singing of 'Those Evening Bells.' Next he sang with exquisite sweetness and pathos one or two of Moore's melodies, after which he repeated 'Those Evening Bells.' At first he sang with great clearness; but gradually his voice became plaintive in the extreme, then tremulous, then thick, as if with emotion. It slowly died, and a dead silence followed. I softly opened the door and went in. His head was bowed upon the piano, and as he raised it on hearing my approach a moonbeam fell upon the keys of the instrument, showing me that they were wet with tears."

He had given up all hope of recovery. He had abandoned himself to weeping and despair while he awaited the end. But now that he was so close to death he was tormented less by his present plight than by his knowledge of its causes. He was in dread of some mysterious Divinity whom he did not understand but in whose existence he believed instinctively. Would his depature from this world mean the finish of his sufferings, or would he have to pay further for his sins in an after life? He wanted desperately

to make atonement before it was too late. He was afraid to
die while he was still at war with his own conscience or
with God.

His mother wrote to him in September of 1832 to say
that she was very ill and to ask him for money in advance
of her allowance. "I am in a strange state of health," she
concluded; "two days before I saw Harry everyone thought
I could not live the night through. I am sorry that I live to
trouble my dear child, and yet I cannot wish to die. *Let me
you see.*"

It was not the first time that she had appealed to his
charity thus, and he was already keeping the Harry Darnleys
and their children. But now he asked her to come to his
house at Richmond, and when she arrived a few days later
"Aunt" Tid left. It was like his childhood over again, and the
exchange was just as unfortunate. For Ann Carey was an
incurable invalid, and incapable of nursing her son. She
spent most of her time in bed. According to Doctor Smith,
"She . . . proved to be a low, dissipated, illiterate woman."

In December, Edmund wrote to his wife:

DEAR MARY,

Let us be no longer fools. Come home; forget and
forgive. If I have erred, it was my head, not my heart, and most
severely have I suffered for it. My future life shall be employed
in contributing to your happiness, and you, I trust, will return
that feeling by a total obliteration of the past.

Your wild but really affectionate husband,

EDMUND KEAN.

But Mary did not reciprocate his sentiments. In her heart
there was no desire for a reconciliation with the man whom
she supposed had wronged her so grievously. Two years
ago she might have gone back to him, had he asked her.
But now her future was secure with Charles. Charles was
a devoted son, and was doing very well for himself. He was
striding forward in his profession. He had recently returned
from a tour of the United States, and at the moment was

engaged to play leading parts at Covent Garden. With
Charles to provide for her comforts, she preferred to remain
alone.

It is true that to please her son she did visit Edmund
once or twice near the end. But it is impossible to suppose
that she brought him much comfort. She had nothing to
give him—neither love nor even pity. Only a few months
after his death she would be accused, in *Fraser's Magazine*,
"of compendiously collecting his vices for the contempt or
execration of the world." And one knows from her letters
to Cornwall that she never learned to respect his memory.

Meanwhile Edmund was having to fight hard for mere
existence. Though his responsibilities were as onerous as
ever, his earnings had dropped alarmingly in the past few
months. He had no savings with which to satisfy his
creditors. His need for ready money was urgent. And he
had to work for it.

His health was now so precarious that he could never be
certain of living through a part. Every time he appeared on
the stage he gambled with mortality. There is a pathetic
story of his physical weakness—typical of many others—
which was told by Johnston, the actor, who once played
Tubal to his Shylock. At the end of the scene Edmund was
too exhausted to make his exit without assistance, and so
he changed the line, "Go, Tubal, and meet me at our
synagogue," to "Lead me to our synagogue." Then, using
Johnston for support, he dragged himself into the wings.

But it was a choice between courting death and starving
to death. So long as he had the power to move he could
not afford to remain idle. During November and December
he gave no less than fourteen performances at Drury Lane,
out of which he played eight times as Othello to the Iago
of William Charles Macready, whom he had affected to
despise and by whom he was hated in turn. It was an
uncomfortable partnership, though it drew the town.
Macready, smug, self-centred, snobbish, superior, had no
understanding of Edmund. He was proud to hold the

conventional view of him—that he was a great tragedian who had sacrificed his talents to his vices. He disliked the experience of appearing on the stage with him. He called him "that low man." In his diary on December 10th he wrote, "Acted well when Kean did not interfere with me." Edmund still regarded Macready as a dreaded rival. Even now he could not bear the thought of being eclipsed by him. He struggled against his ailments to dominate the scene. And by fair means or foul he succeeded at least in holding his own. G. H. Lewes, who as a very young man saw one of these performances of Othello, remembered "how puny Kean appeared beside Macready, until in the third act, when roused by Iago's taunts and insinuations, he moved towards him with a gouty hobble, seized him by the throat, and in a well-known explosion, 'Villain! be sure you prove,' etc., seemed to swell into a stature which made Macready appear small. On that very evening, when gout made it difficult for him to display his accustomed grace . . . such was the irresistible pathos—manly, not tearful—which vibrated in his tones and expressed itself in look and gestures that old men leaned their heads upon their arms and fairly sobbed."

During January and February Edmund played only twice at Drury Lane. On February 19th he went to Brighton to give a single performance of Sir Giles Overreach. At the end of a particularly exhausting passage, midway through the last act, he fainted and had to be carried from the stage. On recovering consciousness he asked exactly when it was that he had broken down. He was told. "I fear it will be my last dying speech," he said. His sense of the dramatic never forsook him.

But he rallied again, and again understood how urgently he was in need of money. His bank balance was not large enough to discharge even his most pressing liabilities. He asked Captain Polhill, who had succeeded Alexander Lee as lessee of Drury Lane, to advance him a loan of £500 on account of his future performances. Captain Polhill

declined. The services of an actor, who might fade out at
any moment, were not sufficient security.

But Edmund was as sensitive as ever to insult. And now
to have been refused a trifling favour by the manager of
the theatre which he had once rescued from bankruptcy,
was a crowning, insupportable affront. It resulted in his
last impulsive action. Heedless of his legal obligations, he
sent a doctor's certificate to Drury Lane and signed a new
contract with Covent Garden, from where the Kembles had
recently departed for a tour of the United States.

He opened at Covent Garden as Shylock on Thursday,
March 21st, and was enthusiastically received. On Monday,
March 25th, he was billed to play Othello to the Iago of
his son Charles. Naturally the announcement caused a
sensation, for the two Keans had never been seen together
in London. "It is mere quackery," wrote Macready in his
diary. But it drew a large, excited and sentimental house.

When Edmund arrived at the theatre he looked very
pale, and he was shivering. It was only after he had swallowed
many glasses of brandy and had listened to the encouraging
words of the theatre officials, who hovered anxiously about
him, that he decided that he had enough strength to act at
all. He changed his clothes and blacked his face.

He was rewarded with a storm of cheering on his entrance.
It was a grand, dramatic moment for which the audience
had been waiting impatiently. Edmund bowed again and
again. Then he took Charles by the hand and led him
towards the footlights. He presented his heir to his public.
The house broke into a renewed frenzy of applause. Edmund
could not have suppressed his tears even if he had wished
to do so.

He struggled feebly through the first two acts. He was
not pleased with himself, but he was proud of his son. He
remarked to someone in the wings, "Charles is getting on
to-night, he's acting very well. I suppose that is because he
is acting with me."

The great third act began. He had warned Charles

"Mind that you keep before me. Don't get behind me in this act. I don't know that I shall be able to kneel; but if I do be sure that you lift me up."

He spoke the farewell speech as movingly as always. John Vandenhoff wrote that his delivery of it never varied. "It ran on the same tones and semitones, had the same rests and breaks, the same forte and piano, the same crescendo and diminuendo, night after night, as if he spoke it from a musical score. And what beautiful, what thrilling music it was! the music of a broken heart—the cry of a despairing soul!"

"Othello's occupation's gone." That was the line which heralded his terrific explosion, beginning, "Villain, be sure thou prove my love a whore," and with which he had dwarfed Young and Booth and Macready and all the other Iagos, who had ever crossed his path. But now the anticipated onslaught never came. Edmund was at the point of collapse, and had lost the power of speech. A deep mist was blotting out his vision and a wracking pain was paralysing his limbs. He flung his arms round Charles. "O God, I am dying," he said. "Speak to them for me." Then he became unconscious.

He was carried from the stage, and later to a neighbouring tavern, where he was put to bed and attended by his London physician, Doctor Carpue. At the end of a week he was strong enough to return to Richmond.

Meanwhile at Drury Lane the audience had not waited to see *Othello* concluded with another actor in the name part. Instinctively they had known, perhaps, that though Edmund was not yet dead, a great and tragic epoch in the theatre had reached its close.

4

He knew that he had played his last part.

Back at Richmond he was tended by James Smith and by his medical advisers from London—Douchez and

Carpue. Within a few weeks he was out of bed again, and was even able to go for drives in his carriage. But though he liked to have his doctors about him, he was really kept alive by the exercise of his own will. He did nothing to rebuild his strength. He refused to eat food, except when it was administered to him in the form of medicine, and he continued to sustain himself on brandy.

Perhaps he fought deliberately for the chance to say good-bye to "Aunt" Tid. She would not come to him now that Ann Carey was at Richmond. So he had to go to her. One day towards the end of April he drove to her lodgings at 4 Camera Street, Chelsea.

The journey imposed too great a strain on his physique. When he returned home that evening he said that he had "caught his death blow," and called for brandy, which made him feel no better. He never left his house again.

On May 1st his doctors realized that there was no hope. On May 2nd Charles and Mary came to take their leave of him. Yet he lingered on for another fortnight. He had done with the world. But his life ebbed painfully away. It seemed to have shrunk and to have become encompassed within the walls of his own room at Richmond. There, on his bed, were piled the classical volumes which he had never had the leisure to read and now had not the strength to open: there, sitting round him, were a few devoted friends to whom he recited Shakespeare and talked of his triumphs and his failures; and there, within his reach, was a supply of brandy which was killing him, but without which he could not survive.

On May 14th he sank into unconsciousness. Throughout the night his secretary, John Lee, and his surgeon, George Douchez, watched over him. In the early morning of May 15th he opened his eyes and seemed to recognize them. But he could not speak. He died a few hours later.

He left behind him no estate—only £600 worth of debts. But, among his papers, they found a document, written in his own hand and headed, "Edmund Kean's last will." It read:

The villainy of the Irish strumpet Ophelia Benjamin, has undone me and though I despise her, I feel life totally valueless without her I leave her my curses.

My property in Bute, with the furniture of this House—Richmond—I leave my mother (with the proviso) that no portion of it, shall be either sold or let if so,—the whole goes to the possession of the Drury Lane Theatrical fund.

My Dramatic Wardrobe with all other clothing I leave to my worthy friend John Lee (forgive me oh Lord and receive my Soul with mercy)

APPENDIX

THERE are four biographies of Kean:—

Life of Edmund Kean, by Barry Cornwall (B. W. Procter), London, 1835.
Life of Edmund Kean, by F. W. Hawkins, London, 1869.
Life and Adventures of Edmund Kean, by J. Fitzgerald Molloy, London, 1868.
Edmund Kean, by Harold Newcomb Hillebrand, New York, 1933

Of these Mr. Hillebrand's book is by far the most authoritative and is documented with meticulous care.

In the following notes I have neither quoted sources which are obvious from the text itself nor have I bothered to prove details which have already been proved. I have confined my attention to new matters which may arouse controversy.

1. Moses Kean's death was reported in the *Morning Post* on January 3, 1793, and in the *Courier* on January 1, 1793, as follows: "Died. A few days since, Mr. Moses Kean, well known for his endeavours in the LOUNGE."

2. Miss Tidswell's age is proved by her death certificate at Somerset House. She died on September 3, 1846, aged 86.

3. A brief account of Miss Tidswell is given in the *Thespian Dictionary,* and in other contemporary biographies of the stage which I found in the library of the Garrick Club.

4. From an examination of the Drury Lane play-bills in Mrs. Enthoven's collection, and of the Liverpool play-bills in the British Museum I find that Miss Tidswell appeared with faultless regularity on the stage between the years 1787 and 1790.
This may for ever dispose of the idea that she was really Kean's mother.

5. The authority for Miss Tidswell's association with Moses Kean is a letter published in the *Sunday Times* on June 2, 1833, from a certain J. Addison. The letter chiefly concerns Edmund Kean *père,*

with whom the author was intimate. But the last two paragraphs read as follows:

"Miss Tidswell was spoken of in the family as the wife of Moses, though not publicly announced as such nor did she reside in the house with him.

"About the year 1787 or 88 my intimacy with Edmund was interrupted by his attention to Miss Carey, daughter of George Saville Carey, and our evening walks generally terminated at the door of Carey's chambers in Gray's Inn. He died about the age of 22 or 23, previous to which he had been disordered in his intellect. . . ."

Mr. Hillebrand—to whom the credit for discovering this letter belongs—quotes it from what he infers is a transcript of the original. According to his version the first paragraph reads: "Miss Tidswell was spoken of as the wife of Moses though not publickly announced as such nor did she reside with him about the year 1787 or 8." There are other differences tending to show that the transcript of the original (if transcript of the original it really is) was very hastily made. I think the letter as published in the *Sunday Times* must be the correct version. Certainly it appeared to satisfy the author.

6. The account of the Duke of Norfolk is drawn from *The Beaux of the Regency*, by Lewis Melville, London, 1908.

7. The name of Moses Kean is to be found on one or two of the Haymarket bills for 1790. A complete collection of these is in the Garrick Club.

8 Among the family papers to which I have already referred in the Preface, there is a letter to Kean from a certain Edmund Hudson. It is dated April 14, 1830. Part of it reads: "It is now more than two years since Mrs. Carey came to my house and having stated to my wife and self the difficulty She was Labouring under on account of her having spent Beforehand the yearly allowance so Bountifully Bestowed on her by you—which Difficulty she said was occasioned by a long and severe illness in Yorkshire—She was an entire Stranger to me But on her producing a letter written by you Sir which said she was to have that allowance for Life I Did not hesitate taking her and the Boy which she brought with her into my house. . . ." Edmund Hudson's address was 66 Marsham Street, Westminster.

9. Tom Dibdin in his *Reminiscences* mentions that Kean asked him to find jobs for two of his relatives. The Surrey Theatre play-bills for 1817 and 18, which I have seen in Mrs. Enthoven's collection, frequently contain the names of Mrs. Carey and Miss Carey. For example, on March 30, 1818, Mrs. and Miss Carey were gypsies in a new burletta.

10. The biographic notes among the family papers already mentioned read as follows:

1789. Born 17 March half past three in the morning. E.K. went to Miss Tidswell & said Nance Carey was with child and begged her to go to her lodgings in Chancery Lane. Miss T and her aunt went with her & found Miss Carey near her time —Have you proper necessaries—nothing. Mrs. Byrne (a friend) begged baby clothes.
He said he was born in Gray's Inn.

1790.

1791. Miss Tidswell took him—Mrs. Carey would not keep him any longer—Aunt Price sister to Edmund Kean!—E.K. put him to Nurse when he was made crooked in knee walked on his ankles—cured by wearing Irons till he was seven—night Irons & day Irons.

1792.

1793.

1794. Six years old—with Mrs. Clarke (*Mrs. Clarke she says ten years old*).

1796 at eight years old Mr. and Mrs. Duncan went out to Tobago Mr. D. sd. he used to sleep with them in irons. *They used to hurt us!!*
He and Mrs. Carey were travelling with Richardsons Company. The Windsor Thea' boys saw and perhaps heard of the little boy. They begged Mr. Heath to let him come there. The King heard of it and Kean recited before him.

1798. 10 years old. Ran away from Miss Tidswell and walked to Portsmouth without a penny—slept in a Barn—eat turnips. probably acted there—*he must in order to live.*

1799. 11 years old spoke Rollas address at Covent Garden for Knight's . . . benefit (manager of Liverpool). He was quite hoarse having spoken so many speeches at the Diorama (Sans Souci)—got no applause.

15. An account of Kean's engagement with Samuel Jerrold was written, for Barry Cornwall's benefit, by Douglas Jerrold. The original of this is among the family papers already mentioned.

16 In the *Era Almanack* of 1875, T. F. Dillon Croker wrote that the Haymarket books, which had come into his possession, revealed that in 1806 the season began on June 9th and ended on September 15th Kean played one hundred and ninety-three times. His parts were as follows: Fifer in the *Battle of Hexham*, Petei in the *Dramatist*, Thomas in *Agreeable Surprise*, John in *Heir-at-Law*, Peter in *The Iron Chest*, Country Servant in *John Bull*, Fourth Planter in *Inkle and Yarico*, Young Goatherd in *The Mountaineers*, Warner in *Poor Gentleman*, Alcaide in *Spanish Barber*, Carney in *Ways and Means*, Waiter in *Mrs. Wiggins*, Dibbs in *Review*, Piero in *Tale of Mystery*, Clown in *Fortune's Frolic*, Fiddler in *Speed the Plough*, Landlord in *Prisoner at Large*, Trueman in *Clandestine Marriage*, Countryman in *Five Miles Off*, Rosencrantz in *Hamlet*, Alguazil in *She would and She would not*, Nicolas in *Sighs*. The books also state:—

"July 10th 1806, Mr. Kean absent from rehearsal being ill. Mr. Stokes played the part of the Countryman in ' Five Miles Off.'

"July 17th, Mr. Kean resumed business.

"July 26th, Mr. Kean absent from three acts of the rehearsal, in consequence of an error in his part of Nicolas in *Sighs*, having only the first act written.

"August 3rd, The part of Nicolas was cast to Mr. Noble, but Mr. Kean having tickets, obtained permission of the managers to play the character."

There is a complete collection of the 1806 Haymarket play-bills in the library of the Garrick Club. Kean's name appears on them frequently, though not 193 times!

17. The gossipy account of Kean's hurried departure from Sheerness is contained in a contemporary biography written by Francis Phippen and published in 1814. A copy of it is in the British Museum.

18. Both Mary and Susan habitually signed their name "Chambres." In the biographies they have always been called Chambers, and I have adhered to this spelling.

1800. Miss Plumptree, one day in Clarges Street, was sp(
this Diorama and said, "I used to be so pleased with th
who spoke the poetry at the Sans Souci." (There were
scenes and a voice was heard coming from behind
poetry descriptive of the scenes that were passing.)
K. "Do you know who it is that was who spouted the
said K. (tumbling over head and heals)—It was I—H(
to get a good deal of money at the S. Souci but Mrs. (
took it away from him."

1801. Kean disentangled himself from Mrs. Carey about this
—at the age of fourteen he was entirely his own master.

1803.

1804. Went to Sheerness Jerrold's company. 16 or 17.
Mr. Jerrold's statement.

I do not suggest, of course, that this confused account of Kean
childhood is consistently accurate! Some of it conflicts with estab
lished evidence. But it may be of passing interest to Kean student;
I would not like to guess its author, but it must have been someone
closely connected with the family.

11. Hawkins writes without apparent authority that Kean was
taught singing by Incledon and fencing by Angelo. It is certain
that Kean and Incledon were old friends. In Mr. Ifan Kyrle Fletcher's
collection there is this letter to Kean, dated Feb. 21, 1827:
". . . The object of my visit was to request you to become a sub-
scriber to my publication. . . . It is my intention to say something
of everyone of my distinguished friends—and shall take the liberty
of introducing my friend Mr. Kean. . . . Your old fencing Master
Henry Angelo, Senr."

12. There is, in the library of the Garrick Club, a short note
from Miss Tidswell to the manager of Drury Lane requesting a
renewal of her engagement. It is addressed from 12 Tavistock Row.
It is, so far as I am aware, the only original Tidswell letter in existence.

13. Mention of Kean's performance before Lord Nelson is made
in *Carmarthen Transactions*, vol. iv.

14. A copy of the evidence collected and of the report made by
the select committee appointed by the House of Commons in 1832,
is in the library of the Garrick Club.

19. The original of Mary's letter of September 5, 1813, to Margaret Roberts is in Ifan Kyrle Fletcher's collection.

20. Mary's letter to Barry Cornwall is in Mr. Ifan Kyrle Fletcher's collection. It refers to other letters which she had written to him. Her age is proved by her death certificate. She died on March 13, 1849, aged 69.

21. The notice in the *Staffordshire Advertiser* was reproduced by *John Bull* in April, 1825.

22. The relevant copies of *The Cambrian* are in the Swansea Library.

23. Information about Andrew Cherry and Ann of Swansea was found by reference to the Swansea and Cardiff newspaper files.

24. The entire account of Grattan's association with Kean may be found in *Beaten Paths; and Those Who Trod Them*, by Thomas Colley Grattan.

25. The information about Grattan himself is chiefly drawn from the *Dictionary of National Biography*.

26. The biographic details of Sheridan Knowles are drawn from the *Dictionary of National Biography*.

27. Molloy publishes Kean's letter to John Hughes, but apparently did not recognize the significance of the address.

28. The letter written from Exeter on July 4, 1812, by Mary to Margaret Roberts reads as follows: "I must own My Dear Margrt your letter was written very hastily—I shall not however comment on it except on the word *passion*—nothing was further from my Bosom than passion of any kind—I was so ill no one expected I should ever get better—the two Boys Dying in Measles & hooping Cough—Edmund entirely ruining his health with drink—I saw nothing but misery before me & the repulse I met with from Mrs. Hunt—when I expected her interest did rouse what little feeling I had—as I expected we had but 6 pound in the House for our Benefit we were out of pocket—I have written to Susan about this Box of things. I wish to God you could get some safe Captain to send them with—as I wish to get them as fast as possible—if once they come to

Bristol & that the Captn would send them immediately by the Coach I would Have them in a day—we leave this this Day three weeks for Weymouth & then the Box would have farther to go & I more to pay—Susan has the direction will you get it—& the Box & send it immediately I beg you will not neglect it—if you knew how much I want it you would send it instantly—I shall rely on you to see about it—as Susan is not in the place—if you have any bits of Silk or Muslin you can send it, or any old thing—little Howard is very delicate the Measles has weakened him much—Mr. Keans Aunt has been trying to prevent his living with me—Oh! you know not half what I am suffering—you will answer this Directly—I am so anxious about these things I hope in God you can send them

believe me ever yours most sincerely

M. KEAN.

The original of this letter is in the collection of Mr. R. N. Green-Armytage.

29. The original of Mary's letter to Margaret Roberts in September, 1813, is in Mr. Ifan Kyrle Fletcher's collection.

30. The account of Doctor Drury is drawn from the *Dictionary of National Biography*.

31. The Drury Lane sub-committee and general committee minute books for the years 1813 *et seq.* are in the library of the Garrick Club.

32. Mary's letter to Susan about Howard's death was actually written from London in December of 1813. The original is in Mr. Ifan Kyrle Fletcher's collection.

33. The play-bill of Kean's last performance in Dorchester is in the Garrick Club.

34. The biographic details concerning Robert William Elliston are chiefly drawn from *Life and Enterprises of R. W. Elliston*, by George Raymond, London, 1857.

35. There is a complete collection of Drury Lane and Covent Garden play-bills from 1813–1833 in the library of the Garrick Club.

36. Mary's letter to Susan of December 1813 mentions, *inter alia*, the dispute with Elliston. She added to it the following postscript: "Have you seen the paragraphs previous to all this trouble which Whitbread put in the *Morning Chronicle*?" It was this which led me to search for the paragraph which I have quoted in the text. All Kean's biographers have vigorously denied that he was "puffed" before his first London appearance.

37. In *Notes and Queries* 6, VIII, 235, a correspondent writes: "About twenty-five years ago (i.e. 1858) I wrote a biographical memoir of my old school fellow and valued friend Charles Kean, *on notes with which he supplied me.* It appeared in a magazine of that date, and I find the following authentic statement 'Who were his (Edmund Kean's) parents he himself scarcely seems to have ascertained: for in later life he was pensioning two women on the grounds of maternal claims upon him. But the truth appears to be that Ann Carey was his real mother, and that Miss Tidswell was his aunt, who showed him much affection and kindness during an ill-used childhood, and that he was consequently always inclined to treat her with filial regard.' "

Proof that Kean made an allowance to Ann Carey is afforded by Edmund Cooper's letter quoted above. Proof that he gave Miss Tidswell money is furnished hereafter.

38. The first-hand stories of Mary and Samuel Whitbread, Kean at Holland House, Kean and Douglas Kinnaird, etc., etc., may be found in *Memoirs of a Long Life*, by Lord Broughton (John Cam Hobhouse). I am indebted to Mr. Derrick A. Sington for drawing my attention to these.

39. Lady Caroline Lamb's note to Kean was first published in the *Athenaeum*, April 30, 1836.

40. Susan's letter to Margaret Roberts was written on March 29, 1814. The original is in Mr. Ifan Kyrle Fletcher's collection.

41. The report in *The Cheltenham Chronicle* of Kean's performance of Richard III is preserved in the Cheltenham Public Library.

42. The original of J. H. Merivale's letter to Doctor Drury is among the family papers already mentioned. It reveals that Kean's decline began much earlier than has been supposed hitherto. The

sentence, "Upon receiving this letter she instantly set off for Woolwich, accompanied by her sister . . .", is conclusive proof that Susan
was staying with Mary at the time. From later letters it is evident that
she continued to live at Clarges Street.

43. Kean's grievances against the Drury Lane sub-committee are
enumerated at the end of Mr. Merivale's letter to Doctor Drury.

44. Jack Hughes' association with Kean was lifelong. William
Chippendale was a strolling player whom Kean helped. He used to
stay with Kean at Bute.

45. The letter of Lord Essex to Mary was first published in the
Athenaeum, April 30, 1836. The date of the letter there given is
June 11, 1817, but it must clearly be wrong, for Whitbread died on
July 6, 1815. No doubt the seven is a misprint for five or four.

46. The story of Sheridan and Beau Brummel may be found in
The Life of Beau Brummel by Capt Jesse.

47 Kean's letter about his annual prize wherry was first published
in the *Athenaeum*, April 30, 1836.

48. On May 17, 1824, *John Bull* published a paragraph making
huge fun of the fact that Kean employed a secretary called Phillips.

49. The original of Kean's letter to the secretary of the Wolves
Club is in Ifan Kyrle Fletcher's collection. It is addressed to the
O.P. and P.S. Tavern in Russell Court. Hitherto it has been supposed
that the Wolves Club met at the Coal Hole in Fountain Court.

50. A copy of *Kean*, a poem by Theodore Norton, is in Ifan Kyrle
Fletcher's collection. The British Museum does not possess a copy.

51. The manuscript of Kean's poem "What is this happiness of
man?" etc., is in Ifan Kyrle Fletcher's collection. It has, of course,
never been published before.

52. The description of the Drury Lane Green Room and of the
sub-committee's management immediately after Whitbread's death is
chiefly drawn from *Memoirs of J. S. Munden* by His Son, London,
1846

53. The original of Kean's letter to Alexander Rae is in the
collection of Mr. R. N. Green-Armytage. It is dated, in error, by

Kean, Wednesday, March 31st. It must, of course, have been written on March 27th, which was in fact a Wednesday. March 31st was a Sunday.

54. Grattan's re-meeting with Kean took place in the summer. Grattan does not state the year, but it was after the Duke of Milan incident, and must have been before the Booth controversy, because Kean took Grattan to the Wolves Club. The only possible year, therefore, is 1816.

55. The original of Kean's letter to Lee (July 10, 1816) is in Ifan Kyrle Fletcher's collection.

56. Anne Wickstead—at the Cox v. Kean trial—thought that Kean met Mrs. Cox at Taunton about 1815. But there is no evidence that Kean visited Taunton in 1815, whereas it is certain from extant play-bills that he went there in 1816 in fulfilment of his promise to Lee. Moreover, while Grattan remembered seeing the Coxes at Clarges Street in the early summer of 1817, he did not meet them there in the previous year.

57. The details of Booth's performances in Brighton and the letter from Kinnaird to Booth may be found in *Junius Brutus Booth*, by His Daughter, New York, 1866.

58. Kean's presence in a box at Macready's Covent Garden début is recorded by Macready himself in his published diaries.

59. There are a good many newspaper cuttings relating to the structural alterations at Drury Lane at the beginning of the 1817–1818 season in the Winston collection at the British Museum. This collection forms quite an instructive survey of the frequent rows and ructions at Drury Lane, and I have drawn from it for various odd bits of information.

60. Elliston announced on the Drury Lane play-bills that the model of Mr. Beasley's design would be on view in the Saloon. This was at the beginning of the 1819–1820 season. Actually he postponed building operations until 1822.

61. The original of Kean's letter to Michael Kelly (July 21, 1819) is in Ifan Kyrle Fletcher's collection.

62. The original of Elliston's instruction to Horace Twiss is in Ifan Kyrle Fletcher's collection.

63. There are letters from Kean to Edward Crooke in Mr. Ifan Kyrle Fletcher's collection, which show that Crooke was a theatrical agent, employed from time to time by Kean, and that he was also the proprietor of a "theatrical reading room." Otherwise the letters are of no particular interest, and therefore they have not been specifically quoted.

64. There are some grounds for believing that Elliston was responsible for the idea of Kean's appearance in *The Admirable Crichton* on June 12, 1820. On October 1, 1824, Kean wrote: ". . . I accede to Mr. Elliston's proposals for the ensuing season, with the proviso—that he does not expect me to act in farce-interlude, etc., on the night of my benefit."

65. The short survey of the American stage is chiefly reconstructed from Hornblower's *History of the American Stage* and Clapp's *History of the Boston Stage*.

66. The manuscript of Kean's poem, "Friends with new faces are common we're told," is in Ifan Kyrle Fletcher's collection.

67. So far as I am aware Elliston was the first manager to use two-colour printing on the Drury Lane play-bills. He printed Kean's name in red after his return from America.

68. Kean ends his letter to Miss Tidswell . . . "I will rather add to your comforts than diminish them . . ." which is proof enough that he was supporting her.

69. The biographic details of Charles Mayne Young are drawn from *Charles Mayne Young*, by Julian Charles Young, London, 1871.

70. In 1908 Murdoch Mackenzie gave a lecture on the subject of Kean's life in Bute. He obtained the bulk of his information from interviews with the oldest inhabitants who remembered Kean. His lecture was subsequently reprinted in *Transactions of the Buteshire Natural History Society*, Vol. I. A copy of this is in the Museum at Rothesay, and I have had access to it.

71. Murdoch Mackenzie saw the lease signed by Kean and Lord Bute. It was a lease of 24 acres for 99 years at £48 p.a.

72. The news of Kean's illness in the autumn of 1823 was conveyed to Elliston by Mary. Mary's letter to Elliston was sent on

November 8th ten days before Kean's letter from Bute to Phillips. It was published by T. F. Dillon Croker in the *Era Almanack* of 1875. It is as follows:—

> SIR,
>
> With feelings of the most acute agony, I write to inform you that Mr. Kean lies still dangerously ill—so ill that I tremble for the consequences. He has within these two days exhibited strong indications of brain-fever; if this takes place the world must lose a great and good man, and a devoted family the best of husbands and fathers.
>
> "I scarcely know what I write—your feelings must excuse the diction of an afflicted wife, in the fear of disappointing that public to which he is bound in so firm a bond of gratitude. He has feebly muttered his wishes, which I as feebly obey."

Kean wrote an earlier letter to Phillips—on November 14th— which began: "Mrs. Kean wrote to Elliston on the 8th, telling him that I have not one week to live. All is well by my keeping away." It seems as if he exaggerated his illness in order to escape Macready.

73. The story of Dunn's visit to Brighton and Kean's subsequent letter to Elliston are published in Raymond's *Life of Elliston*.

74. The story of Kean's performance of Richard III at Boulogne is told by Grattan, who was there.

75. Susan's letter to Margaret Roberts was written in December 1824, and gives details of the journey up to Bute, etc. The original is in Ifan Kyrle Fletcher's collection.

76. Mr. James Agate in his *Ego* 3 (London, 1938) publishes a letter which Kean wrote to Elliston from Belfast in the autumn of 1824. It reads: "There is a very clever Irishman in this company— with the exception of Johnston the best I ever saw. I have no acquaintance with him, nor does he know that I am writing in his favour, but I conceive it a duty to pay the just tribute to talent in whatever garb I find it. The actor's name is Conolly.

". . . How do you do? How goes the Theatre? Where are all my women? Tell Newman to get some good brandy against the fifteenth of January—to drink damnation to whores and Aldermen."

The last sentences of this letter obviously refer to the approaching

Cox v. *Kean* trial. Newman was the name of Kean's dresser at Drury Lane.

77. The mass of *Cox* v. *Kean* literature has mostly been lost, though a fairly complete list of it may be found in Lowe's *Bibliography of the Stage*. A copy of Fairburn's edition of the report of the trial is in the British Museum and also in the library of the Garrick Club. A copy of the *Suppressed Letters* is in Ifan Kyrle Fletcher's collection. A copy of *The Actor and The Alderman's Wife, A Farce in Three Acts,* by Thomas Little, Esq., is in the Birmingham Library. A copy of an illustrated ballad called *Keenish Sport* is in Ifan Kyrle Fletcher's collection. This last is so rare that it is not even mentioned in Lowe's *Bibliography*.

78. The original of Kean's letter to Jack Hughes (July 21, 1825) is in Ifan Kyrle Fletcher's collection.

79. On September 5, 1825, the following paragraph was published in *John Bull:*

"Mr. Kean, wrecked in health and fortune, his spirits broken and his temper soured, is acting 'for a little' previous to his departure for America. . . . His lady, to whom, like another Samson, he instructed all his strength in the shape of a power of attorney, having drawn out £4,000, has retired to Bute."

This drew forth an inspired reply in which it was said that "Mrs. Kean was a close prisoner in Bute," "had been forced there against her inclinations," and was suffering from "a languishing illness contracted through her husband's means." Mary later denied that she had been responsible for this reply, but her letter to Sigell proves that she must have given out that she was suffering from venereal disease.

80. Mary's threat to sell the property at Bute is proved conclusively by the correspondence which passed between her and Henry Sigell. On October 8, 1825, Sigell wrote to her: "Mr. Kean does most certainly peremptorily refuse to have the House or one iota of his furniture or property disposed of. I am most happy that such an idea has been abandoned. . . ."

81. As an instance of Mary's regard for truth it may be noted that whereas she told Barry Cornwall in 1834 that her parting from Kean took place on his returning the last time from America—"That

is he parted very kindly from me when going but on his return I did not see him"—she wrote to Sigell in October 1825 ". . . Why did he not take leave of me?"

82. The originals of all the letters which passed between Henry Sigell and Mary are in Ifan Kyrle Fletcher's collection. Of course, they throw an entirely new light on the cause of Kean's separation from Mary. It is worth while stressing again that Mary knew all about Kean's affair with Charlotte Cox long before she left him. Susan mentions the trial in December of 1824 when she wrote to Margaret Roberts. At that time the trial had not yet taken place, and Mary was with Kean at Glasgow. Grattan says that when the Keans called on him at Boulogne in the early summer of 1824, the approaching trial was discussed openly. Moreover the proceedings at the trial itself show that Mary knew of Kean's infidelity considerably before the Alderman's alleged "awakening." There can be no doubt at all that Mary condoned her husband's infidelity. The idea tacitly accepted by all the biographers—that she left him because her moral instincts were outraged, simply will not do. I had actually reached this conclusion before my fortunate discovery of the Sigell correspondence.

83. The original of Kean's letter to W. Clarke (December 31, 1826) is in Ifan Kyrle Fletcher's collection.

84. The original of Kean's letter to Cooper (April 1827) is in Ifan Kyrle Fletcher's collection.

85. The story of Kean giving a false fire alarm in America was told by his servant—Miller—and repeated by Mary to Barry Cornwall. Barry Cornwall did not use it.

86. Kean complained of Henry Sigell's bill in a letter to William Chippendale. This letter is published in an old catalogue which has been pasted in a newspaper cutting book at the Garrick Club.

87. The original of Kean's letter to the manager of the Scarborough Theatre is in Ifan Kyrle Fletcher's collection.

88. The original of Kean's letter to Emile Laurent (January 1828) is in Ifan Kyrle Fletcher's collection.

89. The original of Kean's letter to the Covent Garden manager (August 27, 1828) is in Ifan Kyrle Fletcher's collection.

90. The criticism quoted of Kean's Virginius appeared in the *Theatre*.

91. Kean called Dan M'Corkindale, "Corkingdale." There is no doubt that he was wrong. Relics of Dan M'Corkindale (he was a heavy drinker!) may still be seen by visitors to the *Bute Arms* at Rothesay.

92. The busts put up by Kean on the front gates of his property at Bute are still there. So, too, is the wall paper with which he papered the walls of his drawing-room. The road which he built has been replaced by a new road.

93. Kean's Moss House at Bute has been pulled down. But I have stood on the mound where it once was.

94. The original of Kean's letter to his tailor (1827) is in Ifan Kyrle Fletcher's collection.

95. Mr. Hillebrand's book contains a letter of Kean's (dated June 13, 1829) in which Kean writes to his new solicitor, Stock, "Mrs. Kean desires her best regards & joins me in the invitation to Paradise."

96. Mrs. M'Fie testified to the fact that Charles would not enter Woodend House while Ophelia was there (*Transactions of the Buteshire Natural History Society*, Vol. I).

97. John Reid testified—among others—to Ophelia's extravagance at Kean's expense.

98. The manuscript of Kean's lines, "I break your slumber, sweet," etc., is in Ifan Kyrle Fletcher's collection.

99. The original of Kean's letter to Bartley (November 19, 1829) is in Ifan Kyrle Fletcher's collection.

100. The original of Kean's letter to Dunn (February 1830) is in Ifan Kyrle Fletcher's collection.

101. The King's Theatre was opposite the Haymarket. It was later called "Her Majesty's." It was the home of Italian Opera.

102. Mr. Hillebrand interprets Kean's last will as meaning that Ophelia stayed with him to the end. But the opposite interpretation is *prima facie* just as likely and according to the evidence must, I think, be correct. No one ever said that they saw Ophelia at Richmond. No mention of her is made in any letters or otherwise while Kean lived there. Moreover, it is inconceivable that "Aunt" Tid would have agreed to sleep under the same roof as the woman who had alienated most of Kean's friends. The "Last Will" is actually undated, but it was clearly written at Richmond. According to one account— unsubstantiated—Ophelia left Kean for a husband and settled in Frith Street, Soho.

103. John Lee's presence on the quay when Kean arrived in America was reported in several newspapers.

104. The original of Kean's letter to John Lee (April 10, 1831) is in the collection of Mr. R. N. Green-Armytage. The word (or name) left out is quite illegible. It looks like a seven-letter word— the last four letters are certainly c o t s.

105. The story of Phelps and Kean is published in *Memoirs of Samuel Phelps*, by John Coleman, London, 1886.

106. The manuscript of Kean's poem, "This is the hour, when sluggards are in sleep," etc., is in Ifan Kyrle Fletcher's collection.

107. All Kean's property was sold to satisfy his debts. His estate at Bute reverted to Lord Bute, the landowner. Even his personal belongings were disposed of. Charles was apparently unable or un- willing to purchase any of them. In the *Era Almanack* of 1875, T. F. Dillon Croker published an announcement which had originally been made a few months after Kean's death. It is as follows:—

TO THE THEATRICAL WORLD AND THE CURIOUS
GENERALLY

THE BEDSTEAD

ON WHICH

EDMUND KEAN THE TRAGEDIAN BREATHED HIS LAST

"This relic, once the property of the greatest Genius that ever graced the *British Stage*, will be raffled for by forty members at 5/-

each at Mr. Phillip's Swan Tavern and Lord Dover Hotel, Hunger-
ford market. . . .

"The proprietor to spend a guinea and the winner a guinea.

"The bedstead can be seen at the Bar, by tickets, sixpence each,
which may be had in refreshments."

108. Charles Kean's tablet in memory of his father was placed in
Richmond Parish Church in 1839. Previously John Lee and others
had attempted to raise public subscriptions for a memorial to Kean.
But there was no enthusiasm for the scheme outside Richmond. In
Ifan Kyrle Fletcher's collection there is a letter from Lord Essex
refusing to head the list of subscribers on the ground of his disapproval
of Kean's habits.

109. As shown in the Pedigree of Kean, printed at the beginning
of the book, Ann Carey died at Richmond eight days after the death
of Kean.

Mary died in her house at Keydell, near Horndean (Hampshire),
on March 13, 1849. The house had been given to her by Charles.

Miss Tidswell died on September 3, 1846 at 4 Camera Street,
Chelsea. No medical attendant was present at her death. The cause
of death was certified as old age. She was 86.

INDEX I

NAMES OF PERSONS

INDEX II

PLAYS, PLACES, THEATRES, NEWSPAPERS, ETC.